THE BOILING FROG

How Complacency and Ignorance
Created our Leadership Crisis
and What We Can Do About It

MICHAEL DARMODY

CONTENTS

DEDICATION

For Liam, Megan and little Brooks

And for the world's children, all of whom deserve a clean, healthy, flourishing planet and a just, fair and prosperous life.

INTRODUCTION: WHY THIS BOOK?

WE ARE IN DEEP TROUBLE.

For the first time in its history, the human race is facing the existential and disastrous threats of climate change, severe income inequality, and a frenetic pace of technological development. And yet societies continue to sleep in ignorance while our 'leaders' ignore or exacerbate these conditions.

While the global Paris Accord on Climate Change in 2015 made significant progress, it is insufficient to address the challenge. "Let us praise the real progress made while we loudly and clearly tell our leaders that goals are not actions, pledges are merely promises, and time is running out. We must build on Paris to strengthen the pledges and implement the policies to realize them. We must *organize against the counter-reaction and denial already underway* [italics mine]".[1]

Scientists agree that should we fail to hold the current increases in temperature to less than 2 degrees C, the consequences will be both devastating and irreversible. They estimate a 'window' of eleven years to do this. The current US Administration *has no plan* to deal with climate change, largely because they deny its risks.

A 2017 US Federal survey disclosed that 40% of Americans cannot withstand a $400 emergency, and 25% stated they have saved nothing for retirement. Four hundred American families own as much wealth as the bottom 150 million citizens. Globally, twenty-six people hold as much wealth as the bottom 3.8 billion people in the world.[2] Income inequality around the globe is at Gilded Age levels known to destroy democracy.

Innovative technology companies around the world forge ahead at a blistering pace in the development of Artificial Intelligence (AI), despite warnings from experts that we should first pause to debate potentially dangerous consequences of runaway AI, and decide proper global standards and regulation to guide the process so as to avoid disaster.

We are standing at the most critical crossroads of human existence. It will take broad awareness and intentional cooperation among all of us, and especially business and political leaders, if we want to avoid the worst case scenario: Extinction.

For fifty years, misdirected, surreptitious and sometimes sinister, forces in government, business and media have quietly and irresponsibly shifted away from important safeguard regulations. By gradually unwinding protective legislation and implementing policies and practices that placate lobbyists and maximize corporate profits, politicians and businessmen have slowly created the conditions that now imperil our very survival.

Unfortunately, societal complacence and ignorance permit it to continue. With a few notable exceptions, the quality of our 'leaders' leaves much to be desired. In fact, in many cases they are simply dangerous to the greater good. As our serious challenges continue to mount, our government and business leaders continue to obsess and squabble over oil, geo-political dominance and quarterly earnings per share. They are simply rearranging the deck chairs on the Titanic while we seem oblivious to even being on the ship.

There is an old adage about the boiling frog, which claimed that if you dropped a frog into a pot of boiling water, it would immediately jump out. But if you placed it in cool water and gradually raised the temperature to a boil, the frog would slowly cook without realizing it. True or not, the metaphor is powerful, and in my view, does describe well how many things have gotten to this critical point and how crucial it is that we jump out of the water. We must wake up, shake off our indifference and take action.

It's worth pausing here to ensure you're not offended by the words 'complacency and ignorance' in this book's subtitle. Though sometimes used as pejorative terms, by definition, neither is. Nor are they used that way here. Complacent simply means self-satisfied and unaware of a danger or full implications of a situation. Ignorance simply means lack of knowledge or information on a given topic. We are all complacent some of the time, and by simple math we are ignorant of far more things in life than those of which we are knowledgeable. No one can know everything. But as we'll later see, complacency and ignorance related to our leaders and their activities has had, and continues to have, serious and debilitating consequences. We must guard against both.

In trying to decide how I might best contribute to a solution for this serious dilemma, I felt compelled to write this book. It struck me that whenever I spoke to people about these troubling, sometimes sinister patterns in business, politics and social behaviour, their muted responses were not so much due to indifference, as to an understandable ignorance of what is really going on. I realized that with incredibly busy lives, most did not have the time, inclination, or energy to follow closely the crazy pace of change occurring in just about every sector of world events. They are just too tired and distracted with their day-to-day lives. It's easily understandable. And yet, we simply *must act*, and *quickly*.

The goal of this book is to inform, inspire and call to action.

The time to act is *now*, and this book will tell you *why* and *how*.

You will read a concise, objective summary of what is going wrong in the world and what our current leaders are doing (or not) about it. You will find useful information, exemplary stories and actions we can individually and collectively take to create positive transformation and a safer future. If we act now, we still have time to avert disaster and together create a much better world. An imperative part of the solution is to elect better leaders and hold them accountable. In some cases, maybe we ourselves will feel the call to step up into a leadership position.

Although I've studied leadership since the mid-Eighties, since the financial crisis of 2008 I have closely followed global business and political events. I have read dozens of books on such topics as business, strategy, finance, economics, organizational development, neuroscience, positive psychology, conscious awareness and mindfulness, and Quantum Science. I noticed some intriguing convergences. I am convinced that we have reached a place where simply tweaking our current systems and behaviours is no longer sufficient to solve our problems. We require the proverbial 'paradigm shift'. In the following pages, I will share with you what I see as the most important developments in those fields; how they can help you and your networks to decide there *is* a better way than the status quo, and that there *is* a very real sense of urgency to act now within our own spheres of influence.

I have attempted to be objective, factual, and constructive when explaining how changing relationships between leaders and followers are a significant and primary cause of what is happening to us, why we need to be concerned about it, and finally, to offer a challenge, and a call to action for leaders. I hope you will consider responding in a meaningful way.

We are in the midst of a leadership crisis.

If one looks back through history, a preponderance of both the major problems and the greatest benefits of society have stemmed directly from the decisions and actions taken by leaders. From earliest times of tribal assembly, we have always achieved progress through some form of organization.

> *"That is the true genius of organizations: they can lift groups of people to punch above their weight, to achieve outcomes they could not have achieved on their own."*
>
> **FREDERIC LALOUX**[3]

Safety, security, food, community, trade and commerce, creative inventions, innovations, and growth all evolved, disseminated and scaled from organizations: Tribes, religions, villages, cities, nation-states, or corporations.

Each of those required some type of leadership to protect, plan, organize and ideally, guide and inspire people towards progress; a better future for all. People either selected, accepted or grudgingly submitted to those leaders depending on the particular situation. And the quality of the leader made a monumental difference one way or another: whether a benevolent dictator like Julius Caesar or Peter the Great, a temporal Abraham Lincoln, who seemed to arise out of nowhere to the US presidency to achieve a monumental task, or a Hitler or Mussolini, who rose to unthinkable power and popularity, wrought unconscionable criminal havoc, and died in disgrace and infamy.

It has been said that societies get the leaders they deserve, and I believe there is some truth to that. Regardless, we continue to move forward largely through organizations in society, and those organizations continue to require effective leadership in order to fulfill their missions.

Do the times create the leader, or the leader create the times? Perhaps it's both. British rule in India certainly affected Gandhi's evolution as a leader, yet his leadership also reshaped a nation, and in some ways, the entire world order. This book outlines my deep concern about our current situation. These times are creating a particular type of leader, and there is great danger that many of them will undo much of what democratic societies have striven to achieve for the greater good over the past century or more. For a variety of reasons, many of which will be explored, we do not now have the luxury of complacency or indifference. For perhaps the first time since the October Missile Crisis of 1962, we collectively face challenges that imperil the entire human race, including that same nuclear threat that was so courageously avoided by Kennedy and Kruschev. And yet in the US "only 18% of Americans trust government to do the right thing at least most of the time."[4] As of July 2018, only 17% of Americans approved of the way Congress was doing its job.[5] Neoconservative movements, fuelled by populist leaders in America and in the EU, threaten further divisiveness within and between countries. When compared to what solid research shows to be the characteristics and practices of excellent leadership, many of our leaders today fall well short of that standard. It is a serious problem that we ignore at our peril.

And yet many of these leaders were elected in democratic countries. What has happened to followers? It appears that a combination of cynicism, indifference, and ignorance have resulted in a public that has neglected to vote. Recent elections in the US saw only 56% of eligible citizens vote, while in Canada it was at 62%.[6] Low voter turnout opens doors for manipulation and illegal system abuses, so we as followers need to examine what we want for our society and how our actions can result in that outcome. Ineffective, and in some cases, dangerous, leaders in democracies are a reflection on us.

These being the times of 'fake news', effort has been made to present factual information in this book from legitimate, reliable sources. Because my professional background has been in leadership development, corporate strategy and effectiveness, much of the

DEALING WITH AMERICA

It's important to establish here the treatment of the United States in this book. While much of the suggestions and criticisms deal with America, it is not because they are any better or worse than any other nation. It is simply that since the fall of the Berlin Wall in 1988 and the dismantling of the Soviet Union, the US has been the unilateral superpower in the world, and hence has wielded a disproportionate influence on world events. Absolute power eventually corrupts, and has resulted in decisions, particularly the invasion of Iraq, that have had serious and major implications for the entire world. As the biggest actor, they will naturally draw the biggest scrutiny. That said, one must consider the outcome were another nation the unilateral global giant. How would Russia, China, Germany or Japan act in such an unchallenged state? My opinion is that, at least until now, the world could have been much worse off had another country with fewer democratic principles embedded in its Constitution, risen to become the sole world power. As China rises in economic clout, we may soon find out.

The second fact to illuminate regarding America is that the current antics of President Donald Trump have resulted in many in the media and public blaming him for the current dangerous state of affairs. This is incorrectly short-sighted. The Trump presidency is only a symptom of the many things slowly shifting in the US during the past sixty years. I believe he is the product of corrupt leadership and a sleeping public.

information will relate to commerce, and corporate leadership, but because of the unavoidable interactivity between business, governments and media, the impact of leadership in all of those sectors is also reviewed. Great care also has been taken to include the thinking and work of credible authors and thought leaders in the fields reviewed to validate all statements.

As a Canadian born resident with naturalized US citizenship, and having lived ten years in the US, much of the commentary and examples relate to those countries because of my first-hand experience in each; but mostly to America, given its disproportionate influence on the challenges of globalization, wars, international finance, corruption and the volatile, uncertain, complex, ambiguous (VUCA) world. The world now more than ever is an interconnected living system, where actions in one sector affect all others, yet rarely have we incorporated that into our planning or decisions. Because the US has been, and for at least a little while longer, remains the 'Big Dog' unilateral superpower, with commensurate influence on global events, much of the book addresses trends and events currently underway there, not least of which is the quality and potential consequence of their current 'leadership'.

The book is organized into three parts:

Part I: What? Provides an overview of our most pressing societal challenges, how we ended up here, and the roles that our leadership, and we as followers, played in that.

Part II: So What? Provides an objective and convincing argument for why we should care about this.

Part III: Now What? Offers a challenge to current leaders to either step up in a better way, or step down and get out of the way. As well, some enthusiastic encouragement is provided to new would-be leaders, along with some research-proven leadership practices for those who wish to step up.

PART I: WHAT?

"Every few hundred years in Western history there occurs a sharp transformation. We cross what I call a 'divide'. Within a few short decades, society rearranges itself – its worldview; its basic values; its social and political structure; its art; its key institutions. Fifty years later, there is a new world. And the people born then cannot even imagine the world in which their grandparents lived and into which their own parents were born. We are currently living through just such a transformation." **Peter Drucker** - "Post-Capitalist Society" 1993

CHAPTER 1

How We Got Here

"Fifty years later, there is a new world." Drucker was right: it's interesting that fifty years ago today was 1968, a year when so much upheaval and seeming chaos can be said to have started us on our path to here. At least that's when social rebellious Western change seriously began, as primarily college educated youth began pushing back against the corporate and government sectors and their policies: the Vietnam War, civil rights infringements, corporate abuses of the environment and labour, and sexual mores, among others.

Technology, with the invention and broad application of the transistor and the silicon chip, fueled rapid economic expansion and created new exciting industries. Yet as the radical excitement of the Sixties gradually subsided, and we trundled through the Seventies and into the Eighties, public scrutiny of, and faith in our institutions seemed to wane. Watergate in Washington, and the proliferation of Wall Street corporate raiders, leveraged buyouts, and the hollowing out of corporations for immediate profit combined to jade those of us who did pay attention, and create cynical indifference among the rest.

It was not so much that people didn't care; they were busy working at their jobs, trying to raise families, and keep pace with a world that was experiencing the unprecedented effects of <u>Moore's Law</u>.[1] We would never look back: the pace of change in the world had taken off, and it would become harder and harder to keep up with it, so, many sought needed relief by simply ignoring it.

Being deep in the trees of day-to-day life, many became unaware of the forest; the macro view of what was transpiring over the longer term. And as the public in some ways went to sleep, especially regarding civic and corporate awareness, some leaders emerged who saw the situation as a ripe opportunity to quietly advance their own agendas. In America, the traditional separation and often adversarial relationships between Congress and Big Corporate gradually dissolved, and in time, policy for business was actually crafted verbatim by groups like American Legislative Exchange Council (ALEC).[2] No one in the middle class seemed to notice or care much.

The financial crisis started by Wall Street tactics in the US and hit markets on September 15, 2008; most people were stunned at the magnitude and depth of the crash. But the steps that led to it began well back in the 1990s, starting with the 1999 legislation Financial Services Modernization Act (yes that's really the name!) that unwound the 1933 post-Depression stop-gap Glass-Steagall law, which prevented, among other things, commercial banks from owning investment banks and brokerages. The average person was at worst completely oblivious, or at best, just shrugged it off as those politicians and Wall Street guys playing around again. This is not to criticize the public (people work hard to raise their families, and cannot be expert in all things), but rather to show that historically, change has often come about without people fully realizing or grasping what is happening until it is upon them. Nazi Germany is a good example. The frog usually boils slowly.

And yet to truly understand what's happening today, how our leaders are selected and what we as followers permit and expect them to do, it's very important to understand how we got here. As a cursory overview, I submit that it is the primarily the result of the evolution of three events and subsequent trends:

1. How leaders rose to power, and how constraints were placed on their power

2. Commerce

3. The impact of the Age of Enlightenment and the Scientific Revolution

Leaders and Constraints

Leadership can be simplified as a relationship between those who choose to follow, and those who wish to lead. Unfortunately, as in the case of Russia's Vladimir Putin, Rodrigo Duterte of the Philippines, and several African nation leaders to name but a few (and for all hapless slaves throughout history), the only 'choice' for some followers is to do or die. But in democratic states, corporations and other institutions, people have agreed to follow in exchange for a leader delivering consistent peace, prosperity, safety, a sense of cultural unity and pride, employment, membership and the like. This arrangement is very important: an implicit or explicit understanding that the leader will deliver on a set of responsibilities in exchange for the people agreeing to accept his or her decisions and direction. Throughout history, there has always been a tension between the two, sometimes positive and harmonious (Queen Victoria's long reign), and other times, violent and rebellious (King Louis XVI lost his head). We will be examining this relationship between leaders and followers later on, in the current context of 2018.

As mentioned earlier, from tribal times forward, humans have achieved major progress through organizations, which must in turn, have leadership. In tribes, and eventually states, the chief may have been the most feared (Genghis Khan), the bravest (Alexander the Great), the smartest (Ramses II), the wisest (Suleiman the Magnificent), or perhaps a spiritual leader; and while different cultures had various means of selecting leaders, a 'royal' or leader class usually emerged. Regardless of how they achieved power, these leaders helped our transition from hunter-gatherers of about 10,000 years ago, into the 'Neolithic Revolution' (New Stone Age), during which the system of settled farmers and domesticated animals created the possibility for division of labour, allowing the evolution of artisans, soldiers, larger religious sectors, and a more diverse society. With this set up, "their numbers exploded, and about 5000 years after the origin of agriculture, true states appeared on the scene ... when the more powerful chiefdoms used their armed retinues to bring other chiefdoms under their control, further centralizing their power, and supporting niches for specialized classes."[3] These autocratic leaders called all the shots, largely because of the people's faith in the strengths for which they were chosen. Often they received higher education relative to that of the general population. There were few restraints on the leaders, such as the rule of law, which followed much later. In the Middle Ages, various forms of feudal systems emerged, with peasants working lands privately owned by the aristocratic leaders of each country. These leaders tended towards mass exploitation, largely through rents and taxes on the huge lands they had acquired, and with few if any limitations to their locally autocratic ways.

Fortunately for all of us, beginning way back in 539 BC, Cyrus the Great of Persia had craftsmen create the Cyrus Cylinder, considered the first charter of human rights, kicking off a long and hard-fought trend towards clipping the wings of self-serving leaders everywhere. It was followed by major documents like the Magna Carta (1215), the Petition of Rights (1628), the US Constitution (1787), the French Declaration of the Rights of Man and of the Citizen (1789), and the US Bill of Rights (1791). All of these served to limit the capacity for oppression and subversion of followers, by leaders in the 'civilized' world, eventually reducing feudal baronies and replacing them with more enlightened forms of society. "Europe had five thousand independent political units (mainly baronies and principalities) in the 15th century, five hundred at the time of the Thirty Years' War in the early 17th, two hundred at the time of Napoleon in the early 19th, and fewer than thirty in 1953" [4] But imagine still having any baronies as late as that!

Thus throughout history, the leader-follower relationship has evolved, impacted by the eventual formal and informal education of the public, which allowed them to better understand what the leaders were doing, and by the actions of the leaders, which began to be further reined in by the rule of law. The notion of governing by a set of laws as opposed to the edict of a leader was around as far back as Aristotle, who suggested "It is more proper that law should govern than any one of the citizens: upon the same principle, if it is advantageous to place the supreme power in some particular persons, they should be appointed to be only guardians, and the servants of the laws"[5] The legal concept can also be found in writings of Ancient Greece, Mesopotamia, India and Rome. It can safely be said that as societies witnessed and experienced the detrimental and irresistible effects of power on anointed humans, they realized that a check and balance system was in order. "Power concedes nothing without a demand; it never did, and it never will."[6]

In 1651 Thomas Hobbes wrote *Leviathan*, using the term to denote "a monarchy or other government authority that embodies the will of the people and has a monopoly on the use of force."[7] His main idea was to establish a system that would use an objective third party (primarily a judiciary) which by inflicting penalties on aggressors, including monarchs and other leaders, could eliminate their incentive for aggression. While Hobbes prescribed a Leviathan system primarily as a means to avoid war by the use of law, war being a prevailing concern of the times, it also served to mitigate damage that might be caused by unscrupulous leaders.

Commerce

The next event to significantly alter the relationship of leaders and their followers, and set us upon the path to our current situation in the twenty-first century was commerce.

Again, please forgive the oversimplifications here, recalling that my purpose is to give a basic overview of forces that formed our current leadership situation.

Feudal times involved a zero-sum game. Land was finite: if you owned most of it, everyone who didn't lost. Wars were often rooted in the desire for more land. And landowners, in acquiring huge wealth, wielded all the power that went with it. The evolution of commerce, from early bartering systems to the introduction of currency, served to shift power from leaders to followers by redistribution of wealth other than land. The Gilded Age of the late 1800s, and our current global trends, represent a reversal of that shift, but much more on that later.

Commerce created what we now refer to as the middle class, while also giving opportunity to the average person to acquire greater wealth. It is based upon the notion of mutual utility, and began to burgeon in the Middle Ages. The feudal system required craftsmanship – carpenters, blacksmiths, stonemasons, potters, weavers, and others – which eventually evolved into the system of guilds. The earlier system of barter was unwieldy and growth-limiting: how many pots does a housebuilder want in exchange for the house? He has no interest in storing and selling the excess above his own needs. And while currency is first recorded in 600 BC in Lydia (now part of Turkey), it was around 1200 AD that Marco Polo returned to Europe speaking of the concept he saw in China. Money fueled the expansion of specialized expertise in crafts, which in turn broadened the variety of available goods and services. The guilds, while existing for centuries, eventually corrupted into a system that unduly enriched a small class of powerful burgher merchants, and so were gradually displaced by what was proposed, particularly by Adam Smith in his famous 1776 book *Wealth of Nations,* as the free market system in which an 'invisible hand' supposedly maximized supply and demand forces, and in so doing, benefitted society. This is highly significant because it evolved into the capitalist system we currently utilize. From *Wealth of Nations* sprang forth the 'science' of classical economics, and it is this subject which has been the source of much prosperity and also much damage to society, depending on what we accept as fact: theory versus empirical observation. It is economic theory that has come to establish the policy beliefs and foundations for political systems (Capitalism, Communism), parties (Republicans, Democrats, Liberals, Conservatives, Greens, Socialists), and corporate strategy (profit maximization, monopoly, oligarchy).

In the 1980s, what became known as Reaganomics or Trickle Down theory, was introduced, based upon economic models that indicated tax cuts to corporations would spur investment in assets and consumption of goods and services, creating jobs and wealth for the middle classes. In the US, it became Republican strategy that is still touted widely, despite ample empirical evidence that it only redistributes wealth to the few. Donald Trump's $1.5 trillion tax cut in 2018 was made with the promise that every family would benefit by around $4,000. Instead, the richest received billions, while the average family benefited by a few hundred dollars. We will revisit this in another chapter.

The degree to which commerce played a role in how we got here should be crystallizing by now. The explosion of commerce in the eighteenth century "ushered in the transformation from the feudal to the market economy, altering the economic paradigm and social construction of Europe."[8] How is this relevant to our topic? Over the past 500 years, capitalism became the most dominant economic system throughout the world, shaping the values, beliefs, assumptions and norms of the societies from which our leaders emerged. If and when some of those beliefs and

Cartoon by Adam Zyglis, Buffalo News

assumptions prove false, then the outcomes of the system will be very different from what was expected, leading to tension, division and eventual dysfunction.

For example, in building their models, early economists accepted the notion that *Homo sapiens* was really *Homo economicus*. "Economic man is a simple creature who makes all of life's choices like a shopper in a supermarket with plenty of time to compare jars of applesauce. If that's your view of human nature, then it's easy to create mathematical models of behavior because there's really just one principle at work: self-interest."[9] Adam Smith was perhaps the most famous proponent of this theory, insisting that rational self-interest and competition would lead to economic prosperity. Yet empirical studies have since shown that it is not that simple; human beings have many concerns beyond narrow self-interest, not least of which is a "working set of moral foundations."[10] Also, the assumptions of free market capitalism assumed fully available and equally accessible information (certainly false), and a level playing field for all (also since proven false).

Around ninety years after *The Wealth of Nations*, in 1867, having witnessed the destructive capabilities of unbridled capitalism, Karl Marx wrote *Das Kapital*, which became the foundational idea for what evolved into the communist form of government; and it is this clash of two politico-economic philosophies, communism and capitalism, that has shaped the last 150 years of global society.

See where all this is taking us? As societies came to embrace governmental systems (capitalist or communist), the mindsets and assumptions that were taken for granted became the source of their expectations. Leaders, as we've seen, are expected to deliver on those followers' expectations; and in some cases, help create them. But what if the underlying premise is wrong? What if the concepts we have accepted as true are, in fact, only partially true, or even false? And what if some leaders manipulate the system for their own purposes? What if *Homo economicus* is simply an economist's fantasy that permits clean, neat mathematical models that look great on paper, but don't reflect reality? What if Russia's Vladimir Putin, North Korea's Kim Jong-Un and China's Xi Jinping are among the biggest capitalists in the world? How did Russia's communist system permit the wealthiest oligarchs on earth, while the standard of living of the average person remained low? When there is a disconnect between what people believe to be happening and what leaders are actually doing (innocently or otherwise), things begin to unravel.

For example, the belief after WWII that the 'other side' (capitalists or communists) was the evil empire, justified both Russian and American leaders to allocate trillions of dollars to 'defense' initiatives of the Cold War, as each side viewed the other with hatred and deep mistrust for the second half of the twentieth century. The result: for much of the twentieth century, the world lived under the policy of Mutually Assured Destruction, with staggering sums of capital devoted to arms; capital that could have done much for society if invested in education, science, health care, research and development. Businesses in the defense industry earned tremendous profits in the western world (war is a very profitable pastime!), and the Cold War enriched communist leaders who, in wielding absolute power, had access to any material items they wished.

Finally, commerce, while influencing the expectations of society for their governments and the type of political leaders that arose, also affected a major shift of power over time to a new type of leader: the wealthy merchant class. The Rothschild family is perhaps the strongest example of how a middle class merchant could rise to unprecedented international power and influence through banking and finance, with kings and aristocrats requiring their help to finance wars and manage estate debts. In democratic countries, commerce and its wealthy titans grew to influence every aspect of government, and that continues to this day. In communist countries, nationalizing the factors of production and commerce served to cement the power base of the leaders, many of whom, as mentioned, live as well as the wealthiest capitalists anywhere.

Without change, there is no need for leaders. Yet if leaders need to foment change, especially painful change; they need to reach followers on both an intellectual and an emotional level. Challenging deeply held values and beliefs among people is a difficult task, and yet as we will later see, it is exactly what is required at this time in 2018. And globally, but particularly in the Western world, two big events in history occurred that shifted traditional beliefs to a new set; one which lasted and formed the foundation of thought and behavior for over 300 years. Today, these sacred 'truths' are proving only partially true, and so merit re-examination.

The Age of Enlightenment and the Scientific Revolution

In keeping with the proposition of this book that we arrived at our present situation through a combination of societal (followers) beliefs and expectations and our leaders sharing those beliefs and acting accordingly, we need to take a quick look at the Age of Enlightenment, also called the Age of Reason, and at the Scientific Revolution.

The Age of Reason (1685-1815), perhaps most famously expressed by René Descartes' conclusion, *cogito, ergo sum* ('I think, therefore I am'), was a period of radical thinking by many gifted minds. The writings of people including Hobbes, Descartes, Locke, Kant, Madison, Jefferson, Hamilton and Mill challenged centuries-old traditions of faith and belief, instead promoting skepticism and rational thinking. "One therefore ought to seek good *reasons* for believing something. Faith revelation, tradition, dogma, authority, the ecstatic glow of subjective certainty – all are recipes for error, and should be dismissed as a source of knowledge."[11] Immanuel Kant used the phrase *sapere aude* ('dare to know' or 'dare to think for yourself') as the motto for the Enlightenment Age; this after centuries of society being told what to think, and forbidden to even question many aspects of life by the Catholic church. The practice of viewing the world through eyes of reason elevated society in awareness and judgement, by helping to illuminate myth and deceit. And a different society produced different leaders.

This hotbed of creative, original thinking overlapped with the Scientific Revolution, and the two movements supported and fed off each other. The 'reasonable man' notion influenced the development of the scientific method, which is still in use today as a means of objectively determining truth in knowledge. In a way, the scientific method served to support democracy, in that no longer could a leader or institution impose their views as absolute truth and expect the public to accept them. Of course, many still try to do just that today, and public skepticism seems to have waned somewhat, as evidenced by the recent emergence of 'fake news'. But we'll visit that in another chapter.

The most astonishing outcome of the Scientific Revolution was the publication in 1687 of *Principia Mathematica*, by the genius Isaac Newton. The impact of the work changed everything about how society viewed the universe, and the Newtonian mechanistic view has influenced every decision made in the developed world since. Newton devised laws of motion and gravity that scientists could rely upon as certain. He introduced the view of the cosmos as a large machine with multiple moving parts. "We have prided ourselves, in all these centuries since Newton and Descartes, on the triumphs of reason, on the absence of magic... We've held onto an intense belief in cause and effect... We really believed we could study the parts, no matter how many of them there were, to arrive at knowledge of the whole. We have reduced and described and separated things into cause and effect and drawn the world in lines and boxes."[12]

Reason and Newtonian science were great gifts in a civilizing world, dispelling many falsehoods and enabling true and reliable progress in all the scientific fields. Their impact reached deep into the nineteenth and twentieth centuries, and contributed immensely to industrial innovation, while also influencing the evolution of military and organizational structure and thinking. They served to advance our standard of living for centuries.

And yet, we are quickly learning that many of our current challenges stem from the fact that neither pure reason nor the Newtonian worldview are completely true. Most of our institutions are still structured according to the underlying assumptions, but favorable results elude us. Man is not a *Homo economicus*; he does not function rationally all the time. "The indispensability of reason does not imply that individual people are always rational, or are unswayed by passion and illusion. It only means they are *capable* of reason,"[13] New research in the field of moral psychology shows that we are actually governed first by emotion. "Intuitions come first; strategic reasoning second."[14] Developments in neuroscience, particularly the functional magnetic resonance imaging (fMRI), have opened up new understanding of the functioning of the amygdala, hippocampus, and prefrontal cortex of the brain. Much of human behavior is governed by the emotions we experience, which may or may not be rational.

Much of the modern structure of corporations, scientific research institutions, and governments has been deeply influenced by the Newtonian machine model; we chunk everything down into discrete parts for examination, analysis and understanding. And until recently, it has served us well. As Wheatley says, "The 'thing' view of the world, therefore, has led to a belief in scientific objectivity. And we prospered with this belief for many centuries, working well in a world of you-me, inside-outside, here-thereness."[15] But then came the quantum subatomic world, where behavior defied Newton's laws and continues to stymie the brightest minds. There are no certain predictions, only probabilities. Newton's laws continue to have their place in the visible world, but underlying that there is much more going on. Consultants like Margaret Wheatley who study organizations and effectiveness, are discovering that agile, resilient organizations with strong cultures act more like the quantum world than a Newtonian one. And leaders play an indispensable role in creating them. Things are changing *very* rapidly!

We got here by decisions taken by our leaders, elected or otherwise, and by the constraints we followers eventually placed on their unlimited powers. We evolved with commerce, to a place where corporations wield considerable clout and influence on political leaders, and on society. We continue to operate in a system that assumes rationality and reason drive behavior, and that a mechanized, Newtonian world still functions best.

But there is a new world emerging, and at a faster pace than ever before experienced, and as Marshall Goldsmith says, "what got you here, won't get you there." [16] Many of the strategies and tactics used by leaders of the past are no longer valid or effective, simply because the needs and wants of their constituents have drastically changed.

Quantum physicist Fritjof Capra and chemistry professor Pier Luigi Luisi write: "there *are* solutions to the major problems of our time; some of them even simple. But they require a radical shift in our perceptions, our thinking, our values. And, indeed, we are now at the beginning of such a fundamental change of worldview in science and society, a change of paradigms as radical as the Copernican revolution. Unfortunately, *this realization has not yet dawned on most of our political leaders, who are unable to 'connect the dots'... They fail to see how the major problems of our time are all interrelated* [italics mine]."[17]

The premise of this book is that the relationship between us, as followers, and our leaders, is critical to the conditions of the society we live in. Our leaders have often failed to 'hear' their followers, failed to inspire visions of positive possibility, and failed to anticipate the impact of the radical change we experience. Some of this failure is innocent, based upon ignorance or capability, and some is by negligence, greed, desire for fame and power, and irresponsibility. However, regardless of reason, *weak leadership is at the root of most of our collective problems.* But weak leadership is also the result, at least in democracies, of the indifference, tolerance and apathy of voters. As all revolutions in history (American, French, Russian, Chinese, Iranian to name a few) have demonstrated, when followers unite around common values and goals, when they're clear and passionate about what they want, new leadership arises and drives the desired changes. If we're dissatisfied with how things are working, we have the power to change it. If we don't care, the frog continues to boil.

Next we will look at the research on effective leadership, and then compare the track records of selected leaders against the excellence benchmark established by that research.

CHAPTER 2

Our Leadership Crisis

"Nearly all men can stand adversity. But if you want to test a man's character, give him power." Abraham Lincoln

GOOGLING 'LEADERSHIP' IN SEPTEMBER 2018 YIELDED 2.1 billion results, but when I began working in the leadership development field back in 2000, the results were around 5% of that number. Since then, the leadership development market has exploded from about US$1 billion to the current estimate of US$14 billion, and is expected to grow at 14% annually until 2021, for very good reasons, which we'll visit in part II.

This is not meant to be solely a business book, but it does seek to examine leaders primarily in business, non-profit organizations and government, given that those institutions employ the greatest number of them. So a short recap of how our leaders in both sectors evolved will be useful. Again, it's a brief overview, but necessary to understand the pressures that helped form leadership practices of the past 100 years.

Business leaders

The study of leadership has been around since ancient philosophers like Plato and Suetonius, and later, Sun Tzu and Machiavelli, all of whom attempted to discern the qualities that differentiated between great, good, and poor leaders. For our purposes, I think we can focus on the twentieth and twenty-first centuries, because aside from monarchies, much of 'modern' leadership practices began within a militaristic context and evolved over the past 100 years, heavily influenced by the arrival of the graduate business school. It is safe to say that many post-WWI and WWII men transitioned from military service, especially the officer class, into leadership roles in business after the wars. They brought with them the same structural, organizational and procedural mindset and practices of a military leadership model, 'command and control', and applied it to the corporate organization. This proved quite effective as long as a) the employee population held the values of the WWII generation: respect for authority, trust in authority, and strong work ethic, and b) events in the world moved *slowly.* Yet as Old Abe cautioned above, unchecked power soon exposed the wanting character of many of those leaders. Working terms and conditions, while better than in the previous centuries, were still far from fair and safe even into the 1940s. With the merger of the American Federation of Labor (AFL) and the Congress of Industrial Organizations (CIO) in 1955, labour union push-back gained momentum, and began to undermine management autocracy; but the freedom of management to create and execute strategy remained quite intact, and by the 1970s unions began to decline.

The early 1900s saw the invention of the Master of Business Administration (MBA) degree, at schools like Wharton, Tuck and Harvard, which introduced a scientific, quantitative analytical approach to running a corporation that included statistics, managerial economics, and operations research. As early as 1910, Frederick Taylor was experimenting with time and motion studies in factories, but it wasn't until the 1950s and 1960s that academic research funding started to flow into the study of professional management, which until recently was used synonymously with 'leadership' (we'll see later that they actually have different purposes and skill requirements).

It was during this period that the concepts of marketing as a discipline (the Profit Impact of Market Strategies (PIMS) study), finance (the Capital Asset Pricing Model (CAPM), Return on Investment (ROI), and Return on Equity (ROE)), profit maximization, and product/brand management went mainstream, fueling the growth of multinational corporations. Tasks traditionally referred to as leadership were actually management functions:

staffing, organizing, coordinating and monitoring/controlling, with a heavy emphasis on profit maximization through quantitative analysis. Managers grew to 'live by the numbers', and somewhere along the way the assumed primary purpose of a business shifted from creating whatever product or service they offered, to maximizing shareholder value. This very important shift in purpose partially explains the poor quality of American cars and electronics of the 1970s that opened the door for the Japanese to gain supremacy in those markets, and is at the root of many of the business problems we currently face. By the 1990s, the practice of companies giving quarterly earnings per share (EPS) 'guidance' to Wall Street had taken hold, pressuring an intense short term focus by management that would eventually damage society. All of these events impacted corporate leaders in often uncontrollable ways. If they didn't play along, and deliver on the narrow definition of shareholder ROI, they were usually replaced. The key takeaway here is that *maximizing returns to shareholders became the ultimate end goal*, and shaped all decisions about strategy, resource allocation, and people. This mindset contributed greatly to our current income inequality crisis.

In 1982, a book called *In Search of Excellence* was published by Tom Peters and Bob Waterman, two McKinsey consultants. It became for many years the best selling business book. It developed what was called the McKinsey Seven S Model for evaluating one's organization, based on common practices discovered from interviewing dozens of companies that met a preset 'excellence' standard. It revolutionized the manner in which corporations were evaluated and provided many valuable insights, but to my knowledge, it was also the first high profile work to allude to

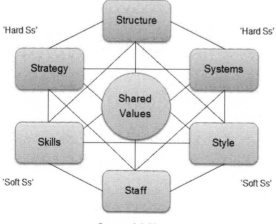

Source: McKinsey

the power of the 'soft' side of people in business: the soft S's. They called it 'shared values' and it was the center of the model around which the other six revolved.

The authors realized that even the most effective strategies are only as good as their execution, and superior execution depends upon people and their level of motivation. This signalled the beginning of the decline (although it's still far more prevalent today than it should be) of top-down, command and control management. What the latter system overlooked is that in the military, one *must* execute orders without much questionning. There isn't much grey: the order is either carried out or it isn't. Obedience is built into the system; the 'follower' soldiers have little if any choice, and both they and their superiors expect and accept that relationship. But in the corporate sector, particularly during strong ecomonic cycles, unhappy talent can always go to the next company. If they don't like the orders, they don't have to stick around. In 1997, a now famous McKinsey article declared an upcoming 'War for Talent' that described the coming talent shortage and a shift in bargaining power to the employee. There is a big difference between dealing with an assembly line worker and a software coder. Command and control is losing it's effectiveness. The 'Soft S's' are essential. In the October 2018 issue of Forbes magazine, an article on soft skills stated that "Last year, Google announced the findings from an internal study that looked across teams to determine the most innovative and productive groups within the company. They found that their best teams weren't the ones full of top scientists. Instead, their highest performing teams were interdisciplinary groups that benefited heavily from employees who brought strong soft skills to the collaborative process."[1] Further research revealed that important predictors of success within Google were skills like good communication, insights about others, and empathetic leadership. But it's not just top tech companies that are finding value in these types of skills. A Twitter poll from TedX found that most people think teamwork and collaboration are the most helpful soft skills in the workplace, followed by critical thinking, public speaking and persuasive writing."

This is where leadership skills become increasingly indispensable, yet many organizations are just now starting to learn the difference between them and management skills. Harvard's John Kotter is considered among the top (if not *the* top) authority on business leadership and organizational transformation. Below is his concise and invaluable chart highlighting the differences between management and leadership functions. There are two very important observations here.

1. The tasks of management and leadership differ greatly; the former focus on control and quantifiable, measurable operations: numbers. Those of leadership require people skills, emotional intelligence, passion and vision. *The skill sets are almost opposites!*

2. The desired, successful outcomes of each function are also polar opposites: management seeks to exercise tight control, and *minimize changes*. Leadership seeks to *produce dramatic change*, innovation, creativity, and energized, engaged workforces. Carefully read the last two bullet points in the model below, to compare.

MANAGEMENT

- **Planning and Budgeting:**
  Establishing detailed steps
  and timetables for achieving
  needed results, then
  allocating the resources
  necessary to make
  it happen.

- **Organizing and Staffing:**
  Establishing some structure
  for accomplishing plan
  requirements, staffing
  that structure with
  individuals, delegating
  responsibility and authority
  for carrying out the plan,
  producing policies and
  procedures to help guide
  people, and creating
  methods or systems to
  monitor implementation.

- **Controlling and
  problem solving:**
  Monitoring results,
  identifying deviations
  from plan, then planning
  and organizing to solve
  these problems.

- Produces a degree of
  predictability and order and
  has potential to consistently
  produce the short term
  results expected by various
  stakeholders (e.g., for
  customers, always being
  on-time; for stockholders,
  being on budget).

LEADERSHIP

- **Establishing direction:**
  Developing a vision of the
  future – often the distant
  future – and strategies for
  producing the changes
  needed to achieve that vision

- **Aligning people:**
  Communicating direction in
  words and deeds to all those
  whose cooperation may be
  needed so as to influence
  the creation of teams and
  coalitions that understand
  the vision and strategies and
  that accept their validity

- **Motivating and inspiring:**
  Energizing people to
  overcome major political,
  bureaucratic and resource
  barriers to change by
  satisfying basic, but often
  unfulfilled, human needs.

- Produces change, often
  to a dramatic degree,
  and has the potential to
  produce extremely useful
  change (e.g., new products
  that customers want, new
  approaches to labor relations
  that help make a firm more
  competitive).

Source: From Kotter, John P. *A Force for Change: How Leadership Differs from Management*, Free Press, 1990. With permission from John P. Kotter

When the world moved slowly (steady interest rates over long stretches, national and limited competitors, slow and lengthy product innovation cycles, etc.) management science and skills worked beautifully to mitigate risk. Detailed five and ten year strategic plans comforted (deluded?) managers into believing that they had it all under control.

The real challenge today is that the management-leadership dichotomy is critical to success. *Both* skill sets are absolutely necessary, and at high competency levels, but because budgets rarely afford two sets of people (e.g. managers *and* leaders), the managers must acquire leadership skills to supplement their management abilities. This is a very difficult undertaking, and explains the rapid growth of the leadership development field.

Government Leaders

Though perhaps a simplistic, sweeping assumption, undemocratic governments are basically militaristic command and control systems. 'Leaders' (Putin, Jong-Un, Duterte, Erdogan, El-Sisi) have the full support of the military, which cements their position of power through coercion. They are not leaders by the definition we will offer later, because there is a one-way relationship between them and their 'followers', who have little or no choice. Heavy surveillance and physical brutality take place with regularity. That said, the domestic decisions of those leaders nevertheless still impact the world, as we'll see in the next chapter. Sometimes, as in the cases of Egypt, Turkey and Saudi Arabia, the leaders present a world profile as tough but fair guardians of their people, but the underlying principle is one of terror, coercion and threat. The chief problem with that system is that in a high tech world that's racing ever faster towards new methods of existence, they are suppressing much of the brainpower, innovative potential and skill contribution of their populations. In the long run, that is very dangerous for them and the world. For now, we'll leave them aside in our look at government leaders.

In democracies, the leadership role is far more complex. We have already done a surface review of how tribal and royal rulers evolved into leaders who had some constraints eventually placed upon them. The United States is perhaps the most important experiment in democratic government because their founding fathers had the wisdom to acknowledge and set checks and balances against the vagaries of human nature. They realized that select morals and principles of law transcend the individual, and are necessary to protect advances in civilized societies; to prevent us from regressing, to avert demagogues. It feels somewhat strange writing that statement in September of 2018, given what's happening now in the US and the world, but at least we can still revert to those solid foundations if we so choose.

As democracies matured, there evolved camps of like-minded people, usually based upon conservative or liberal value sets; our modern parties. Leaders ran for election based upon their embrace of the particular values, and promised if elected, to move the city, state, province, nation in the general direction of that party's values through policy. Separated functions of executive, legislative and judiciary were intended to work independently yet in concert to effect smooth government. This worked OK for awhile too. Because the first constraint on any proposed policy was that it comply with existing laws, governments tended to attract lawyers into the system. American president Franklin D. Roosevelt (often called FDR) was a lawyer and visionary who used his knowledge and skill to establish the New Deal, and helped pull the country out of the Great Depression. He was an exemplary leader in that he placed the welfare of the nation ahead of his own, an act that caused the wealthy class (of which he was an Establishment member) to label him 'a traitor to his class'.In the following decades, as lawyers, politicians and coporate leaders became more and more cozy with each other, and much less transparent, the quality of our leaders generally declined, with an increase in the practice of placing their own fame, wealth and desire for power ahead of the public service ethic.

We have now arrived at the place where, referring to our oligarchy of leaders, George Monbiot of The Guardian writes, "Those to whom we look for solutions trundle on as if nothing has changed. As if the accumulating evidence has no purchase on their minds. Decades of institutional failure ensures that only 'unrealistic' proposals – the repurposing of economic life, with immediate effect – now have a realistic chance of stopping the planetary death spiral. And only those who stand outside the failed institutions can lead this effort." [2]

Becsause the subject of leadership is so vast, it's best to present some definitions proposed by leading thinkers on the subject, as well as some research-based traits, characteristics and best practices of excellent leaders, followed by some examples of leaders who exhibited these traits in varying degrees. The idea is to leave you with a general understanding of good and not-so-good leadership; a feel for how some leaders measure up against the benchmarks, while others do not. You be the judge.

In Chapter 3 I'll attempt to explain what went wrong.

Leadership Definitions

Here are some widely respected definitions and types of leadership:

- "Leadership is the art of mobilizing others to want to struggle for shared aspirations. It is a reciprocal process between those who aspire to lead, and those who choose to follow."[3] (Kouzes and Posner)

- "Leadership is about setting direction, aligning people, and motivating them. It's about learning how to cope with rapid *change*."[4] (Kotter)

- "A leader is best when people barely know he exists, when his work is done, his aim fulfilled, they will say: we did it ourselves. To lead the people, walk behind them." (Lao Tzu)

- "Motivation and efficacy are the power of leadership that produces significant change." (James MacGregor Burns)

- "Leaders surpass limitations of current reality to create a new one." (Francoise Morissette)

- Authentic Leadership: "Authentic leaders demonstrate a passion for their purpose, practice their values consistently, and lead with their hearts as well as their heads. They establish long-term meaningful relationships, and have self-discipline to get results. They know who they are."[5] (George, Sims, McClean, Mayer)

- Adaptive Leadership: involves helping employees respond quickly and positively to complex, systemic problems with no easy answers, called "adaptive challenges". Adaptive leaders recognize that solutions reside not in the executive suite but in the collective intelligence of employees at all levels. They ask hard questions, knock people out of their comfort zone, then they manage the resulting distress, creating an environment of high standards and also high support and care.[6] (Heifetz)

- Transformational Leadership: research indicates that this is the most effective yet most difficult form of leadership. It exists when "leaders and followers make each other advance to a higher level of morality and motivation."[7] (MacGregor-Burns) Such leaders "garner trust, respect and admiration from their followers."[8] (Bass) They ensure constant attention to four areas: walking their talk for followers, connecting followers emotionally to the vision, addressing individual needs of followers, and encouraging followers to apply their skills and energy to the cause. Organizations with this type of management achieve results superior to those of other leadership styles.

Notice the words in the defintions above: shared aspirations, motivation, passion, heart, support, care, morality, trust, respect, admiration. Earlier in the century, these would not have been found in management or political literature. Yet as the command and control style became less and less effective for managing in a faster-paced global environment, those skills and attributes became essential because organizations discovered they were too rigid and bureaucratic to respond to the new world. Successfully functioning in the new world requires agile, resilient and engaged people in all organizations. We are not there yet.

Effective Leadership Characteristics, Traits, and Practices

The following are a few select research-based leadership characteristics, traits and practices that yield proven results in business, government and other forms of organization. Because there is such a large quantity of research, I've selected what I believe to be the most critical, and ranked them subjectively.

1. Honest, Competent, Forward-looking, Inspiring:

   In a study conducted roughly every ten years since 1987, business and government executives were asked "what they most look for and admire in a leader; someone whose direction they would *willingly* follow."[9] In thirty years, the four attributes listed above held the top four spots, in that order, every time. In data from North America, Mexico, Western Europe, Asia and Australia, honesty was *always* number one, with 88% of respondents ranking it so. Can you start to see why we have a leadership crisis?

2. Emotional Intelligence:

   This includes self-awareness, self-regulation, social awareness (motivation and empathy) and relationship management.[10] One of the absolute best executive programs in transformational leadership is at INSEAD business school in France. Seasoned CEOs must pass a rigorous series of interviews just to be accepted. The program seeks to develop long-term change in the mindset and behaviour of the executives, and "underscores the illusion of rationality, the challenge of seeing what's happening beyond the level of consciousness, the impact of the past on current behaviours and thinking, the importance of transference…the role of emotions, and the *motivational need systems* important for human functioning."[11] The core exercise for each participant is a life case study, which is discussed and analyzed by the group of peers. Heavy psychological stuff! No business analysis, financials, six sigma or strategy on the agenda; just an intense deep dive into their behaviour, in order to raise awareness of self, and its impact on decisions and people. It's about those 'Soft S's' again. Check out any job description for any company or organization today, and see the emphasis on emotional intelligence skills.

3.   Credibility:

There has been increasing research done on the impact of trust in organizations. It is not rocket science, yet real trust remains rare. In 2017, the Edelman Trust Barometer survey discovered "a staggering lack of confidence in leadership: 71% of survey respondents said government officials are not at all or somewhat credible, and 63% said the same about CEOs. The credibility of CEOs fell by 12 points in 2018, to 37% globally."[12] Pretty serious situation, wouldn't you agree? Credibility is critical to trust, and trust drives loyalty. Frederick Reichheld of Bain & Co. found that "the center of gravity for business loyalty - whether it be the loyalty of customers, employees, investors, suppliers or dealers – is the personal integrity of the senior leadership team and its ability to put its principles into practice."[13] Leadership authors Kouzes and Posner go so far as to declare that "credibility is *the* foundation of leadership".[14] These findings perfectly support those on honesty shown above, and also integrate with emotional intelligence: self-aware people recognize the importance of credibility in relationships with followers.

4.   Purpose and Values:

The INSEAD transformational leadership program spends considerable time exploring the personal purpose and values of participants through their life stories. Why? It has to do with authenticity.

Temet Nosce ('know thyself'). Harvard Professor Bill George found that "Your life story provides the context for your experiences, and through it, you can find the inspiration to make an impact on the world. Leadership emerges from your life story".[14] His research determined that authentic leadership requires a commitment to developing oneself, and to do that, it is imperative to start with defining your own purpose and values. Richard Barrett is known for his work in helping create values-driven organizations. He defined seven levels of consciousness (See p. 166) from basic Survival to Service, and then determined the values that tended to be present at each level. So the highest level, seven, Service, included concern for social responsibility, for future generations, and compassion. Level five included trust, commitment, honesty, integrity, and enthusiasm. The lowest level, Survival, holds values such as financial stability, profit, and employee health. For leaders the trick is to first align their individual values and beliefs with their own actions and behaviours, and then to seek mission alignment with those they lead: "the alignment of an individual's sense of purpose, mission or drivers with the groups (organizations) stated purpose or mission."[16].

Doing so creates what is known as a positive culture in an organization, and a growing body of research indicates that such organizations outperform their competition by large margins.[17] That is because a culture of shared purpose and values generates intrinsic motivation in every employee or member. It's because they come to emotionally care about the outcome of their work.

Try to recall a favorite boss, teacher or mentor in your life, and check to see if they embodied these traits. Were they clear about their purpose? Did they hold and live out values that exceeded mere survival? My sense is that they most likely did.

5. Humility and Will:

It is always fun to read about a study that found results surprising to the the original hypothesis. That was the case in Stanford Professor Jim Collin's blockbuster book *Good to Great*, where he examined leadership traits. Collins, in an attempt to isolate the factors that made a company great, instructed his team to "ignore the executives." But they kept encountering evidence that could not be ignored. To his and his team's surprise, "the good-to-great executives were all cut from the same cloth. It didn't matter whether the company was industrial or consumer, in crisis or steady state, offered services or products…all the good-to-great companies had Level 5 leadership at the time of transition."[18] In his model, Level five is the highest and rarest calibre, and "a study in duality: modest and wilful, humble and fearless." Level five leaders *give credit for successes to their people, yet assume personal responsibility for failures and poor results.* (How many of our current political or business leaders behave like this?) As well, they "act quietly, calmly, and determinedly – relying on inspired standards, not inspired charisma, to motivate."[19] As perhaps the highest compliment to these types of leaders, Collins says, "Good-to-great transformations don't happen without Level 5 leaders at the helm. They just don't." Personal humility and fierce professional will.

6. Vision:

Excellent leaders *have an intense drive to take people to a better place.* American President Franklin Delano Roosevelt (FDR) saw devastation of a country, people in deep distress, a seemingly impossible situation that his predecessor, Herbert Hoover, had neither the vision nor resolve to address. FDR had ideas, and more importantly, the adaptability and persistence to keep trying new ones as others failed. He used vibrant language to paint a picture in words of more propserous times, and used rhetoric and soaring langauge to raise the hopes, dreams and energy of a suffering society: "The only thing we have to fear is fear itself." Vision does not mean take one's place as CEO for the usual three to five year stint, maximize shareholder value (including your own) at the expense of eveything else, and avoid bad press and all risk until taking one's golden parachute and stepping down. It does not mean entering Congress, as former Grand Old Party (GOP) House Speaker, Paul Ryan, did, with a net worth of $365,000, and leaving eight years later with $7 million. Such people leave their organizations the same or worse than they found them. Good leaders foresee a more ideal condition for their organizations, picture incredible possibilities, and generate excitement through the entire organization as a vital influence on the behaviour of all employees. *They identify and work for something larger than themselves.* Good vision creates positive culture, which moves us to better places. In her fabulous book *Leaderhip and the New Science,* Margaret Wheatley compares vision to a scientific field: "recoginze that in creating a vision, we are creating a power, not a place, an influence, not a destination. (People) have picked up the messages, discerned what is truly valued, and then shaped their behaviour accordingly."[20] Where are our visionary leaders today? Some do exist for sure, but are we elevating them to positions of maximum effectivenes? The evidence is sketchy.

7. Challenge the Status Quo:

Because they usually have an emotional and intellectual connection to a vision of a better condition, good leaders tend to reject the status quo and rally others to first understand and then embrace their vision. Henry Ford didn't want a better horse; Elon Musk is passionate about clean energy; inventor Dean Kamen felt deep compassion for war veterans who had lost arms in action, and created an incredible prosthetic.[21] Martin Luther King Jr (MLK) and Robert F. Kennedy (RFK) sensed pursuit of their visions might cost them their lives, yet forged ahead anyway, waking us up in the process.

And they're usually impatient about getting it done. They tend to have what Peters and Waterman called 'a sense of urgency'. In the summer of 2018, a 28-year-old woman from the Bronx, Alexandria Ocasio-Cortez, challenged and unseated the powerful incumbent Democratic Caucus Chair and seven term Representative Joe Crowley for the Democratic nomination. Ms. Ocasio-Cortez said that trips to places like Flint, Michigan, and Standing Rock in North Dakota, left her feeling a deep urge to bring about positive change. Further inspired by a stint with Bernie Sanders' 2016 organizing campaign, she decided to enter the arena herself. Using brilliant social media techniques and incredible energy and enthusiasm, she spent $194,000 of small donor money to defeat Crowley, who spent $3.4 million. Her story is reverberating throughout America right now, energizing her generation to get more politically involved for the causes they care about. Right out of the gate, she is challenging the status quo in bold ways.

Leadership Examples

As mentioned, many studies have identified other valuable attributes of good leadership, but the seven listed above are always present in some form. Keeping them in mind, here are a few profiles of government and business leaders against which to compare. These extreme examples are intended to highlight the different outcomes that can occur when the positive leadership traits are present or absent.

- **Tommy Douglas**: In 2004, CBC television ran a nation-wide survey of viewers, who voted Douglas "The Greatest Canadian" for his role as the father of Universal Healthcare in Canada. As a child, Douglas was spared an unnecessary leg amputation only because an expert surgeon offered to treat him for free provided his students could observe the several surgeries required.

His parents were unable to pay. He retained his leg, and the experience formed his later views on Medicare as an entitlement. While doing his PhD at the University of Chicago, he witnessed firsthand the devastation of the Great Depression on society, again an experience that reinforced his later socially democratic views. Rising to Premier of Saskatchewan in 1944 as leader of the first social democratic government in North America, and after fighting off much opposition from governments, doctors and businesses, he eventually implemented universal healthcare in the province.[22] The successful experiment gradually persuaded critics that it was economically viable and equitable, and the entire country soon followed suit. His persistence in a vision of healthcare as a right, despite fierce opposition and frequent ridicule, benefitted every Canadian citizen of his time and every generation since.

- **George W. Bush**: Following the 9/11 incident, President Bush pushed a concerted attempt to persuade Congress and allied countries that Saddam Hussein in Iraq was connected to al-Qaeda, was developing weapons of mass destruction, was complicit in the 9/11 event, and was planning further attacks on America. All of these claims have since been proven completely false.[23] Yet Bush (influenced by a crew which included Paul Wolfowitz, Richard Perle, Dick Cheney, Donald Rumsfeld, and Condoleeza Rice, and had been determined to invade Iraq even prior to his election) decided to invade Iraq, with no plan for governance post-invasion, launching chaos in the middle east that severely impacts the world today. Labelling it the 'War on Terror', and spending $5.6 trillion on subsequent 'wars' in Afghanistan, Iraq, Libya, Syria, and Pakistan, (none of which have been formally declared), Bush blurred the legal lines of war and torture. Much of the equipment and reconstruction contracts were awarded without tender bid to Defense and other contractors like Halliburton (Cheney was former CEO). Using the situation to justify the restriction of civil rights in America with the Patriot Act, Bush set the stage for the current global refugee crisis, and left the

US in a perpetual state of war. Bush instigated the need for the astonishing $700+ billion annual Defense budget that prevents funding
for badly needed domestic social programs and infrastructure repair.
A recent Forbes[24] report (other mainstream media failed to cover
it) revealed that the Pentagon, which failed the first ever general
accounting audit in 2018, *could not account for $21 trillion since
2001!* Never did Bush stop to ask why America was so hated that
people would be willing to blow themselves up to attack it? There are
a growing number of critics who believe that the real reason behind
the War on Terror lies in an unstated imperialist American strategy. I
adhere to that theory. Regardless, the actions of Bush and his administration have played a major part in creating the turmoil we face in
the world today. A CBS News ranking placed Bush at 33 out of 45;
the twelfth worst President of the US.[25]

• **Herb Kelleher**: founder and former CEO of Southwest Airlines, was
  a proponent of the power of people well before it became mainstream. He recognized that his strategy to be the lowest fare airline depended upon high productivity, and that that could only be
  consistently achieved with a highly motivated workforce. His own
  personality traits of humour, humility and obsessive customer focus
  infected all employees, and he became a legendary figure. Passing
  through airports he was known to have jumped behind the ticket
  counter to tag bags and help customers if his staff were backed up.
  Kelleher believed that work should be fun, and that treating people
  with dignity and respect was a must.

  During his forty years as CEO or Chairman, Kelleher built the successful no-frills service airline that many others around the world
  copied. His goal was to make air travel available to the average
  person, and he created a culture among employees that customers
  found most comforting. But his 'softness' did not preclude stellar
  performance; rather it enabled it. Despite the periods when volatile
  fuel costs ravaged the entire industry, Southwest plugged along to

become the fourth largest airline in the US, with thirty consecutive profitable years, something no other airline has even come close to achieving. Shareholder returns for the same period were almost double those of the S&P 500, and Southwest's market capitalization grew to exceed that of the remaining American airlines combined. An incredible track record especially for such a long-tenured CEO.[26] His advice to aspiring young leaders? "Be humble; work harder than anyone else; serve your people. Your spirit is the most powerful thing of all."[27] Kelleher is widely considered to be among the top echelon of business leaders.

- **Martin Winterkorn**: the 2015 scandal at Volkswagen occurred on the watch of CEO Martin Winterkorn. Upon his selection as CEO in 2007, Winterkorn set an ambitious vision for VW to become the world's largest auto manufacturer. While a laudable goal, it is said that his style created an extreme pressure on employees to avoid failure and meet growth targets. The most important market for growth was the US, which led to engineers installing software that would 'fool' the emissions testing machines in California. Although initially the company did almost double global annual sales to 10 million cars, and $225 billion, the cheating software was discovered in 2015, and both VW and Winterkorn were eventually indicted. The scandal has cost VW $2.8 billion in fines, and an estimated $20 billion in costs to retrofit vehicles and compensate owners.[28] Winterkorn stepped down as CEO.

An engineer by education, he was known internally at VW as a competent and respected manager. But his autocratic, authoritarian style is said to have created a culture of fear and intimidation. It was well known that he did not tolerate failure. A senior labour official on VW's supervisory board said afterward, "We need in future a climate in which problems aren't hidden but can be openly communicated to superiors. We need a culture in which it's possible and permissible to argue with your superior about the best way to go."[29]

Winterkorn has been described as a micromanager, strong in the command and control style, but likely deficient in the leadership skills of emotional intelligence. The VW case is unfortunate, because Winterkorn had the courage to embark on the challenge of being the largest in the world. What he failed to recognize was that in leadership, *how* goals are achieved matters too. That oversight cost him his job, and reputation, and severely damaged the brand image of VW. In April 2019 the German government charged Mr. Winterkorn with fraud related to the diesel emissions issue.

- **Winston Churchill**: Few political leaders can be described as "the saviour of their country",[30] but few disagree in the case of Winston Churchill. And in a way, had Britain collapsed to the Nazis, the result could have been a much different and horrific world. His many famous speeches have been repeated countless times over the decades, and he is remembered for his fierce will and determination, and reassuring optimism during the darkest days of the war. And yet, Churchill as a younger man was mostly responsible for a disastrous attack campaign against Turkey in the Dardanelles, during WWI. The battles at Gallipoli lasted nine months until allied forces retreated in January 1916 having failed to achieve their objective, and incurring 46,000 deaths and 220,000 casualties. Although Churchill always maintained that the effort saved millions of lives that otherwise may have been lost, most historians see it differently. The slaughter at Gallipoli matched that of the Western Front; waves of men senselessly sent into machine gunfire for no real gain, and due to a rigid strategy that failed to take changing realities into account.

This event, often referred to as 'Churchill's Folly', haunted him for his entire life. But at that time, he demonstrated resilience by eventually accepting responsibility, leaving his high post to go lead a battalion on the dangerous Western Front, and later resurfacing to lead Britain through WWII. As an aristocrat in those times, there was no pressure on him to assume any role of real responsibility, yet his personal ambition and love of country drove him to do so. His courage and intense commitment gained him trust and credibility with the public, and loyalty and cooperation during the most difficult of times. The Gallipoli experience helped him with humility, and to reflect on the meaning of responsibility, especially for the lives of others in his charge. By the time he was elected Prime Minister in 1940, he was sufficiently self-aware to declare "all my past life has been a preparation for this hour and for this trial".[31] Churchill's emotional intelligence and earlier experiences left him a shrewd judge of character, able to ease American President Franklin Delano Roosevelt (FDR) into the war, and later, recognize Stalin's deceptive post-war plans, and take steps to corral his expansionist ambitions.

Perhaps Churchill's greatest talent was his ability to inspire. Time Magazine wrote, "He best personified the type of leadership Britain needed during WWII; a larger-than-life figure who pronounced dreams of victory when all seemed lost."[32]

- **Stephen Harper:** In May 2011, Canada's flawed 'first-past-the-post' electoral system resulted in Stephen Harper's re-election as Prime Minister of Canada, gaining a 100% majority government from only 39.62% of the popular vote. With this majority, Canada's twenty-second PM embarked on a four-year term of secrecy, disdain for other parties, disregard for parliamentary law and procedure, scandal and corruption. Although his government's initial election in 2006 resulted largely from a public knee-jerk response to a corrupt Liberal government, Harper's Conservatives quickly erased the Liberal's $13 billion surplus, and ended his two terms with a $1.5 billion deficit. At a time in 2008, when Canada could have stepped forward on the world stage as a balanced stable country that had largely avoided the global financial meltdown, Harper ran the country as a dictator, with a litany of governmental abuses too long to list here. A few notables: he reversed investment in Canada's high tech programs, reverting the country to a resource driven economy at the time when oil and other commodity prices hit all time lows. He reneged on climate change initiatives to which Canada had committed. Prior to his second election, his party engaged in 'robo-calls' to opposition voters, giving incorrect instruction on voting booths. He spent $500 million of taxpayer money on pre-election advertisements for his government, muzzled scientists on climate change, illegally spied on environmental and indigenous activists, and 'prorogued' (shut down) parliament to avoid non-confidence votes when he held a minority position and when the opposition was investigating scandals.[33]

Harper brought an arrogant and autocratic attitude to the job, tightly controlling how party members could vote, and strengthening the Prime Minister's Office (PMO) to wield far more power than a parliamentary system permits. Following nine years of Harper 'rule', many Canadians felt that the Harper government had taken the country backwards in many areas of world status, and the 2015 election saw the Conservative party suffer a massive defeat, causing Harper to resign as Prime Minister and also as leader of the party.

"I would say it has been an unmitigated disaster. I don't think we've ever had a prime minister who's failed to articulate, to the extent this one has, a vision of the country. He's essentially ruled the country as a CEO and given Canadians zero inspiration. I would be hard-pressed to find one moment where Harper has made us feel proud of Canada."[34]

- **Louis Gerstner Jr.:** In 1993, International Business Machines (IBM), lost $8 billion; a whopping sum even by today's standards. Since it's 1911 inception, IBM had grown to become the leviathan of the computer industry. But as with all things successful, human nature is such that complacency eventually sets in, the eye comes off the ball, and the mighty can fall. The search for a saviour CEO resulted, second time around, in persuading Nabisco CEO Lou Gerstner Jr to accept the monumental turnaround task. Where he at first felt he lacked the technical expertise to tackle the problem, he eventually realized that his experiences as CEO of American Express, a huge IBM customer, gave him valuable perspective. Gerstner was a 'numbers guy': engineer and MBA, former McKinsey consultant, and an expert manager. Upon his arrival at IBM, he faced an already-underway program to break up the company and sell off some of the smaller businesses. After intense full-time travelling in the field for his first few months, listening to and gathering feedback from IBM top performers in all departments, Gerstner made the gutsy decision (which he later referred to as the most important of his entire career) to keep the company together, but shift its strategy and change the culture from an insular bureaucracy, to a market-driven, customer obsessed, IT services consultant and integrator. He realized that while IBM still offered value as a hardware and software developer and supplier, its greatest value-add to clients was its deep expertise in IT systems, integration and problem solving. Yet this transformation required a massive shift in culture; no easy task. "Until I came to IBM, I probably would have told you that culture was just one among several important elements in any organization's makeup and success – along with vision, strategy, marketing, financials, and the like. I came to see, in my time at IBM, that culture isn't just one aspect of the game; it *is* the game. In the end, an organization is nothing more than the collective capacity of its people to create value."[35] On the management side, Gerstner changed the incentive bonus and the promotion criteria, to reward collaboration and information sharing, as opposed to individual performance and hording. As a leader, he realized an intense and relentless communication effort would be required to explain the What and Why of the transformation, engage people in the effort, and support them in the difficult early years.

"Changing the attitude and behavior of thousands of people is very, very hard to accomplish," Gerstner writes. "You can't simply give a couple of speeches or write a new credo for the company and declare that a new culture has taken hold. You can't mandate it, can't engineer it. What you can do is create the conditions for transformation, provide incentives."[36]

On Gerstner's departure from IBM nine years later in 2002, the company generated an $8 billion profit, was solidly repositioned in the market as an important IT player once again, and most importantly, had embraced a culture that would allow it to thrive in a much faster paced world. In his words, he had "taught the elephant to dance."[37]

- **John Stumpf:** Wells Fargo Bank was cited by Jim Collins in his bestseller *Good to Great,* as one of those companies, that, beginning in 1983, began a transition to great performance largely based upon an obsession with hiring the very best people, and the discipline to face the realities of new bank deregulation. By 1998, one dollar invested in Wells Fargo in 1983 appreciated to $74, against a general stock market appreciation of $20, and a comparator Bank of America growth of $16.[38] Very impressive, and much of the performance was credited to CEO Carl Reichardt. The company was so impressive that the shrewd Warren Buffett took a 9% ownership position. In 1998, Wells Fargo merged with another bank, Norwest, that has been credited with the invention of aggressive product cross-selling to customers. John Stumpf came with the merger, and rose to become Chairman and CEO of the new Wells Fargo in January 2010. In 2011, the LA Times reported stories of intense pressure on line employees to meet sometimes impossible sales targets. The aggressive sales culture, in addition to creating health issues for employees, resulted in 3.5 million fraudulent accounts of deposit, checking, and credit cards, and often involved employees moving client's money from account to account without the customer's permission, or knowledge of their existence. It should be noted that in 2012, 54% of Stumpf's $22 million pay package was impacted by company share price. After negative press from the Wall Street Journal and LA Times continued, the Consumer Financial Protection Bureau investigated and levied a $185 million fine, although I've yet to read the amount of revenues generated by the 2 million fraudulent accounts. Stumpf's initial response was to blame the line and branch employees, firing 5300 people, and a refusal to resign. But by October 2016 he had agreed to forfeit $41 million of his pay packages related to the term, and resigned as Chairman and CEO. His tenure as leader resulted in, among other things, the Federal Reserve placing asset growth restrictions on Wells Fargo until the Fed was satisfied the bank had implemented the proper controls to prevent future abuses, and the departure of large customers such as the states of California, Seattle and Illinois, and many cities and municipalities.

What did you think of these leadership stories? Were you able to detect a pattern between the proven traits and characteristics, and the leaders whose work you admired? While the research is ongoing, reliable and valid correlations between leadership attributes and organizational effectiveness are increasingly being identified.

We get things done through our organizations and institutions, and leaders deeply impact organizations and institutions in major direct and indirect ways. Consider the implications of a culture where fear of the 'messenger being shot' permeates (e.g. Volkswagen), versus one where people are vying with each other in a healthy way to contribute their best ideas, because loyalty to and the expectations of their leaders encourage it (e.g. Southwest Airlines). Which institution will generate better results?

So far, we've looked at how leadership organically evolved; at how developments in government, commerce, and science influenced our definitions and expectations of leaders and followers. We've checked out the latest research and facts about what constitutes effective leadership, and we've seen some examples of outcomes, given varying levels of leadership proficiency. You might ask, what is so different today from past decades, or even centuries, that portends a leadership crisis? The answer lies partially in old Abe's admonition about character and power. When Caesar reached a certain level of power, he came to believe he transcended the value of institutions, as did Napoleon, as does Putin, Trudeau, and Trump, to give but a few examples. When leaders seek, for their own agendas, to undermine or destroy the institutions they lead, and in which we must trust for integrity, society becomes imperiled. "The most ominous danger we face comes from the marginalization and destruction of institutions, including the courts, academia, legislative bodies, cultural organizations, and the press, that once ensured that civil discourse was rooted in reality and fact, helped us distinguish lies from truth, and facilitate justice."[39]

This is happening today, but with one simple yet indisputable difference: humankind now faces the threat to its very existence: in climate change, in use of nuclear and biological weapons, in the development and abuse of AI. Poor leadership decisions in the past had tragic yet *finite* consequences. Millions of dead and damaged soldiers and civilians in world wars were the horrific result of unfortunate decisions made in 1914, 1938, 1963 (Vietnam escalation) but afterwards, families reunited, new generations grew up, economic and social progress returned. This is different; the decisions our global leaders take at this unprecedented cross-road can have irreversible, terminal consequences for the human race. Therein lies our crisis.

And yet, at a time when trust and transparency between leaders and their followers is most desperately needed, when a concerted international effort of collaborative discussion, planning and action are most urgent, we are moving in the opposite direction. Leaders, particularly a toxically partisan executive branch and Congress in the US, are quietly passing legislation in the name of national security that dangerously impinges on human freedoms (the Patriot Act, reversal of Net Neutrality, Citizen's United). Nationalist movements in Britain, France, former eastern bloc countries, and even in Germany, promote isolationism, xenophobia, and racism. Although public awareness has just lately started to shift, the societal frog continues to boil. A public obsessed with the daily dramas of the Kardashians ignores or shrugs off their government's separation of immigrant children from their parents, and incarceration in cages in camps. It is not just Americans; people everywhere can name winners of *'Whichever-Country's' Got Talent*, yet remain oblivious to the civilian murder and destruction in Yemen. Leaders globally have taken advantage of the detached boiling frog to forge and install their own agendas. Demagogues return, corruption in government results in laws that channel wealth, and consequently power, to a tiny 0.1% of the population. Meanwhile, the middle class diminishes, the percentage of the poor grows, and when we do think about it at all, we delude ourselves that we are still living free in a democracy.

To convince you of that, we need to examine what went wrong in the last century.

CHAPTER 3

What Went Wrong?

"Power tends to corrupt; and absolute power corrupts absolutely"
Lord Acton

RECENTLY, I WATCHED AN INTERVIEW OF A MAN WHO HAD allegedly left the mafia to live a law-abiding life. (I didn't think they let you do that either.) His father had been a capo in the mob, and the man, Michael Franzese, 67, was asked his opinion about government corruption in his father's and his own earlier times, versus today. He replied, "no comparison"; that earlier corruption was always present in varying amounts, but that today it is more widespread and generally accepted than even he can believe. Sadly, we should not at all be surprised.

So what did go wrong? Many, many things, and it's difficult and simplistic to reduce them all into one specific cause. But was I forced to do so, I'd submit that the underlying cause has been the gradual erosion of trust in our leaders and institutions, and that erosion is a result of the quality and actions of our recent leaders. Despite brilliant science, advances in medicine, complex economic models, even our rule of law, everything in our society is based upon trust. What is fiat currency? Simply a promise to honor a piece of paper or digital unit as being worth a certain value. It's based on trust in the issuer. Rule of law has both the letter and the spirit, and we trust our appointed judges to apply both with wisdom, justice, and fairness. We trust in the competency and compassion of our doctors. Commercial brands are simply promises in which we trust: in the 1980s we trusted Japanese cars for reliability and value – American cars, not so much.

Recall the famous Charles Schultz *Peanuts* cartoon, where Lucy continuously promises Charlie Brown that she won't pull the football away as he kicks, yet always does so. Our trust is created by our experiences, and when

they're predominately positive, when people generally deliver on what they promise, they earn our trust, and we will usually cut them some slack in difficult times when things don't go well for them. Leadership research shows we admire and follow people we trust, because they earn it.

In his brilliant book, *The Speed of Trust,* Stephen M.R. Covey suggests trust has four main components, each of which are in play in any relationship: Intent and Integrity (which he says are Character based) and Capability and Results, (which are Competence based).[1] Ranking each of the four yields the degree to which we will trust someone or an organization, and obviously affects our attitudes and actions with them. Choose any one of the leader profiles listed in the previous chapter, and apply this model to their story. Its effect on our relationships becomes apparent. Covey also demonstrates the cost of trust to businesses and societies, showing the inverse relationship between trust and cost, and between trust and time required to accomplish projects.

Trust in our leaders and institutions have eroded, particularly over the past 100 years. Again, I suggest that erosion is caused by a combination of public apathy in democracies, and in communist and dictatorship countries, a life of fear and intimidation caused by oppressive leaders. But any apathy has been created in large part by repeated failure of leaders to deliver on their promises. In the Western world, politicians have come to be tolerated as necessary annoyances. Cynicism, particularly among the young, is embedded and widespread. People have decided, 'I'm not going to fall for that old football trick again. Get lost!'

And yet, deep within there remains a yearning. We *want* to trust; but only in people who are true leaders. Recall Obama's Audacity of Hope campaign, and the excitement it generated. View videos of Bernie Sanders' rallies during the 2016 Democratic Primary. People still hope.

To get a sense of what went wrong, we need to examine why and how trust has disappeared, and a good place to start is at the turn of the nineteenth century, with the Gilded Age.

"The Bosses of the Senate" (1889). Reformers like the cartoonist Joseph Keppler depicted the Senate as controlled by the giant moneybags, who represented the nation's financial trusts and monopolies.

In the late nineteenth century, America and Europe experienced what was known as the Second Industrial Revolution. Author Jeremy Rifkin posits that whenever there is a simultaneous, step-function technological shift in three key areas – energy, communication, and transportation/logistics – we experience a revolution in society; the clichéd 'paradigm shift'.[2] According to Rifkin, in the First Industrial Revolution, the invention of wind and water power led to unprecedented improvements in productivity, and "a new force of small-manufacturing entrepreneurs" that eventually displaced the guilds, and shifted society away from a feudal economy "structured around proprietary obligations, to a market economy, which was structured around property rights."[3] Water power was soon deployed as steam in engines that allowed the invention of trains, textile mills, and heavy steel production among other things. Railroads revolutionized travel in scope, cost and time, the benefits of which all flowed into economic growth. The invention and explosion across Europe of the printing press in 1436 was the communication marvel that had positive implications far too numerous to explore here; but just the ability to mass produce books and legal contracts accelerated the pace of government and business. And when steam was applied to printing presses, literacy actually grew due to the availability of cheap printed matter.

Wind and water power, printing presses, and better roads, railroads and steam powered boats all radically changed the world from the fifteenth to the eighteenth century.

Jump ahead to the late nineteenth century, and we again witnessed a similar leap through technology in those three sectors: the Second Industrial Revolution. As Rifkin says, "the discovery of oil, the invention of the internal combustion engine, and the introduction of the telephone gave rise to a new communication/energy/transportation complex that would dominate the twentieth century."[4]

It is the parallels between the Second Industrial Revolution and today that are most striking, so we need to look back at what happened then. The collective impact of those three inventions (again, somewhat oversimplifying) drove a migration of rural agricultural workers into the fast growing cities for manufacturing work. Industrious, intelligent businessmen like Andrew Carnegie (steel), Cornelius Vanderbilt (railroads), John D. Rockefeller (oil), John Jacob Astor (real estate), Henry Frick (railroads), William Clark (copper),

J. Pierpont Morgan and Andrew Mellon (Finance) and many others, saw the possibilities in advance, and moved quickly to capitalize on the new economy. While often since vilified for their cutthroat tactics, it is fair to recall that at that time, because there had never been any precedent, there were few if any laws prohibiting most of their monopolistic activities. Much of what they did was, if unethical, not necessarily illegal. It was simply unharnessed free-market capitalism at its best and worst. Nevertheless, their brutal suppression of smaller competitors, their purchase of corrupt politicians, and their heartless exploitation of immigrants, child laborers, and employees, soon resulted in an American oligarchy of a couple of dozen ultra-wealthy families. "It was a period where greedy, corrupt industrialists, bankers and politicians enjoyed extraordinary wealth and opulence at the expense of the working class. In fact, it was wealthy tycoons, not politicians, who inconspicuously held the most political power during the Gilded Age."[5]

Any of this sound familiar? The Third Industrial Revolution, according to Rifkin, is now well underway, with radical new technologies driving ferocious change in communication (the Internet, Internet of Things, Mobile), energy (sustainable low or near-zero cost wind, solar, geo-thermal, and other forms of power), and transportation (self-driving trucks and cars, smart roads, delivery drones, robots, etc.).

The prescient entrepreneurs who acted first to create and capitalize on the new technologies were also rewarded with staggering wealth: Bill Gates, Jeff Bezos, Larry Ellison, Steve Jobs, Mark Zuckerberg, Elon Musk, Sergei Brin and Larry Page, Jack Ma, Carlos Slim, and Mukesh Ambani are just a start. These are our new oligarchs. It is unlikely, because of current legislation, that they are as blatantly ruthless or corrupt as their Gilded Age counterparts, so perhaps should not be labelled negatively; but they still wield enormous clout with both local and federal politicians in their respective countries, and some are known to follow regressive employment and competition policies.

But there is another subtle difference with this revolution. Those in the Gilded Age may be partially excused for their bad behaviour due to the fact that they were the first to experience such an explosive growth phenomenon; it all happened so quickly that the law fell behind the pace of change. It was a Wild West of activity with many unknowns. No one had 'been there, done that' before. Not so today. Fool me once shame on you; fool me twice shame on me. We today have forgotten and/or ignored the lessons learned from the Gilded Age. With the election of Teddy Roosevelt in 1901, the US found a leader with an agenda greater than his own wealth and power. What did he do? With the help of the press (labelled 'muckrakers' for their efforts to expose the corruption and illegal behaviour of the Robber Barons), Roosevelt determined that the monopolies, called Trusts, were damaging to democracy and the public, and proceeded to break them up, starting with Rockefeller's enormous Standard Oil.

Income inequality was such that a few super wealthy citizens continued to gain while the majority of workers and their families lived in disgusting tenements and slums in the cities, working outrageous hours in unsafe conditions.[6] Roosevelt implemented restraints to the power and influence of the elite wealthy, and also made positive changes in the areas of labour reform, fair labour standards and unions, tax reform, women's suffrage, election reform and food and medicine regulations. By the time America entered into WWI in 1917, Roosevelt's Progressive Movement (though his term ended in 1909) had restored a healthier balance of power between government and wealthy corporate moguls. Standards of living improved considerably and the public perceived a higher level of fairness in society.

So it can be said that at least partially due to quality leadership, America recognized and remedied a severely imbalanced and dangerous social situation, caused by unchecked capitalism, restoring some semblance of fairness and balance, and creating a better quality of life for the average citizen. We made it out of the mess. But not for long.

Geopolitically, after WWI, a group of well-intended yet somewhat arrogant and naïve allied victors, led by America's Woodrow Wilson, Britain's Lloyd George, and France's Georges Clemenceau, undertook to create and ratify the Treaty of Versailles, and equally important, to carve up Europe and the Middle East into what they saw as a more equitable map, especially for their empires. Through Wilson's Fourteen Points, they honorably attempted to recognize the national rights of sovereign nations that had been previously conquered or annexed. They established the League of Nations in an effort to prevent future catastrophic wars. While what happened in Paris in 1919 had many serious repercussions for the future of the world, three things are pertinent to this book: 1) the austere punitive terms of the treaty fomented extreme bitterness and resentment among Germans, and planted the seed for the rise of the tyrant, Hitler, 2) they quickly realized that nationalism was still deeply felt among even the smallest of countries, and that racial animosities would only be fueled in future, and 3) they arbitrarily decided "the establishment in Palestine of a national home for the Jewish people…"[7] This was done despite protests from the Palestinian people, many of whom were displaced by the mandate. For our purposes, it set the stage for the seemingly insoluble political issue that exists to this day.

America became richer and more powerful on the world stage following WWI, but it is since WWII that it not only rose to supreme dominance, but also sought global hegemony.[8] As the only major country to emerge from the war economically and militarily strong, it was able to influence policy, setting up the global financial system still in use, and the North Atlantic Treaty Organization (NATO), an alliance against the Soviet Union. Following the 1991 collapse of the Soviet Union, the US did not pull back from any of the seventy countries in which it had previously established 800 military bases.[9]

It can be fairly claimed that the trust of the 'following' public in their leaders post-WWII was quite high. FDR was revered, having died while in office fighting for victory over the Nazis, General Eisenhower was eventually elected president, Churchill was lionized in Britain. Big corporations had stepped up to deliver quality armaments in time for victory. Scientists had developed the atomic bomb that supposedly saved the day. These leaders had delivered upon the expectations of the public, and were celebrated, as people exhaled and returned gratefully to peacetime.

In Chapter 1, it was asked what happens if a set of assumptions and beliefs upon which our expectations rest turn out to be false? For example, it was generally accepted by western societies after WWII, that they needed to adopt a defensive strategy to stem Soviet communist expansionism. It was the stated intent of most democratic governments, especially the US, and there was plenty of evidence to justify the strategy. But what about after the collapse of the Soviet Union? There was no longer a rationale for huge defense budgets, yet the US continued to expand and spend. We believed and trusted government in their defense against communism; we did not trust their rationale for invading Iraq. From our belief in economic theory, to belief in the motives of a government, a corporate sector, and intelligence agencies, I contend that this is where we went wrong: *what our leaders ask us to believe and what is true are often at odds, yet we only recently have started to question it.*

Beginning in the 1950's, a series of signature events has served to erode public trust, sow seeds of apathy, and reflects an agenda of our leaders that is often not what it purports to be. It is why I believe we are experiencing a leadership crisis.

Let's take a brief walk through some of what I believe are the most critical events that brought us to our 2018 situation. It's beyond the scope of this book to attempt to determine *how* or *why* these things happened, but rather to simply state factually *what* has happened. You will draw your own conclusions.

Try to view the events within the context of the relationship between leaders and their societies, and the impact of those events on trust. Did the actions and explanations strengthen or weaken trust in the leaders?

- January, 1961. Dwight Eisenhower gave a speech[10] warning of the dangers of what he called the Military Industrial Complex, and the possibility of their gaining undue influence and power over governments and the people. The current Defense budget in the US exceeds $700 billion *annually*, and the sum of the defense budgets of the next seven largest countries.

- The US, with an understandable concern about the spread of communism, established military presence in West Germany, South Korea, and Europe among other places, as a deterrent to Soviet aggression. Using Stalin and his drastic tactics as proof of tyranny, the western governments convinced the public that communism must be avoided at all costs. The Cold War began.

- Wartime Office of Strategic Services (OSS) morphed into the Central Intelligence Agency (CIA) and began covert operations around the world to protect against communism and guard other US interests, interfering in Iran's government in 1953 to overthrow elected Prime Minister Mosaddegh, and install the puppet Shah Pahlavi. At the time, Mosaddegh was opposed to Britain's harsh demands regarding oil, and nationalised the Iranian oil industry. The CIA would later meddle in the political affairs of Guatemala, Cuba, Chile, Nicaragua, Venezuela, and others, helping to topple legitimate governments, and even participating in murders. This was done in complete secrecy, under the assumptions that any action to protect against communism was justified (e.g. McCarthyism and the House Un-American Activities Committee of 1953-55).

- 1963, after firing CIA chief Allen Dulles for the botched Bay of Pigs Cuban invasion, and alarmed by the military's cavalier attitude toward the use of nuclear weapons, President John F. Kennedy (JFK) became highly distrusting of the military and the CIA, and decided to begin recall of the 'advisers' in Vietnam. Some historians believe this was an indication of his intent to exit the war, though it is hotly contested.[11] Regardless, JFK was removed from office shortly after. If you believe the Warren Commission's 'Oswald as lone gunman theory', you can access the reams of recently available and credible research.[12] The Warren Commission did much to damage public trust in government leaders, as almost no one believed their report. The Commission included Allen Dulles.

- The Vietnam War escalated under President Lyndon B. Johnson (LBJ), causing deep rifts among the public, particularly with students who disagreed with the draft, and with the government's stated 'domino theory' motive for war. Civil unrest spread over the war; civil rights, women's rights, and what many saw as oppressive laws against freedom of speech. The military industrial complex owners became extremely wealthy.

  In the 1970s, with many of the idealistic dreams and hopes of the 60s since dashed, and disillusioned by untimely and mysterious deaths of Martin Luther King Jr. (MLK) and 1968 presidential candidate Robert F. Kennedy (RFK), and the ongoing Vietnam war, a Boomer generation experienced the Watergate scandal and eventual resignation of President Richard Nixon. With the help of the media, government lies and cover-ups came to the light of day. The 1973-74 oil crisis, caused when the Organization of the Petroleum Exporting Countries (OPEC) placed an oil embargo on the US for supporting Israel, highlighted American vulnerability regarding oil supply, and impacted policy as a national security issue. The 1980s witnessed the Iran-Contra Affair in the Reagan government, where the CIA illegally sold weapons to Iran to gain funds to support rebel groups attempting to overthrow the Nicaraguan government. Documents later released showed a cover-up to protect Reagan, and the phrase "post-truth politics" was coined.[13]

- Capitalism in the 1980s prompted the line 'greed is good' from Michael Douglas' character Gordon Gekko in the movie *Wall Street*.[14] By this time, the western approach to business was primarily quantitative, where assets were simply assessed for market value as either a whole company, or as parts to be spun off. MBA degrees had flooded the business sector, and particularly Wall Street, where the notorious and outrageous bonuses were implemented. Mergers and acquisitions, and leveraged buyouts (the most famous of which at the time was RJR Nabisco) became the plays of the day, driven by greed, debt, and power. The early versions of hedge funds and private equity firms were companies like Kohlberg Kravis Roberts (KKR), Drexel Burnham Lambert, and Bain Capital. The financial services sector grew in size and clout, as a percentage of the total economy, from 2.8% of Gross Domestic Product (GDP) in 1950, to 4.9% in 1980, and 8.3% in 2006, when their antics almost destroyed the world economy in 2008.[15]

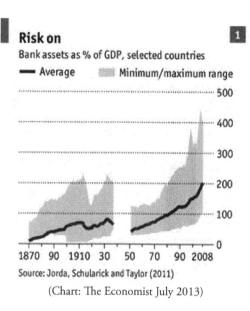

Risk on

Bank assets as % of GDP, selected countries

━━ Average   ▨ Minimum/maximum range

Source: Jorda, Schularick and Taylor (2011)

(Chart: The Economist July 2013)

- During the 80s, another trend began which has contributed greatly to our current leadership dilemma: the cozying-up of the three sectors of government, business, and the media. In the Gilded Age, the 'Muckrakers' like Ida Tarbell and Lincoln Steffens wrote powerful articles that helped Teddy Roosevelt gain public support for his progressive policies. Later, Woodward and Bernstein played a dogged and risky role in exposing the Watergate scandal. While the press has been guilty of many sins (William Randolph Hearst's yellow journalism, tabloid newspapers), the so-called Fourth Estate has historically played a very important role in framing issues to help the public to understand, in exposing corruption and scandal in government and business, and raising awareness of otherwise ignored important issues. They played to some degree the role of protector of the public; foil of tyrants. Yet for the past thirty years, we have seen global consolidation of television, cable, newspapers and entertainment media into giant oligopolies (eight huge conglomerates now own the vast majority of US television and entertainment media)[16] and an increasing tendency towards political bias and corporate interference. The Internet has enabled a disturbing increase in the proliferation of 'fake news'. Where before there was a relatively healthy separation and independence between government, business and media, we currently see a revolving door of people moving from government posts into lobbying firms representing corporate interests, and into the media as talking heads, and then back into government.[17] Both the Obama and Trump administrations are filled with former Wall Street alumni (especially Goldman Sachs). Corporations spend $2.6 billion annually lobbying in Washington.[17] Jeff Stein of the Washington Post notes: "Ten years after the financial crisis brought the U.S. economy to its knees, about 30 percent of the lawmakers and 40 percent of the senior staff who crafted Congress' response have gone to work for or on behalf of the financial industry".[18] This dangerous alliance is quietly dismantling decades of democratic progress while the unsuspecting, distracted public sleeps. It is quietly turning up the heat on the frog.

Later we will examine the serious issue of income inequality and its effect on world events. Two important triggers of that trend occurred in 1999, when President Clinton repealed key elements of the 1933 Glass-Steagall Act, passed after the Great Depression to prevent future abuses by Wall Street that could again endanger the public. The changes carried in the Gramm-Leach Bliley Act, reversed Glass-Steagall, and allowed mixed ownership of commercial, investment banks, brokerages and insurance companies, and kicked off the merger spree and reckless financial activities of the next seven years. The second major trigger was the Commodity Futures Modernization Act, passed by Clinton in 2000, which exempted derivatives from government regulation. Derivatives represented a major risk, and caused the 2008 financial meltdown. Texas Senator

Phil Gramm was the driving force behind both Acts. He left the Senate in 2002 to take a high level job at UBS bank, and opened his own Washington lobbying firm, Gramm Partners.[19] His wife Wendy Lee was head of, you guessed it, the Commodity Futures Trading Commission, under Reagan.

- In 2001 energy monolith Enron filed for bankruptcy and stunned the public with their illegal accounting practices. Their bankruptcy caused the instant collapse of Arthur Andersen, one of the most prestigious audit and accounting firms in the world. Soon after, Worldcom, a giant telecom company, also went under, with the CEO convicted of accounting fraud. Both failures were caused by and typical of the attitudes and mindset of many leaders in a deregulated capitalist system and fed public cynicism about big business and corruption and lax government oversight.

- The late 90s and early 2000s saw the explosion of the internet as the newest and most powerful medium, shifting power away from traditional news and entertainment media behemoths, and allowing infinite opinions and viewpoints to be posted. Services like Google and Wikipedia offered free content for those interested in learning about issues. The arrival of the mobile smart phone in 2007 expanded accessibility even further. The power of the Internet as a tool for public awareness and education has prompted fierce lobbying efforts to gain control by Bell, Rogers and Shaw in Canada, Comcast, AT&T, and Verizon in the US. The issue of Net Neutrality should be one of, if not *the* most important of our day, due to its empowering ability to let us speak to each other, spread truth, and mobilize to demand positive change. In 2017, under the 'leadership' of former Verizon lawyer lobbyist Ajit Pai, the FCC repealed the net neutrality laws set in place by the Obama administration, ignoring 99.7%[20] of hundreds of thousands of citizen's comments against the move.

- The 9/11 tragedy is rife with disagreement about who, what and why, with more and more facts coming forward from credible people. A film I found most interesting is *Architects and Engineers for 9/11 Truth*, and I strongly encourage everyone to see it prior to forming their final opinion. The official 9/11 Committee Report "avoided even mentioning the complete, symmetrical, and rapid collapse of WTC 7, although that collapse was unprecedented in the 100-plus-year history of steel-framed skyscrapers."[21]

Regardless of how 9/11 occurred, one certain fact is that the Bush Administration used it as justification to invade Iraq. Using false information about weapons of mass destruction (WMD) to garner UN and other support, the US went in with no backup plan for post-invasion governance, and created far-reaching negative repercussions in the entire region, while spending at least $2 trillion and costing thousands of lives. The military industrial complex of which we were forewarned by Eisenhower flourished, and the move initiated the 'War on Terror' that guarantees ongoing conflict (and hence MIC revenues), and spawned the Patriot Act as an excuse to restrict human rights. Once again a false premise by American and British leaders served to damage trust among their populations.

- Perhaps the biggest recent betrayal of public trust by government and business leaders peaked in 2008 with the global financial meltdown of that year. Since deregulation in 1999 and 2000, mergers of financial institutions exploded. Actually, *before* the repeal of Glass-Steagall, Citibank CEO Sanford Weill audaciously merged Citibank with Traveller's Insurance Group, despite its illegality. He already knew from his Washington contacts that it would be blessed after the fact. He was right: Clinton's Secretary of Treasury (and a former co-chair of Goldman Sachs) Robert Rubin worked hard to push through the repeal, then left Treasury to accept a job with the new Citigroup, earning over $100 million as an adviser during the next ten years.[22] Following the mergers, the mega-banks began using securitized sub-prime mortgages as part of what is called a collateralized debt obligation (CDO), which essentially shifted risk away from the banks and onto investors and taxpayers. The CDOs were rated by supposedly independent rating agencies like Standard & Poors, Moody's and Fitch, that were paid big sums by the banks to rate the CDOs softly. The term 'moral hazard' refers to the practices of bankers to enrich themselves through reckless risky decisions, because of the realization that should all things collapse, the government would have no choice but to bail the banks out. This introduced a new level of negligence and corruption, and is exactly what came to pass. As homeowners who never should have received mortgages began the inevitable defaults, the credit markets froze and we risked another Great Depression. So the government issued the troubled assets relief program (TARP) and loaned $700 billion to the very banks that had created the catastrophe. These banks – JP Morgan Chase, Goldman Sachs Citibank, Bank of America, Wells Fargo, and Morgan Stanley – were considered too big to fail at that time, yet are even 80% bigger today.[23]

Table: Assets and Profits Since 2008 of the Five Biggest US Financial Corporations

Name	Headquarters	Assets	Profits Since 2008
JPMorgan Chase	New York, NY	$2,609,785,000,000	$188,264,000,000
Bank of America	Charlotte, NC	$2,328,754,000,000	$81,908,000,000
Citigroup	New York, NY	$1,922,104,000,000	$68,810,000,000
Wells Fargo	San Francisco, CA	$1,915,388,000,000	$174,008,000,000
Goldman Sachs	New York, NY	$973,546,000,000	$70,262,000,000
TOTAL	-	$9,749,577,000,000	$583,252,000,000

Commondreams.org Public Citizen's Congress Watch

They continue their activities in CDOs, and have added another risky instrument called collateralized loan obligations (CLOs, which are largely composed of corporate bonds) and the derivative activities continue unregulated. This poses almost the same risk to society as in 2008. A major difference now though, is that Congress does not have the same massive monetary and fiscal stimulus to bail them out next time, should another disaster occur. It is worth noting that during the build up to the failure, many sane honest voices raised alarms (notably Brooksley Born), both with senior bankers and with government agencies like the Treasury, the Securities and Exchange Commission (SEC) and Commodities regulators. No one listened to them. Ten years after the crash, no bankers or negligent government officials have been charged or imprisoned. Each of the major players, including the reckless CEOs of failed Lehman Brothers (Richard Fuld Jr) and Bear Stearns (James Cayne), still have an individual net worth of nine figures or more. This uniquely complex travesty is beautifully explained in the July 2013 article in *The Economist* magazine.

• In 2010, the Supreme Court, under Bush appointed Chief Justice John Roberts, ruled 5-4 in favour of Citizen's United, supporting unlimited 'non-donation' funding as political free speech. Predicated on a 1976 ruling of Buckley vs Valeo, "which sanctioned billions of dollars of independent campaign spending," it soon resulted in a proliferation of super political action committees (SPACs) that "may raise unlimited sums of money from corporations, unions, associations and individuals, then spend unlimited sums to overtly advocate for or against political candidates." That permitted the flow of money, supposedly at arm's length from candidates, into campaigns on their behalf. Further, it protected an earlier ruling that corporations have the right to free speech. But the most serious problems are the Federal Election Committee loopholes, that facilitate the flow of dark money into campaigns,[24] with Congress blocking proposed legislation that would demand total transparency from political donors. As it currently stands, the public has no way of determining who is contributing to a politician's election, even a foreign power. An extremely narrow legal definition of corruption by Justice Kennedy in the Citizens United ruling further enabled shady funding of candidates. The Supreme Court does not make the laws, it only interprets them; but in this ruling interpretation, they have erred on the side of money, power and influence. Justice John Paul Stevens, a sitting dissenter at the time, stated "that the Court's ruling threatens to undermine the integrity of elected institutions across the Nation. The path it has taken to reach its outcome will, I fear, do damage to this institution. A democracy cannot function effectively when its constituent members believe laws are being bought and sold."[25] As a post-script to this section, this very day when writing about the Supreme Court, the GOP voted cloture on Brett Kavanaugh's Supreme Court nomination, 51-49, despite the fact that he repeatedly lied to the Senate Judiciary Committee under oath. He was eventually confirmed despite enormous public objection. So much for political leadership. (Yes, I'm letting my own bias show through clearly here!)

• If research shows repeatedly that honesty is the most important characteristic of effective leadership, then transparency becomes an important factor in educating and facilitating public opinion. To that end, the release of the Panama Papers in 2016 and the Paradise Papers in 2017 had a very damaging effect on public trust of leaders. Remarkably, an insider in Panama leaked vast volumes of data from a Panamanian law firm, Mossack Fonseca, to a German news reporter, Bastian Obermeyer, at newspaper *Suddeutsche Zeitung*, claiming that he (the leaker) could not divulge his identity for fear of his life. Given the size of the project, Obermeyer was able to convince the International Consortium of Investigative Journalists (ICIJ) to assist in vetting the information for veracity.[26] So 107 reporters from eighty countries collaborated, and when satisfied, published the full report on their website. This added objectivity and credence to the project, and exposed tax evasion by a multitude of world leaders, while protecting the lives and safety of the journalists. The following year, the Paradise Papers were leaked by a different source, researched and vetted by the same ICIJ, and exposed further tax evasion and specific corruption by thirty-eight countries, multiple large companies like AIG and Apple, and many world leaders. While many of the shelters were not technically illegal, the ethical question inevitably arose: how can leaders advise and expect regular citizens to pay into a tax system, when they themselves dodge personal responsibility through loopholes and shell corporations, that *they* created in response to lobbying and sometimes payoffs from the same corporations seeking the loopholes? The actions that aren't illegal are only so because the lawmakers themselves are corrupt. Both of these sets of Papers exposed high level politicians, business people, entertainment stars and even monarchs, who were sheltering investments in the obscure shell corporations, set up and sold to them by Mossak Fonseca or similar financial and legal advisers. They served to validate the perception that there exist two sets of rules: one for the 1%, and another for the rest of us.

The Panama Papers exposed 47 countries ranging from Armenia to the United States. The information resulted in the Prime Minister of Iceland stepping down, difficulties for Prime Minister David Cameron in Britain, and eventually in March 2018, the disbanding of Mossack Fonseca itself, given charges of money-laundering and reputational damage. Now 380 journalists continue to work on the Paradise Papers, and issue news as it is verified, of the activities of law firm Appleby and corporate services companies Estera and Asiaciti Trust. These set up offshore companies that larger companies like Apple, McDonald's, Seimens, Nike, and wealthy individuals use for tax dodging.

The leaks from both the Panama and Paradise Papers startled an already cynical world because they confirmed what many always suspected but could not prove: that there is a cabal of wealthy people and companies around the world that share the same information and clandestine practices for personal gain. The participation in the schemes by many of our high level 'leaders' around the world, capitalist and communist alike, signals a level of corruption that threatens our democratic society. Most troubling about this is the fact that despite the personal risk taken by the reporters, the information about both Panama and Paradise Papers splashed into the world media, but were met with a global shrug by the populace. Where was the rage, indignation, protest, street marches? There were none, and it predictably disappeared from digital and actual front pages rather quickly. The frog was already in lukewarm water and drifting further into dangerous sleep.

• The oldest continuously operating non-governmental institution on earth is the Roman Catholic Church. It is also the largest non-governmental provider of education and healthcare in the world today, and has 1.3 billion members. For centuries it exercised powerful influence over Western politics, science, art and culture, much of it in highly beneficial ways. Its contributions to civilization and learning have been considerable and positive. Those, like me, raised as Catholics were taught to trust the church completely, and that the Pope is infallible "when, in the exercise of his office as shepherd and teacher of all Christians, in virtue of his supreme apostolic authority, he defines a doctrine concerning faith or morals to be held by the whole Church."[27] This is an incredible expectation of trust and faith on behalf of church leaders, and followers in return have a right to expect the highest level of behaviour by their church leaders.

As is well known now around the world, in 2002, the *Boston Globe* newspaper, in a city deeply ensconced in Catholic American history, exposed several priests who were guilty of pedophilia during their ministries, and who, more egregiously, had been transferred around by their bishops to different parishes when complaints had been received at an existing parish. Over the past 16 years, similar acts have been exposed in almost every country in which the church exists. The crimes against children have been committed systematically for decades, and covered up by the highest levels in each country and in the Vatican. Church weekly attendance has dropped 6 percentage points to 39% since 2008, when the scandal spread globally, and down from 75% in 1955.[28] For the purpose of this book, the scandal is included as yet another recent example of leaders failing to deliver on the promises to their followers, of failing to consistently live the stated values of their organization, and also, how when followers' expectations are misguided and unmet, cynicism and apathy set in. To any Catholic, the duration, seriousness and cover-up of the *global* abuse represents the epitome of betrayal, and the final impact on the effectiveness of the Church remains to be seen.

- As mentioned earlier, the consolidation of the media into a corporate oligopoly presents a dangerous potential for biased news reporting. Yet in many ways, professional journalists continue to provide valuable service to the public, and often at great personal risk. Since the start of 2017, seven European journalists have been murdered, all but one for their investigations and exposure of corruption in their countries. Since 1992, 1322 journalists have died in the course of their work. While many died from crossfire in war zones like Iraq, Afghanistan and Syria, the majority were murdered in places such as the Middle East, eastern Europe, African countries, and Mexico.[29] The trend has eased since 2016, but still averages seventy deaths annually. During the time of this writing, *Washington Post* reporter and self-exiled Saudi critic Jamal Kashoggi entered the Saudi Embassy in Turkey to obtain papers for his marriage and never left. The Turkish investigation concluded he was murdered, and his body dismembered and removed from the embassy, yet the US refused to sanction Saudi Arabia because it did not want to jeopardize a $100 billion arms sale to the Saudis. That same week, Russian opposition newspaper *Novaya Gazeta* received a funeral wreath along with a severed goat head in a basket; warnings that their reporters were in danger. Since 2000, five reporters from the paper have been murdered for their anti-Putin work. The obvious risk to the public is the expansion of corruption that can result from the intimidation and silencing of the major force for transparency: the press.

• As a final example, Abraham Lincoln once reminded Americans of the biblical saying "a house divided against itself cannot stand." In the US, polarization could be said to be at the highest levels since the Civil War. Global movements in many European countries promote xenophobic, neo-Nazi, fascist views, exacerbated in many cases by the influx of refugees fleeing their war-torn countries. Earlier in this book, we did not encounter in the research intolerance and rigidity as qualities of good leaders. And yet populists like Nigel Farage in Britain, Marine LePen in France, Geert Wilders of the Netherlands, and Alex Gauland of Germany's Alternative for Germany's (AfD) party, have gained alarming support and media attention recently, causing a divided house in their countries and in the EU in general. In October 2018, Brazilians elected Jair Bolsonaros, an extreme right wing politician and former paramilitary soldier. The US, under the Trump Administration, has antagonized allies and enemies alike, with bullying rhetoric, lies, dog whistle comments and offensive insults. At a time when we face the greatest challenges in history, a time when our very existence likely depends on our capacity for col-laboration, understanding, compassion and unified action, we are a global house divided. Even worse is the quality of leader that seems to be emerging globally. It still astounds me that in 2016, out of a possible 229 million Americans who were eligible to run for office, the 'best' two presidential candidates the system could cough up were Hillary Clinton and Donald Trump. This speaks volumes about the state of politics in America: a dynastic candidate with a milque-toast Senate voting record and clouded for decades by scandals and rumour, or a narcissistic sociopathic mendacious buffoon. Take your

pick. Really? That's the best we could do? I cannot blame the disen-
franchised for rejecting Clinton (in my view she is far more dangerous to society than Trump because of her political power and media
favor that obscures her corruption) because the Congressional
Swamp had ignored them for decades. But they (we) can be held

accountable for igno-
rance and gullibility; for
buying Trump's empty
promises without forc-
ing more detailed expla-
nations, and without
delving more deeply into
his background. Where
are his tax returns? Why
do we tolerate his
'in-your-face' disregard
for emoluments? We
must own responsibility
for our own decisions if
we want better leaders.
Holocaust survivor
Victor Frankl, in his

Note: the statue was actually designed and
a foundation set up to raise funds for its
eventual construction.

marvelous book *Man's Search for Meaning*, calls for a Statue of
Responsibility to be erected on the west coast as a necessary comple-
ment to the Statue of Liberty. He rightly points out that freedom
without responsibility leads to arbitrariness and autocracy. We must
constantly guard against the boiling frog.

PART II: SO WHAT?

"The World Geographical Society finally settled on the end of World War II as the onset of the Anthropocene-sharp escalation and destruction of the environment, not only global warming, carbon dioxide, other greenhouse gases, but also such things as plastics in the ocean, which are predicted to be greater than the weight of fish in the ocean not far in the future. So we're destroying the environment for organized human life. We're threatening a terminal disaster with regular nuclear confrontations." Noam Chomsky, July 2018

CHAPTER 4

Why Change? Burning Platforms and Inspiring Visions

So WHAT? YOU MAY SHRUG. SO THINGS AREN'T GOING SO well right now. Why should I care? It's just the human condition: we've been saddled with saints and sinners, scoundrels and saviours throughout history. There is nothing new under the sun. Up until recently, that argument might have held water. Not today. Several critical developments imperil our very existence, for the first time in that existence. Without doubt, the most serious is climate change. Next is the nuclear threat that we've so far been able to avoid unleashing since 1945, but that still looms large, and with far more devastating capability.

We'll visit both of those, and others, but first a word about change.

In business, my field of leadership development and organizational culture deals with change. It's actually transformation. Change is when a process or situation is approached differently for some period of time, but things could eventually revert back to the old ways. Transformation signals a need for *permanent* change; for a new and often completely different way of operating. This is what's required in most cases today. The demand for structured transformation programs during the past thirty years has resulted in several excellent, effective clinical systems, most notably the Eight Stage Change Model by Harvard's professor, John Kotter.

This model evolved in response to bureaucratic organizations' struggle to keep apace with an increasingly accelerating world beginning in the 1980s, as technology, driven primarily by computers, shifted business norms. While there are other good models too, this one is perhaps the most widely adopted. Kotter emphasizes the extreme difficulty of change by noting that an

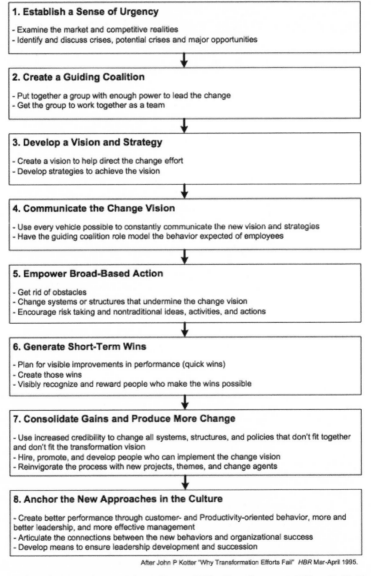

1. Establish a Sense of Urgency

- Examine the market and competitive realities
- Identify and discuss crises, potential crises and major opportunities

2. Create a Guiding Coalition

- Put together a group with enough power to lead the change
- Get the group to work together as a team

3. Develop a Vision and Strategy

- Create a vision to help direct the change effort
- Develop strategies to achieve the vision

4. Communicate the Change Vision

- Use every vehicle possible to constantly communicate the new vision and strategies
- Have the guiding coalition role model the behavior expected of employees

5. Empower Broad-Based Action

- Get rid of obstacles
- Change systems or structures that undermine the change vision
- Encourage risk taking and nontraditional ideas, activities, and actions

6. Generate Short-Term Wins

- Plan for visible improvements in performance (quick wins)
- Create those wins
- Visibly recognize and reward people who make the wins possible

7. Consolidate Gains and Produce More Change

- Use increased credibility to change all systems, structures, and policies that don't fit together and don't fit the transformation vision
- Hire, promote, and develop people who can implement the change vision
- Reinvigorate the process with new projects, themes, and change agents

8. Anchor the New Approaches in the Culture

- Create better performance through customer- and Productivity-oriented behavior, more and better leadership, and more effective management
- Articulate the connections between the new behaviors and organizational success
- Develop means to ensure leadership development and succession

After John P Kotter "Why Transformation Efforts Fail" *HBR* Mar-April 1995.

Source: Adapted BPTrends.com John P. Kotter, "Why Transformation Efforts Fail", Harvard Business Review, March-April 1995. Reprinted with permission.

organization *must* follow the eight steps in order, and even should they do so, chances of successful transformation are only 30%!

There are at least two approaches to both change and transformation, which can be used in tandem, when working to persuade groups of people to change. One is called the 'Burning Platform', and is used when a failure to achieve radical change will likely result in serious damage to, or even the survival of the organization. I believe it is borrowed from the oil industry, where the worst possible scenario is an off-shore oil rig afire. The situation is dire and urgency is imperative to survival; if we don't change, we're screwed – put out the fire or jump into the ocean. It uses some degree of fear to motivate action. This one fits under Kotter's first step; Increase Urgency. At times, the fire is only small, so only a moderate level of fear is needed to produce the desired level of change.

A famous National Hockey League (NHL) coach recently said, "sometimes a little fear isn't a bad thing in helping our guys work just a little bit harder." The burning platform approach is best applied as an adrenaline booster, not to paralyze with fear, but rather to add that positive 'Yikes!' factor and incite fast action.

More powerful, and used most often when an organization is not in peril or urgent need of reform, is the Inspiring Vision. This entails painting a picture of the ideal future state of the company, organization or even nation state, and appeals to the shared values (recall those from the Soft S's model?) of all constituents, ideally to raise excitement and commitment to moving things forward. It taps into positive enthusiasm, creativity and imagination, and uses the resulting inspiration to drive action. It falls into place in Steps three and four in the Kotter model.

Sometimes, the two are used together. In our Lou Gerstner Jr example, he had to first convince employees that the mighty legacy IBM was on a burning platform. Having lost $8 billion the prior year, and more importantly, having faded from market supremacy, thousands of IBMers needed to be shaken out of their complacency, and quickly. But once that was done,

Gerstner canvassed hundreds of loyal employees, and crafted a new inspiring vision of IBM not as a legacy hardware manufacturer, but as a comprehensive software solutions provider. This was a *major identity shift* that required much sacrifice by many people. But using the two transformation approaches together, they pulled it off.

The key takeaway here is that change, especially transformational change, is extremely difficult to achieve, but the good news is that we *do* have case studies from which to learn, and these can expedite our approach and reduce risk of failure. But we *must* embark on the change initiative, or accept dire consequences. And if our current leaders fail to respond, we must change our leaders, and elevate better ones.

So far, I've tried to keep a positive, yet factual tone as we walked through how we arrived here and what went wrong. Hopefully, though several patterns and events have definitely been discouraging, you have not found the story overly negative. If so, remember we're only half way through it; where we go from here can be incredibly positive, if we only resolve to consciously create our future. The next part of the book will offer examples of what I believe to be the most important issues we face, of Burning Platforms and of Inspiring Visions, that we can achieve if we are open and committed to positive change. From here forward the intention is to first inform as to the challenges and possibilities, then to persuade you that we must collectively act, and act now. Finally, my intent is to inspire and energize discussion among *you* and your networks about averting the worst case scenario, and instead creating the amazing future we can build together.

The three Burning Platforms are: 1) Climate Change, 2) Income Inequality and 3) Chaos in the VUCA world. They will be followed by three Inspiring Visions: 1) the Third Industrial Revolution, 2) Conscious Capitalism, and 3) Human Potential and Fulfillment.

Prior to embarking on discussions of each though, I want to address the nuclear threat separately. While certainly as lethal to our civilization as the other threats, there is a subtle yet important difference. There are eight countries in the world today that have nuclear weapons: US, Russia, France, UK, China, Pakistan, India, and North Korea – nine if Israel, as highly suspected, also has them. However, not only are current international checks and balances in place, including the Treaty on the Non-Proliferation of Nuclear Weapons, and the Strategic Offensive Reductions Treaty, but the momentum during the past forty years has been toward restraint and reduction (from 68,000 active warheads in 1985 to 4,000 in 2016) rather than belligerent proliferation. So far, the concept of Mutually Assured Destruction (MAD) which gave pause to aggressive leaders of nuclear nations with the notion that attacker *and* defender would both be annihilated, has served its purpose. Globally, politicians, even tyrants, seem to have accepted that a nuclear war would leave very little of the planet left to enjoy. Pyrrhic victory. Despite the recent impulsive departure of the US from the Iran treaty, all other participating countries have fortunately decided to remain. So the difference is that if we continue on the present path of global détente, with rational leaders, the status quo does not pose an immediate threat to the world. In other words, if everyone 'does nothing', the threat does not increase. In that sense it does not qualify as a burning platform situation.

This is clearly not the case, as we will see, with the others below.

CHAPTER 5

Burning Platform 1 – Climate Change

"There is no documented historic precedent for the action needed at this moment in order to address the incredible crisis that we're facing in terms of climate change." Intergovernmental Panel of Climate Change, UN Report October 2018

A WEEK BEFORE I STARTED TO WRITE THIS CHAPTER, Canadian Green Party leader Elizabeth May requested that the Parliament House Speaker call an emergency debate to discuss the October 6, 2018 report of the Intergovernmental Panel on Climate Change (IPCC). The debate was held on October 15, and one result was the acknowledgement that Canada is not on track to hit our committed CO2 reduction targets. May's impassioned speech[1] highlights the current threat without mincing words. The IPCC report used 'burning platform' language (unusual for reports issued from the broad scientific community), likely in an effort to shock heretofore apathetic politicians worldwide out of their dangerous complacency. The report stated that humanity has about

> "Every time there has been a warning from scientists, the alarm bell rings, and society hits the snooze button."
>
> **ELIZABETH MAY, LEADER, GREEN PARTY OF CANADA**

twelve years to act if we are to limit global warming to a 1.5°C increase over pre-industrial levels, and that current governmental plans agreed to at the Paris Accord are not aggressive enough to achieve this limit. Further, most countries are not even on pace to hit those lower targets. This is the most serious threat we face at the moment, because the science indicates that should we surpass a 2°C degree increase, the results will be irreversible and far more severe.

To mobilize towards an effective solution, there are four major obstacles to overcome. First, with all the noise in today's media frenzy, it is harder than ever before to get one's message heard. Any marketer today will verify the difficulty of landing their message with the right group at the right time.

Add to that our tendency to turn away from news we'd rather not deal with right now, and it becomes apparent that the scientists trying to get our attention are fighting an uphill battle. Achieving widespread knowledge and acceptance of climate change is only now happening, and no doubt explains the alarming language used in the IPCC report.

Second, even if we drive the message through all the other noise, it is often difficult to persuade a distracted public of a need for transformation, primarily because we humans tend to prefer our comfort zone of familiarity; change causes some level of anxiety, and who wants that? When we see videos of others suffering from the effects of climate change, powerful hurricanes, earthquakes, tsunamis, we may feel compassion for them, yet because we do not feel the distress ourselves, we are not prone to act. So generally speaking, if we ourselves are not directly affected by an issue, we are loath to take up the cause.

Third, the most looming and intransigent obstacle is the combination of comfortable governments and their oil industry sponsors. It has been a historical reality that politicians tend to kick the controversial issue can down the road for the next guy to handle. It's long been part of democratic life, and for most issues the timing isn't do-or-die, so we shrug and live with it. An example in Canada is electoral reform. The Liberals recently came to power on a promise to deliver it to the people, but once ensconced as a majority, decided the old system served *them* well, so announced further 'study' was required. With climate change, there is a double whammy of inertia for governments and oil companies that is stalling change. First is that it will take enormous planning and coordination to effect the necessary change to sustainable energy, and most governments in the world want neither the hassle nor the risk. Second, there are trillions of dollars in 'sunk costs' (stranded assets) of infrastructure; refineries, pipelines and distribution, and oil inventories above and below ground, as well as a large industry labour force. Globally, the oil industry has ruled supreme since the 1920s and wielded disproportionate clout over governments. In Canada and the US, politicians face the enormous task of retraining oil industry workers in new skills for new industries so they will be able to transition to new work. They continue to kick that can. Again, poor leadership. Then there's the understandable reluctance of oil industry leaders to change. Why should they jeopardize their own wealth and status, when doing the 'right thing' for humanity will severely reduce their own industry to a shadow of its current size and impact, and possibly eliminate their roles?

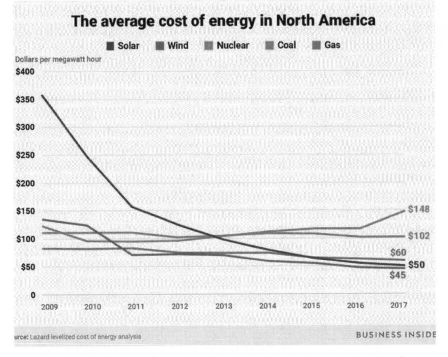

The average cost of energy in North America

■ Solar   ■ Wind   ■ Nuclear   ■ Coal   ■ Gas

Dollars per megawatt hour

$148
$102
$60
$50
$45

2009 2010 2011 2012 2013 2014 2015 2016 2017

urce: Lazard levelized cost of energy analysis   BUSINESS INSIDE

And finally, there is the issue of developed countries assisting developing countries to reach a standard of low cost energy for their people. As China began to rise as a world economic power in the 1980s, staggering investments in cheap coal energy created a serious pollution problem, and also garnered global criticism from developed countries. China (rightly) responded that those countries had polluted the world for 200 years as they rose to industrially developed status, so why should China and other developing countries not enjoy the same economic advantage? It was 'their turn' so to speak. The same situation exists in India, and in most of the African nations. However, China has recently announced a commitment to spend $360 billion on clean energy projects by 2020, reflecting an aggressive plan to eliminate pollution in the country.[2] As the cost of solar energy rapidly descends, developing countries may even be able to leapfrog the investment in infrastructure for coal and oil fired energy plants, and move directly to a clean energy system. The cost of a megawatt hour of solar is now around $50, versus the same for coal of $102.[3] Yet this will likely require cooperation and assistance, including financial, from developed countries; quite the challenge given current trends toward nationalism and isolationism. And yet transform we must.

For any remaining skeptics, let's return to the trust concept. While blind faith in anything, including science, is not always wise, over the past three centuries we have found that placing trust in the scientific community has been a generally sound practice. The adoption of the scientific method, coupled with peer review of published works, has kept the scientific community highly reliable. Why would 97% of climate-related scientists today agree that climate change is real, serious, and is caused by human activity, were it not true? If nothing else, each would risk reputational damage by taking a contrarian position in light of the reams of existing data pointing to the problem.

And further for skeptics, consider this analogy. Let's assume you happen upon a child playing upon the railroad tracks. You look off in the distance and notice a train approaching from about five miles away. Do you think "it's a ways off so I'll let the child play for a few more minutes," or immediately remove the child from the tracks? Most of us would immediately remove the child, for two main reasons: first, the consequences of the train hitting the child are near 100% fatal. Second, the consequences will be irreversible. Who would risk the life of a child under such dire circumstances? The consequence of being wrong is just too high to risk.

This is where we currently stand with global warming: the probability that disastrous weather patterns resulting from warming above 2°C will dangerously alter living conditions globally for future generations is 100%. If we surpass a 2oC rise, we cannot go back.

So why are our leaders hesitating? Certainly for the reasons listed above, but perhaps also because they do not fear being voted out of office by a concerned public that demands aggressive action? Is the frog quietly boiling here as well? I believe so. We must raise the pressure on our political and business leaders to make this *the* priority.

Still not convinced? The following are select facts taken from the October 2018 IPCC report, and some facts from recent severe weather events that we have already experienced:

- "A3. Climate-related risks for natural and human systems are higher for global warming of 1.5°C than at present, but lower than at 2°C (high confidence). These risks depend on the magnitude and rate of warming, geographic location, levels of development and vulnerability, and on the choices and implementation of adaptation and mitigation options (high confidence)."

- "B1. Climate models project robust differences in regional climate characteristics between present-day and global warming of 1.5°C, and between 1.5°C and 2°C. These differences include increases in: mean temperature in most land and ocean regions (high confidence), hot extremes in most inhabited regions (high confidence), heavy precipitation in several regions (medium confidence), and the probability of drought and precipitation deficits in some regions".

- "B3. On land, impacts on biodiversity and ecosystems, including species loss and extinction, are projected to be lower at 1.5°C of global warming compared to 2°C. Limiting global warming to 1.5°C compared to 2°C is projected to lower the impacts on terrestrial, freshwater, and coastal ecosystems and to retain more of their services to humans (high confidence) "

- "B4. Limiting global warming to 1.5°C compared to 2°C is projected to reduce increases in ocean temperature as well as associated increases in ocean acidity and decreases in ocean oxygen levels (high confidence). Consequently, limiting global warming to 1.5°C is projected to reduce risks to marine biodiversity, fisheries, and ecosystems, and their functions and services to humans, as illustrated by recent changes to Arctic sea ice and warm water coral reef ecosystems (high confidence)."

- "B5. Climate-related risks to health, livelihoods, food security, water supply, human security, and economic growth are projected to increase with global warming of 1.5°C and increase further with 2°C."

- Arctic sea ice is diminishing, as are glaciers: besides replenishing global water supply, arctic ice serves an important role of reflecting sunlight back into the atmosphere. Without it, the sun warms the ocean water at a faster rate, causing sea rises and damage to corral reefs and various sea ecosystem species.

- Melting permafrost: in 2018, for the first time, deep permafrost in the Siberian Arctic did not freeze during the winter. The 17 million tons of methane released there in 2013 was 325% higher than in 2006. Methane is a significantly more damaging greenhouse gas than CO2, increasing the effect at a faster rate.[4]

- Ocean heat content is increasing: The top half-mile of most major ocean waters is getting warmer. The amount of heat absorbed by the oceans has increased significantly over the past two decades.[5] Warmer ocean water damages coral reefs, threatens marine ecosystems, and disrupts global fisheries.[6]

- A change in ocean heat content can also alter patterns of ocean circulation, which can have far-reaching effects on global climate conditions, including changes to the outcome and pattern of meteorological events such as tropical storms, and also temperatures in the northern Atlantic region, which are strongly influenced by currents that may be substantially reduced with CO2 increase in the atmosphere.[7]

- Rising global sea levels and coastal flooding: As sea levels rise, high-end developments in coastal cities will spread the costs of insurance over all customers, even those inland. If no mitigating action is taken, many businesses and homes will have to be abandoned. In poor countries and communities, displacement will cause major disruption, economic hardship, and likely political unrest.

- Longer and more devastating forest fire seasons: Earlier spring run-off leads to drier land conditions for longer periods. Combined with higher temperatures, the frequency and scope of forest fires increases. In 2015, 10 million acres in the US burned. Major blazes erupted in Indonesia and Russia in 2015, Canada and Spain in 2016, and Chile and Portugal in 2017. In 2018, raging fires destroyed the Greek resort town of Mati, and a combined 4 million acres in Arizona, Colorado, Idaho and Oregon. In northern California, three major fires (Camp, Woolsey, and Hill) destroyed 204,000 acres, the entire town of Paradise, and killed forty-four people. Climatologists are noticing global fire patterns as opposed to the usual localized patterns.[8]

- Increased destructiveness of hurricanes: Hurricanes like Maria, Irma, Harvey, Sandy Katrina and Andrew have ravaged the US in the past twenty-five years. New research has shown that climate change has made a previously once-in-a-hundred-year storm such as those, now a once–in-a-sixteen-year event. Since the 1970s, the number of Category four and five hurricanes has roughly doubled.[9]

A few years ago, I was diagnosed with rheumatoid arthritis. My doctor recommended a medicine that had the potential for what I felt were some pretty serious side effects. I replied that I'd prefer not to go on the medicine. He empathized, but told me that it was still the most effective drug available, and that, more importantly, whatever damage the disease might inflict in the drug's absence, would be irreversible. So, he said, the disease may not advance strongly, but he could not estimate the probability of that; and going on the medication once damage has been sustained could arrest further damage, but not heal existing damage. Though not happy about it, I chose the risk of side effects over the chance of permanent damage.

Climate change is an even worse alternative. There is very high probability that inaction within the next twelve years will cause severe and irreversible damage to human civilization.

It is *the most serious issue we face today.* Since the 1980s, our leaders have had plenty of time to address this challenge, but we have all hit the snooze button. It's long overdue for us to wake up.

Bear in mind that over future millennia, the earth will still be here; but we might not.

Photo: Nature vs. Man: guess which one endures?
Michael Darmody

Note: One week after writing this chapter, the Ontario legislature, under a Conservative government that won control of Parliament with less than 40% of the popular vote, actually voted to reverse Ontario's commitment to Canada's climate change promise in 2016, and began to unwind the existing pollution mitigating cap and trade law. See what I mean about a leadership crisis?

CHAPTER 6

Burning Platform 2 –
Income Inequality

"The billionaire boom is not a sign of a thriving economy but a symptom of a failing economic system. The people who make our clothes, assemble our phones and grow our food are being exploited to ensure a steady supply of cheap goods, and swell the profits of corporations and billionaire investors."

Winnie Byanyima, Executive Director of Oxfam International

PRIOR TO THE LAUNCH OF THE 2018 WORLD ECONOMIC Forum in Davos, Switzerland, Oxfam International released its report on global Income Inequality. The report included the following observations:

- 82% of the wealth generated last year went to the richest 1% of the global population, while the 3.7 billion people who make up the poorest half of the world saw *no increase* in their wealth.

- Billionaire wealth has risen by an annual average of 13% since 2010 – six times faster than the wages of ordinary workers, which have risen by a yearly average of just 2%. The number of billionaires rose at an unprecedented rate of one every two days between March 2016 and March 2017. (By Davos 2019, it was 1 new billionaire per day.)

- It takes just four days for a CEO from one of the top five global fashion brands to earn what a Bangladeshi garment worker will earn in her *lifetime*. In the US, it takes slightly over one working day for a CEO to earn what an ordinary worker *makes in a year*.

- It would cost $2.2 billion a year to increase the wages of all 2.5 million Vietnamese garment workers to a living wage. This is about a third of the amount paid out to wealthy shareholders by the top five companies in the garment sector in 2016.

- Oxfam estimates a global tax of 1.5% on global billionaire wealth could pay for every child to go to school [1]

The earlier mentioned cozy collaboration between governments, business and media has enabled this trend to grow out of control. We are in the midst of a Gilded Age 2.0, where once again a relatively few people and corporations have amassed disproportionate power and wealth, and use it to influence and in some cases even write government policy for their own benefit. The loosening or elimination of restrictions on money in politics has allowed the elite to 'own' politicians around the world.

"Politics is a game of fear. Those who do not have the ability to frighten the elites do not succeed... The platitudes about justice, equality and democracy are just that. Only when ruling elites become worried about survival do they react. Appealing to the better nature of the powerful is useless. They don't have one." [2]

When I first read the above statement, I was startled at the harshness of it. I did not, and still don't, want to believe it. Yet from my experience in leadership research and activities particularly during the past ten years, it seems far more true than not. To the degree that the elites are our leaders, (not always, but often the case) the recent behaviour of the much written about 0.1% tends to further verify the comment. One sad example is the lack of restrictive gun legislation despite the slaughter of children at Columbine, Sandy Hook and Stoneman-Douglas schools. Another is the silence of many countries while a US supported United Arab Emirates (UAE) and Saudi Arabian coalition destroys Yemeni civilians through bombing and starvation. Money wields astounding influence. Where huge amounts are at stake, moral action often suffers.

Thus the second most urgent Burning Platform issue we face, for a variety of reasons, is income inequality. A case can easily be made that the second, or even *most* urgent issue is Net Neutrality, for how can we quickly and efficiently mobilize against climate change (or any other significant problem) without a vibrant and free internet? But threats to the internet are simply a component of the global mindset and surreptitious movement towards gross Income Inequality. If we can solve that problem, many others will diminish in threat.

Investopedia defines Income Inequality as "the unequal distribution of household or individual income across the various participants in an economy. It is often presented as the percentage of income related to a percentage of the population. For example, a statistic may indicate that 70% of a country's income is controlled by 20% of that country's residents." The Gini Index attempts to measure this with a 100-point scale. A zero rating reflects the extreme of perfectly equal income per capita, while 100 would mean one person received all the income; so in 2013, Sweden had a 23 rating, rather egalitarian, while the US was 42.3 More recent data, as we'll see later, shows an even more disturbing widening gap.

Why is this so important? When examining the American, French and Russian revolutions, there are several common characteristics, but two stand out: 1) a wealthy and elitist class that oppressed the general population through unfair and extreme taxation and legal manipulation, and 2) the disinterest and inaction of governments to address the imbalance. Could we be headed for future revolutions? Over two thirds of the 70,000 people Oxfam surveyed in ten countries believed their governments need to take urgent action to address income inequality. In the US in 2018, Senator Bernie Sanders used his public platform to shame Amazon and Disney into raising their minimum wages to $15 per hour. Both companies had a disproportionate number of their employees dependent on food stamps, subsidized housing, and medical care. Sanders (rightly) charged that they were consciously engaging in corporate welfare: using taxpayer funded public programs to subsidize their payrolls. He tabled the BEZOS Act (stop Bad Employers by Zeroing Out Subsidies), named after Amazon founder Jeff Bezos, who at the time was earning $126 million *a day*, while some employees were sleeping overnight in their cars in the company parking lot. Although the Act has yet to pass, it will tax corporations for every dollar of public subsidy above the average, that their low wage workers received in government assistance. A clever and fair solution. The widespread and shaming publicity was part of what caused Amazon to raise its minimum wage to $15 an hour. Disney had followed suit, and Sanders is now drawing public attention to Wal-mart.[4]

A few more facts that you've no doubt already encountered:

- Eight men (Bill Gates, Amancio Ortega Gaona, Warren Buffet, Carlos Slim Helu, Jeff Bezos, Mark Zuckerberg, Lawrence Ellison, and Michael Bloomberg) own the same wealth as the 3.7 billion people who make up the poorest *half of humanity*.

- A different set of data compiled by Credit Suisse in 2017 concluded 42 people owned the same wealth as the bottom 50% and Oxfam recalculated their numbers based on the same data set and found 61 people as the number. Regardless, 8 or 42 or 61 versus 3.7 billion; the argument and crisis remains the same.[5]

- As of 2012, the share of national income, including capital gains going to the richest 1% of Americans, has doubled since 1980, from 10% to 20% – the level it was at in the first Gilded Age. The share going to the richest 0.1% quadrupled – from 1% to 5% – which is larger than it was in the 1880s.[6]

- CEO pay in the 1950s was 20 times the salary of an average worker. In 2018, the CEO of a typical S&P 500 Index company earned 361 times the salary of an average worker, around $13,940,000 annually.[7]

- The recent multi-trillion tax cut issued by the Trump GOP flowed almost exclusively to the top 1% of people and corporations. No 'trickle down' effect occurred (and never in history has). Wages remained flat. Further, as extreme wealth accrued to the 1%, purchasing power of wages also remained flat over the past fifty years.

Americans' paychecks are bigger than 40 years ago, but their purchasing power has hardly budged

Average hourly wages in the U.S., seasonally adjusted

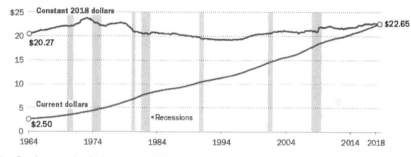

Note: Data for wages of production and non-supervisory employees on private non-farm payrolls. "Constant 2018 dollars" describes wages adjusted for inflation. "Current dollars" describes wages reported in the value of the currency when received. "Purchasing power" refers to the amount of goods or services that can be bought per unit of currency.
Source: U.S. Bureau of Labor Statistics.

PEW RESEARCH CENTER

OK, enough statistics; you get the point. And again, you may ask why it's such a dangerous situation.

The simple answer is that if one accepts the premise that democracy – flawed as it is – is still preferable to autocracy, dictatorship, fascism or communism, then unregulated capitalism, by its very design, guarantees an eventual income inequality and therefore disaster for democracy because it eliminates the middle class. There are primarily three reasons why we need to revamp our current capitalist system: 1) the inherent imbalance in the system itself, r > g, 2) the impact of human corruption, and 3) the welfare of those who lose the 'ovarian lottery'. Let's take a quick peek at each.

1. Thomas Piketty: Return on Wealth Greater Than Economic Growth Rate: r > g

In 2014, a French economics professor, Thomas Piketty, published an exhaustive, scholarly book called *Capital in the Twenty-First Century*, a brilliant work. Without getting too economically technical, we can summarize his claim that the capitalist system is inherently flawed because it *assumes* that economic growth (g) will usually exceed the rate of return on capital (r). But he asserts that "the central thesis (of his work) is that when the rate of return on capital (r) is greater than the rate of economic growth (g) over the long term, the result is concentration of wealth, and this unequal distribution of wealth causes social and economic instability."[8]

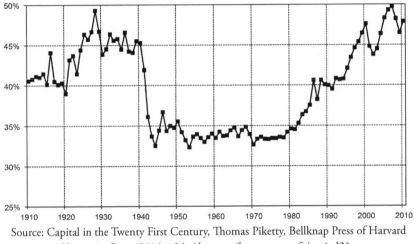

Source: Capital in the Twenty First Century, Thomas Piketty, Bellknap Press of Harvard University Press, 2014, p24. Also see piketty.pse.ens.fr/capital21c

The chart shows the percent of U.S. national income that went to the top 10% over the past 100 years. Notice that just following the Gilded Age and through the Roaring Twenties prior to the Great Depression, the top 10% received the same 45-50% of GDP as they did in 2010.[7] Notice that during the mid-century, when FDR's New Deal and other policies placed restrictions on capitalism, the imbalance dropped and flattened, building a healthy middle class, until 1980 when the Reaganomics legislation began the financial deregulation and tax cuts for the wealthy that continue to this day.

And since 2010, the trend has worsened. We are most definitely in the Gilded Age 2.0.

But more importantly, Piketty shows that throughout recorded history (and he examines global records covering three centuries primarily in the United States, Japan, Germany, France and Great Britain) the rate of return on capital (r) *usually exceeds that of economic growth* (g), thus automatically further enriching idle generations of wealthy families, and guaranteeing inequality and social instability.

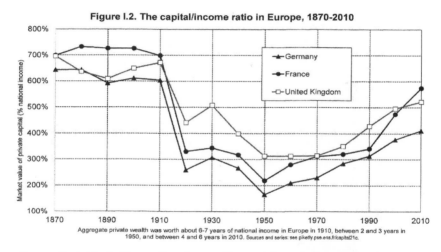

Figure I.2. The capital/income ratio in Europe, 1870-2010

Aggregate private wealth was worth about 6-7 years of national income in Europe in 1910, between 2 and 3 years in 1950, and between 4 and 6 years in 2010. Sources and series: see piketty.pse.ens.fr/capital21c.

Source: Capital in the Twenty First Century, Thomas Piketty, Bellknap Press of Harvard University Press, 2014, p26. Also see piketty.pse.ens.fr/capital21c

In his own words: "The overall conclusion of this study is that a market economy based on private property, *if left to itself*, [italics mine] contains powerful forces of convergence, associated in particular with the diffusion of knowledge and skills, but it also contains powerful forces of divergence which are potentially threatening to democratic societies. The principal destabilizing force has to do with the fact that the private rate of return on capital, r, can be significantly higher for long periods of time than the rate of growth of income and output…the entrepreneur inevitably becomes a rentier, more and more dominant over those who own nothing but their labour. *Once constituted, capital reproduces itself faster than output increases. The past devours the future.*"[9]

Traditional economists criticized Piketty's suggested solutions as being naïve or unrealistic, and sadly, they are not possible given our current leadership situation. But I italicized "if left to itself" above, to emphasize that there *are* viable solutions. There is no reason to discard the many positive incentives and benefits of a capitalist system simply because an unregulated version is damaging to society. Piketty makes a strong case for a progressive annual tax on accumulated capital (not on income); suggesting perhaps 0.1 percent on fortunes below 200,000 euros, and 0.5 percent net wealth between 200,000 and 1 million euros. He prescribes a net wealth tax of 2 percent or greater on fortunes of 5-10 million euros, and perhaps 5-10 percent on hundreds of millions or billions of euros. These taxes would replace the current property taxes, and would not adversely affect the economy. [10] But to do this would require global government policy collaboration to ensure capital didn't simply flee tax regimes for shelters.[11] We have learned from the Panama and Paradise Papers leaks that many 'club members' are business and governmental leaders themselves. It is difficult to imagine them agreeing to a plan that thwarts their own personal wealth agenda. That said, income inequality, while a serious threat to democratic freedom, is not insurmountable. In Chapter 9 we'll explore a different and very viable form of capitalism that is already working well in some companies.

2. The Impact of Human Corruption

Next, traditional economic theory assumes people are rational actors and are clear on what is best for their self-interest. Theories and models did not account for corrupt behaviour or an un-level playing field, where some players have access to the timing and content of information that others do not. The founding fathers knew about the potential danger; Adam Smith wrote about it in his *Theory of Moral Sentiments*: "All constitutions of government are valued only in proportion as they tend to promote the happiness of those who live under them. This is their sole use and end." Smith added a cautionary note, however: "[The] disposition to admire, and almost to worship, the rich and the powerful, and to despise, or, at least, to neglect persons of poor and mean condition…is the great and most universal cause of the corruption of our moral sentiments."[12]

As we've seen in this book so far, there are many indicators that our global political and business leaders are promoting an agenda that is more self-serving than for the good of the general public. Beginning in the mid-eighties, and largely driven by Charles Koch of Koch Industries, wealthy people with deep libertarian beliefs (minimal government and completely 'free' markets) set a strategy of funnelling tax deductible money into foundations. The foundations then donated funds to innocuously titled think tanks and non-profits – like The Heritage Institute, the American Enterprise Institute, and the Cato Institute – to finance 'research', white papers and policy advocacy, all under the umbrella of charitable philanthropy. While tax policy governing philanthropy intended an arm's-length approach, Koch and his colleagues tightly controlled the output of the think tanks. They eventually even opened programs in the law and business schools at Ivy League universities, pouring in millions of dollars in an attempt to influence academic thinking. All of these activities were an attempt to create a movement of political thought and leaders who would eventually enter government and sway policy to that which served the wealthy. It expanded to include the creation of PACs, and flowed significant money into GOP candidate campaigns. Unfortunately, these clandestine efforts have proven remarkably effective over the years. Democrats like the Clintons soon followed suit with their own foundations, which have also been accused of similar covert activities and influence. In her acclaimed book *Dark Money*, Jane Mayer outlines the correlation of Washington tax policy and the influence of these foundations set up by people like the Koch brothers, John M. Olin, Harry Bradley and others. "There were some legal boundaries. By law, tax-exempt charities…must refrain from involvement in lobbying and electoral politics and serve the public rather than their donor's interests. But such laws are rarely enforced… Critics began to complain that the Kochs' approach to philanthropy subverted the purpose of tax-exempt charitable giving. A 2004 report by the National Committee for Responsive Philanthropy, a watchdog group, stated, 'these foundations give money to non-profit organizations that do research and advocacy on issues that impact the profit margins of Koch Industries.'"[13] Their efforts have yielded billions in income (Charles and David Koch are each worth $47 billion as of 2018) and contributed greatly to the tax policies – starting with Reagan – that began to funnel wealth to the 1%, and facilitated the election of Donald Trump, whose $1.3 trillion tax cut in 2017 went primarily to the wealthiest in society. Trump's own foundation was immediately closed down in December 2018 for inappropriate activity.

We're also witnessing a resurgence of fascist ideology in former Eastern Bloc countries, in European countries like Germany, France and Italy, and most disturbingly, in the United States.

Writer Thom Hartmann states, "Instead, unregulated markets — particularly markets not regulated by significant taxation on predatory incomes — invariably lead to the opposite of a healthy middle class: they produce extremes of inequality, which are as dangerous to democracy as cancer is to a living being."[14] Former President Jimmy Carter expressed his own concerns in 2015, when discussing the Citizens United Supreme Court ruling that permitted dark money to flow into political campaigns: "It violates the essence of what made America a great country in its political system. Now it's just an oligarchy with unlimited political bribery". He added: "We've just seen a complete subversion of our political system as a payoff to major contributors…"[15]

Pretty strong criticism from a former President.

Even Aristotle was keenly aware of the need for a healthy middle class in a thriving society: "Thus it is manifest that the best political community is formed by citizens of the middle class, and that those states are likely to be well-administered in which the middle class is large, and stronger if possible than both the other classes, or at any rate than either singly; for the addition of the middle class turns the scale, and prevents either of the extremes from being dominant."[16]

As discussed earlier, a combination of quiet collusion between government and business in the US in particular, coupled with a corporate, biased mainstream media, led to the 2008 financial meltdown that perfectly represents how real income inequality truly is. Rolling Stone Magazine writer, Matt Taibbi, on the tenth anniversary of the catastrophe, wrote:

This… "The bank-state merger brokered 10 years ago this week socialized the risks of the financial sector, and essentially converted Wall Street into a vehicle for annually privatizing a big chunk of America's GDP into the hands of a few executives. The same people who were minutes from being (deservedly) destitute 10 years ago are now a permanent aristocracy."[17]

And this… "compensation levels were one of the first and most urgent priorities of the bailout. Bonuses on the street were back to normal within *six months*. Goldman, which needed billions in public funds, paid an astonishing **$16.9 billion** in compensation just a year after the crash, a company record."[18]

And this… "outside Manhattan, the pain was just starting. In 2008, **861,664 families lost their homes**, and homeowners **lost a breathtaking $3.3 trillion** in home equity (coincidentally, this was the **TARP inspector's estimate** for the entire net outlay of the bailout). By 2011, a full **11.6 million homeowners** were underwater on their homes."[19] Bankers saved by taxpayers; taxpayers abandoned to foreclosures. All these decisions and actions were taken by government and business leaders, driving income inequality even higher, and seriously diminishing the middle class, as the frog continues to boil.

3. Welfare of Those Who Lose the 'Ovarian Lottery'

One of the wisest, most humble and respected billionaires is Warren Buffet. Known for his integrity and sense of fairness, he has called for higher taxation on himself and others like him. You may be aware that he gave upwards of $30 billion to the Bill and Melinda Gates Foundation.

Once, while being interviewed, Buffet was asked about his success and what he did to achieve it. His answer (See Youtube link in Endnotes) involves what he calls the 'Ovarian Lottery.'[20] He asks his audience to imagine that, prior to being born, they were granted the power and opportunity to create the world in any way they wanted. The only caveat was that they would not know how, when or where they would be born. He likened it to the lottery, where a ball pops up, and that's your lot to deal with. Race, gender, IQ, nationality, lineage and parents, social class, wealth: all are simply probabilities. What kind of world would we create? He suggests we'd hedge our bets, and invent one that allowed for success and wealth, but also one that softened the burden for those with an IQ of 70, physical and mental disabilities, poor parents, and developing countries. It makes sense: by regulating against extremes on both ends of the societal spectrum, we would mitigate our own chances of being really badly off if our lottery ball was not the best. Buffett claims that much of his success is due to the fact that he won the Ovarian Lottery: he was born to affluent parents in a safe city of the United States just as they rose to become a world power, was a white male with higher than average IQ and had a gift for growing capital. He had access to excellent education, met brilliant mentors, and became expert at investing just as the Boomer economy launched.

But he asks what about those who drew a different lottery ball? What about those born with a lower IQ, or to struggling or single or addicted parents, or in developing countries where poverty is inescapable? What about those people?

I find Buffett's humility and compassion refreshing. While I'm puzzled and annoyed that he has invested in Goldman Sachs and Wells Fargo bank, I still find him exemplar to the financial industry. The second wealthiest man on earth believes and advocates for a fairer capitalist system that taxes people like him sufficiently to support a healthy middle class and the less fortunate of society. The money is there, and a healthier society yields a healthier economy.

So there we have it. Capitalism by its very nature as a system, when unregulated, leads over time to income inequality and destroys democracy. And even when regulated, if the leaders in government and business are corrupt, it fails again. Finally, income inequality, by weakening the middle class and oppressing the poor, leads to unstable societies, and often towards fascism and oligarchy.

This, in my view, is our second most perilous Burning Platform issue and only high quality authentic leadership, cooperating around the globe will properly address it. The concept of the tax shelter must be eliminated, along with the carried interest loophole and similar scams.

The final Burning Platform argument for necessary, immediate, and radical transformation is the VUCA world and its ensuing chaos. Let's visit there now.

CHAPTER 7

Burning Platform 3 – Chaos in the VUCA World

"This is the moment for all living systems when new birth is available. The critical thing that leads to what comes next out of chaos are the values we choose to organize around." Margaret Wheatley, 1999

RECALL IF YOU WILL, THAT THIS WHOLE BURNING PLATFORM exercise is an attempt to convince you that the world is changing quickly and drastically, and that we must find the will and adaptability to act differently if we wish to avert several disasters. The third burning platform is the VUCA world; the acronym seeks to capture the characteristics of today's business and political worlds (Volatile, Uncertain, Complex, Ambiguous). It is slightly different than the other two in that it's a two-edged sword that can affect things on a smaller scale. Climate change and income inequality are macro issues that require action at large scale: we must deal with them together, *as the human race,* or else face pervasive damage. This is because if only a few countries and companies take action while others do not, the *solution cannot be achieved.* It's a zero sum game. But with VUCA world, individual organizations *can* decide a course of action independently, without imperiling humanity or democracy. On the down side, things are changing so radically and quickly that organizations that fail to keep up will face a high probability of perishing. On the upside, those organizations that *do* transform will reposition themselves perfectly to capitalize on amazing possibilities. The choices to change or not can be and are being made independently by many organizations.

Anyone who has worked in the business world during the past twenty-five years has encountered the acronym VUCA world. It's other things too, but the VUCA four cover a lot of what companies, governments, and we, are up against. Management guru Tom Peters wrote:

"The tough old union militant remembers. Not 1870. (Of course.) But 1970. (Not exactly an eon ago.) Took 108 guys some 5 days to unload a ship full of timber. And now? Container daze: Eight guys…one day. (!!!) No big deal. It happened on the farm. It happened in the distribution center and in the factory."

Peters wrote that in 1990! No Internet, PCs just starting to catch on, no iPhone, no virtual reality (VR), no AI, no first generation robots.

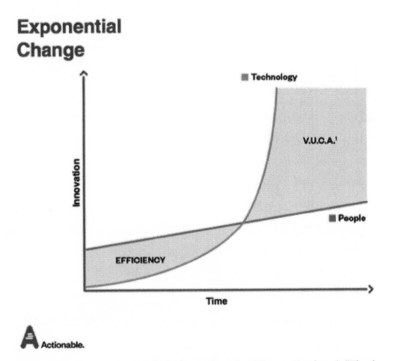

Source: Eric "Astro" Teller's idea explained in Thomas Friedman's "Thank You for Being Late, 2016.

Twenty-eight years later we are simply flying along at great speed of innovation and disruption. Intel co-founder, Gordon Moore is partly famous for his Moore's Law, which predicted back in 1970 that the speed of a silicon chip would double every twenty-four months, and the cost would roughly halve. While the pace has slightly slowed today, it is only by a small amount.

The chart is most interesting too. The curved line shows the exponential growth of technological innovation, while the straight line shows the capacity of people to keep up. Prior to the lines intersecting, we humans were able to understand, harness and apply the technology, which yielded higher productivity growth and efficiency. However, as the pace of tech development took off, our ability to stay abreast of, understand, and apply it grew at a linear, not exponential pace. This created the gap you can see, and the result has been VUCA world. Tech changes faster than many of us can keep up.

In Jim Collin's *Good to Great*, the smash best-selling business book published in 2001, he applauds eleven 'great' companies that managed the transition from good to great.[1] Today, one has gone out of business (Circuit City), two have been shamed and fined for unethical and illegal activity (Fannie Mae, Wells Fargo Bank), one (Gillette) has been bought out by a larger company (Proctor & Gamble). So in seventeen years, 4 of 11 outstanding companies have fallen from the list. These and all companies have experienced disruption; not simply a tweaking of the old ways, or a slight innovation on a standard, but complete disruption. (Barnes and Noble and Best Buy became brick and mortar showrooms for Amazon, as people would go to their stores to physically check out the book or product, learn about it from sales staff, then leave and order it for cheaper online at Amazon.)

3D printing has only begun to turn the manufacturing and tool and die industries upside down. The mobility of our world today makes it hard to believe that the first true smart phone, the Apple iPhone, (sorry Blackberry fans; no offense intended) has only been with us since 2007. Imagine you're the CEO of Canon or Nikon, and you heard Apple was making a phone. It would be completely excusable if you dismissed it as non-threatening. After all, it's a phone, and we make cameras! And yet… I can clearly recall my son showing me the camera in his iPhone 4S, and me asking him why the hell would anyone want a camera in their phone. I've since eaten my words (many times), as he sends me a short video of my new grandson every couple of days. The technology lets me watch him grow up in Alexandria, Virginia, from my home in Mississauga, Canada. Marvellous!It is difficult to remember how our world worked prior to smart phones, yet it's only been eleven years.

A couple of years prior to the 2007 iPhone launch, journalist Tom Friedman was already astounding the world with his best-selling book *The World is Flat*. A three-time Pulitzer Prize-winning journalist for *The New York Times*, Friedman's expertise lies in foreign affairs, the Middle East and global trade. He had taken a trip to India to "understand why the Indians I met were taking our work, why they had become such an important pool for the outsourcing of service and information technology work from America and other industrialized countries."[2]

Similar to our Boiling Frog analogy, Tom named his first chapter 'While I Was Sleeping'. Following 9/11, he spent many years in the Arab and Muslim worlds trying to make sense of events, and interpret them for his readers. During this time, he says, he wasn't really sleeping; just otherwise engaged, and "lost the trail of globalization." But in India, after a meeting with CEO of giant Infosys, Nandan Nilekani, Friedman came to the conclusion that the world had become much smaller and "flatter". He suggested there had been three major globalizations: Globalization 1.0 was from 1492 to around 1800, when Columbus opened up the world for *countries* to expand trade. Globalization 2.0 was from 1800 until 2000, and was driven primarily by multi-national *corporations*. Globalization 3.0, enabled and fueled by the global fiber-optic cable network, the Internet and e-commerce, began in 2000, providing newfound power for *individuals* to collaborate and compete globally.

Friedman goes on to identify what he calls the ten flatteners of the world (Fall of Berlin Wall, Launch of Netscape, Work flow software, Open-sourcing,

Outsourcing, Offshoring Supply chaining, Insourcing, Informing and Digital/Mobile/Virtual). He takes time to point out also, that Globalization 3.0 is not driven (unlike 1.0 and 2.0) by Western white people and companies, but rather by Eastern, non-white, individuals. While all these forces are still contributing to the VUCA condition, it's important to remember that his book came out in 2005. A hell of a lot has happened since then to intensify the VUCA situation. Blockchain, cryptocurrency, robotics, virtual reality, and AI, and other inventions have since arrived, and will inevitably disrupt (at the very least) banking and finance, medicine, law, manufacturing, transportation and agriculture.

In my view, the biggest challenge presented by Burning Platform 3 is the required reinvention of our organizations into a form that understands and leverages culture. This involves an enormous leap, primarily because of current entrenched bureaucratic structures, and the type and style of leadership that has traditionally run that type of organization. But that type of organization simply *cannot* move quickly enough to even keep pace, let alone gain advantage and capitalize on opportunities. For that, organizations need agility and resilience, seamless teamwork, and a culture of inclusion, ownership and responsibility.

And those can only be achieved through those old 'Soft S's', people skills and a different style of leadership. It's glaringly apparent: our organizations need to transform. At the 2018 Peter Drucker Forum, the success of companies experimenting with new forms of organization was discussed. Many in the audience were surprised to learn that not only were these companies more profitable than their 'old school' competitors, but that their profits were the result, not the purpose, of their existence. Furthermore, their remarkable resilience and agility grew from a bottom-up as opposed to top-down approach; one that recognized, included and celebrated the interconnectedness of stakeholders, particularly employees. "In any ecosystem, there are many different perspectives: Not everyone agrees on everything and each of these perspectives has a certain value. The community needs to grow, but this is something that cannot be directed or managed. It needs to be nurtured and inspired. We need to be developing the conditions that enable that growth".[3]

If you pay attention to the business world, you've no doubt heard the alarming statistics from the regular Gallup Polls on employee engagement. Here's the latest from the 2017 Global Poll:

> *"According to our recent State of the Global Workplace report, 85% of employees are not engaged or actively disengaged at work. The economic consequences of this global "norm" are approximately $7 trillion in lost productivity. Eighteen percent are "actively disengaged" in their work and workplace, while 67% are "not engaged." This latter group makes up the majority of the workforce – they are not your worst performers, but they are indifferent to your organization. They give you their time, but not their best effort nor their best ideas. They likely come to work wanting to make a difference – but nobody has ever asked them to use their strengths to make the organization better."[4]*

Eighteen percent "actively disengaged"! That's almost one fifth of our workforce. And it speaks volumes about the leadership of our organizations globally, because there are dozens of studies that prove the <u>direct co-relation and causality between employee engagement, performance, and quality of leadership.</u>[5] If leadership drives culture and culture drives capability and performance, then the Gallup findings not only support my contention of a leadership crisis, but also raises a red flag about our organizations' ability to survive as the world becomes even more VUCA. In my own consulting experience, the percentage of what I would call emotionally intelligent managers remains disturbingly small, at a time that may well be the most turbulent change in history. We have old school

> *"We cannot solve our problems with the same thinking we used when we created them."*
>
> **ALBERT EINSTEIN**

command and control leaders running rigid, bureaucratic organizations, in an environment that changes almost monthly (daily?). It's Burning Platform 3 for sure.

And our governments, already too unduly influenced by that same business leadership, are trying to use the same old solutions to solve these unique, challenging problems.

So they continue to apply outdated fiscal and monetary policies, which are at best a short-term, Band-Aid remedy, and will leave them woefully unprepared to deal with what is coming. The Canadian Economic Growth Advisory Council, headed by McKinsey Consulting Global Director, Domenic Barton, recently released an opinion which stated, "roughly 40% of existing jobs in Canada will disappear within the next decade, due to automation, and that *governments need to craft 'new social contracts' with Canadians to avoid deepening income inequality over time* [italics mine] ".[6]

Barton said the gulf between rich and poor could become wider as those Canadians who aren't on the leading edge of technological change are left behind. That is going to require governments to figure out what to do with older workers who are expected to lose their jobs to technology, and to focus their energy and finances on a few key areas instead of trying to be great at everything. The market should decide what areas to invest in.

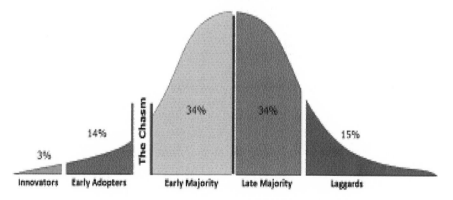

But, there is also a very sunny side to this situation. Fortunately, in experimenting with new forms of organization, society is not at the very beginning of the learning curve. Many companies have been testing and refining more fluid (I call them enlightened) structures and policies; and I believe we are in the early adopters stage, meaning the rest of us can go to school on them.

Of course, for the vast majority, the scary 'Chasm' remains ahead, but at least there is a roadmap, and they can reduce risk by learning from those who have forged ahead. When one learns of the amazing capabilities of these new types of organizations (sometimes called Teal Companies, sometimes Holacracies), it is nothing short of exhilarating. People in these organizations are highly engaged, trusted, challenged, and are given input and expected to contribute to decisions. Leaders see their role as creating other leaders; as developing their people to reach their full potential. The results show up as strong corporate cultures that are vibrantly 'alive' and constantly changing with the flow of events as required.

Consider two examples:

- Auto Electric Supplies (AES) is an American energy company that is one of the world's largest electricity production and distribution companies with 40,000 employees. Its co-founder and former CEO, Dennis Bakke, began experimenting with new organizational structure and process back in the 1980s and refined it through trial and error over the years. One of their unique systems dealt with self-management and was called the 'advice process.' Basically, any employee could drive a decision forward, with the proviso that they *must* seek advice first from experts within the company, and also from *all* parties that would be affected by the decision. The bigger, riskier or more costly the decision, the wider the net of people to be included.

  So one day a recently hired financial analyst, Shazad, went to see the CEO Bakke (how often does that happen in traditional organizations?) and said he wanted to go back to Pakistan as an agent of AES and convince them to build a power plant. Bakke was honest and informed Shazad that AES had had professional consultants look at the opportunity and all had concluded that a) AES didn't know enough to do risky business in Pakistan, and b) given AES's high ethical standards, they felt the corrupt culture of business there would be too onerous.

Here's the exciting part:

"Despite the CEO's recommendation, the advice process meant that the decision was Shazad's. He decided to go to Pakistan, effectively creating a new position for himself as business developer, retaining his previous salary. Six months later, the former financial analyst invited Bakke to meet the Prime Minister. Two and a half years later, a $700 million power plant was running. In line with AES's principles, the decision that AES would invest $200 million of its own equity wasn't made by Bakke or the Board, but by Shazad and people with less seniority (who of course, given the amounts at stake, asked Bakke and the board for advice.)"[7]

To me, this is an incredible story that is both exciting and uplifting. A control mechanism is in place, but one that encourages dialogue, smashes silos, builds relationships and networks, and offers everyone a chance to contribute in as big a way as they are willing to take on the responsibility. In a sense, they're saying, 'you feel strongly that we should be doing something? Make your case and go do it!' Most importantly, consider how a squad of Shazads on your team would handle a VUCA world for your company or government department.

• Morning Star is the largest tomato processing company in the world, with over 40% of the US market for tomato paste and diced tomatoes. It has 200 trucks, three state of the art processing plants, and 2400 employees. Started by a newly minted MBA, Chris Rufer, in 1970, with one truck and one employee, it was agreed that two social values would inspire every management practice at the company: *Never use force* against other people, and *honor your commitments*. This philosophy grew into their Colleague Principles, which are used for conflict resolution with excellent results. All of their management principles revolved around the belief in self-management, and over the past forty-eight years, each colleague focused on his/her own self-development and what they can contribute to to company. This is highly unusual even today, let alone in 1970.

The result is "23 teams (called Business Units), no management positions, no HR department and no Purchasing Department. Colleagues can make all business decisions, including buying expensive equipment on company funds, provided they have sought advice from the colleagues that will be affected or have expertise."[8]

The encouraging news here is that these two organizations handle VUCA issues with much greater ease because of their highly developed, self-managing people. Two other necessary and common ingredients: an attitude of wholeness, where people are encouraged and supported in bringing their full selves to work (not just a professional persona); and a constant listening for purpose. They ensure they stay focused on the true reasons for the business to exist, not simply making money or maximizing shareholder returns.

So already we have the tools and examples to follow in the effort to transform our current organizations. There are large and small companies already thriving under these structures. Transformation is incredibly difficult, but in the coming years, organizations, rigid hierarchies, cultures, command and control leadership methods and employee productivity will endure enormous strains and stresses as the VUCA world intensifies. Those that can flex and bend will survive. It's worth the effort to transform because there is no choice, but we will need leaders with the characteristics outlined in Chapter 2. As Jordan Peterson so eloquently suggests: "To stand up straight with your shoulders back is to accept the terrible responsibility of life, with eyes wide open. It means casting dead, rigid and too tyrannical order back into the chaos in which it was generated; it means withstanding the ensuing uncertainty, and establishing, in consequence, a better, more meaningful and more productive order."[9]

A final word about chaos. This may sound weird to many readers, but please stay open-minded. As mentioned earlier in the book, my interests range from business and leadership, to layman's quantum physics, to the sages and mystics of ancient times, to conscious awareness and mindfulness, to neuroscience, human potential, organizational culture and the like. While researching, I encountered similar ideas and descriptions in books from each discipline; I began to see a common thread, one which supports the notion of singularity (that we are all one), that there is an interconnectedness and a networked ecosystem of all things on earth and in space. Some of these notions have yet to be proven by science, but there is strong evidence for many of them, with much more research underway. Some of it will be shared in the coming chapters. But for now, some thoughts on chaos. Margaret Wheatley has long been considered one of the top Organizational Theory and Practice consultants in the world. In the late 1980s, dissatisfied with the results of her work helping her large clients manage change, she happened upon a book, *The Turning Point*, by quantum physicist Fritjof Capra. It was the beginning of Wheatley's journey to explore how the realities of the quantum world might apply to our organizations and

Source: Mario Markus, Reprinted With Permission

their behaviour. Her fascinating resulting work, *Leadership and the New Science*, opened the door to new thinking in her field. She looked primarily at three areas: Quantum physics, self-organizing systems, and chaos theory, and how new discoveries in those fields might apply to organizational theory. For example, she looked at current science in biology and chemistry, and noticed that "*self-organizing systems demonstrate the ability of all life to organize into systems of relationship that result in increasing capacity. These living systems also demonstrate a different relationship between autonomy and control, showing how a large system is able to maintain itself only because it encourages great amounts of individual freedom.*"[10]

She became convinced that there must be a simpler way, much less stressful, to lead organizations, and her book offers many insights as to how the three areas can be applied to do that. The picture above is called a chaotic strange attractor and is a computerized self-portrait drawn by a chaotic system. Wheatley notes that the system appears to be wandering chaotically, always displaying new and different behaviour, yet over millions of iterations, a deeper order or shape is revealed. She says, "this order is inherent to the system. It was always there, but not revealed until its chaotic movements were plotted in multiple dimensions over time."[11]

She observed that all organizations are similarly fractal in nature. That is, a recurring pattern of behaviour, which is identical to the culture of an organization. A company's value system, when lived out authentically, feeds back on itself and creates a pattern of order. Thus, we can see how the Teal Organizations like AES and Morning Star, Zappos, and Patagonia pull it off, using self-management and values instead of command and control systems. The laws of chaos actually teach us that there *is* underlying order, but it evolves not from leaders telling people what to do and when, but rather from clarifying beliefs, values, and the purpose of the organization, and then leading by example to bring them to life. Painful as it is, VUCA world may just have the silver lining of dragging us kicking and screaming into learning an entirely new way of organizing, leading, and achieving a better standard of living.

CHAPTER 8

Inspiring Vision 1 – The Third Industrial Revolution

"If I had told you 25 years ago (1989) that in a quarter century's time, one third of the human race would be communicating with each other in huge global networks of hundreds of millions of people-exchanging audio, video, and text – and that the combined knowledge of the world would be accessible from a cellphone, that any single individual could post a new idea, introduce a product, or pass a thought to a billion people simultaneously, **and that the cost of doing so would be nearly free,** [emphasis mine] *you would have shaken your head in disbelief. All are now reality."* Jeremy Rifkin, 2014

AT THIS POINT, I HOPE YOU ARE STARTING TO AGREE THAT it's wise and prudent to be deeply concerned about our leadership crisis, about our long-entrenched assumptions and expectations about leaders that brought us to this point and about whether we will take the more difficult but imperative action to remedy it. The looming damages of climate change, income inequality and an increasingly VUCA world simply must be addressed, and quickly, if we desire health and happiness for our children. But the second half of this book will show that there is also great cause for excitement, optimism, and positive thinking if we do choose to meet those challenges.

While the Burning Platform approach to change and transformation does have its uses, far more powerful is the use of shared values and vision.

Effective vision is powerful because it is inclusive and connects with both the intellect and the emotions of everyone involved.

By addressing the Burning Platform issues, we also face extraordinary opportunities to create a better world. Let's call these non-fear driven methods Inspiring Visions, because if we become truly aware of those new possibilities, it's difficult not to feel an inspired urge to participate in the creative process. Three very important inspiring visions we'll examine are: the Third Industrial Revolution, Conscious Capitalism, and recent discoveries in human conscious awareness, potential and fulfillment.

Once again, though, we must ensure that we find and appoint the right people to lead us to those better conditions. The choices we face and the work ahead require leaders with courage, conviction, integrity and above all, a vision of something greater than their own well-being and personal gain.

But first, what is this 'vision thing' that's been thrown around for the past twenty years? We don't want to get bogged down in academic theory here, so I'll offer you what I believe is an excellent definition by Jim Collins and Jerry Porras, and then a couple of excellent examples to illustrate. They say that an organization's vision is a combination of *Core Ideology* (which comprises core values and its core purpose or mission), and a *10- to 30-year ambitious goal* (they call it a Big Hairy Audacious Goal: BHAG), expressed with *vivid descriptions*.[1] While the time period of 10-30 years is far too long in a VUCA world corporate context, effective shifts to sustainable energy to combat climate change solutions will likely take that much time to fully materialize. But the idea is to select a challenging project that best reflects the next progression for the organization and its mission; one with a bit of a 'gulp factor', and then to inspire followers with emotional language and intellectual arguments to get on board, buy in, and help make it happen.

Here are a couple of famous examples:[2]

1. Ford Motor Co. Vision (early 1900s): "Democratize the automobile"

Henry Ford's visionary vivid description: *"I will build a motor car for the great multitude…it will be so low in price that no man making a good salary will be unable to own one – and enjoy with his family the blessing of hours of pleasure in God's great open spaces… When I'm through everybody will be able to afford one and everyone will have one. The horse will have disappeared from our highways, the automobile will be taken for granted…and we will give a large number of men employment at good wages."* P.97

2. Sony Corporation (1950) Vision: "To experience the sheer joy of innovation and the application of technology for the benefit and pleasure of the general public and to become the company most known for changing the worldwide image of Japanese products for being of poor quality." (Akio Morita, 1952) p239

Sony Vivid Description: *"We will create products that become pervasive around the world…we will be the first Japanese company to go into the American market and distribute directly…we will succeed with innovations like the transistor radio that American companies have failed at… Fifty years from now our brand will be as well-known as any on earth and will signify innovation and quality that rivals the most innovative companies anywhere… Made in Japan will mean something fine, not shoddy."* P239

When you read those two examples did you think, 'wow, those were both super ambitious undertakings?' Could you feel the 'gulp factor' that they must have felt at the time? And yet despite the odds against, they both pulled it off!

It's worth noting a few of things here:

- Both companies faced long odds. Ford was tinkering with a completely new, unproven and intimidating product, with a 'horse-comfortable', skeptical society. Sony was still smarting from global fury, racism and disgust, only seven years following WWII. These were bold, courageous visions.

- The combination of very specific detailed language to appeal to the intellect (e.g. get people thinking, 'maybe, just maybe, we could do this'), and emotional language to appeal to the heart and soul. We'll revisit this in the quantum stuff in Chapter 10, but for now the key takeaway is to appeal to both head and heart to gain full personal commitment to the cause.

- Notice neither one (nor do any excellent vision statements) mentioned money, profitability, return on shareholder investment, or the leader's personality or role. While they've had their ups and downs, both companies are still globally functioning, and profitable; Ford 118 years old and Sony 65 years old. Many companies have long since come and gone in that time. Companies with great visions earn better returns and stick around longer, largely because they exist to achieve some purpose; profit is a necessary result of whatever they exist to accomplish. They believe in the old adage 'profit is like oxygen; you absolutely need it to survive, but it is not why you exist'.

By now you've noticed that I contend we're in a global situation that demands big courageous visions. Alexandria Ocasio Cortez (D-NY) and Senator Ed Markey (D-MA) sponsored a resolution in March 2019 for a Green New Deal. It called for broad strategic initiatives to address climate change and income inequality by re-training fossil fuel industry workers, and creating jobs in sustainable energy. This is exactly the type of vision we need, similar to that which pulled America out of the Great Depression, and it requires bold, new thinking, and the courage, integrity and discipline to accept facts and let go of past practices. This is never easy, but offers growth and progress along with any pain. Of course, it was voted down, due, in my view to the entrenched fossil fuel lobby, and its beholden politicians. They refuse to accept that climate change is real and human created, and have vested obligations to their powerful sponsors. Hiding behind a feigned concern for fiscal responsibility, they ask "How will you pay for that?" But they are presuming (insisting?) that the current paradigm remain intact. They are thinking within the myopic context of a $735 billion annual 'Defense' budget and accepting it as a 'given'; 'we cannot cut defense spending for climate change programs!' It is old paradigm thinking, and more than a little influenced by greed and power.

I read somewhere that one cannot jump a chasm in two leaps. We now face unprecedented existential challenges that an incremental change approach will not solve. We must think and act big, and these new technologies, properly managed, will allow us to do that. We must support leaders like AOC and Markey who have the courage to recognize truth and call for a massive visionary solution that benefits the greatest number.

With this understanding of vision as a foundation, let's examine one of the most thrilling opportunities we face today. Ironically, it arises from the very same forces that are causing our current VUCA world. According to consultant Jeremy Rifkin, and many others who study trends, we are in the midst of the Third Industrial Revolution.

Recall from Chapter 3 that Rifkin posits that whenever technological innovation impacted three areas simultaneously (communication, energy, and transportation/logistics) they converged and created a new general purpose technology platform, and we experienced an industrial revolution that disrupted and transformed society in radical ways, destroying some industries while simultaneously inventing new ones.

To recap:

First Industrial Revolution – 1760-1850

- Communication: steam powered printing presses, telegraph

- Energy: coal powered steam infrastructure

- Transport/Logistics: steam powered locomotive trains, distributed rail infrastructure

Second Industrial Revolution – 1880-1990

- Communication: telephone, radio, television

- Energy: electric lighting and commercial applications, oil-fueled combustion engines

- Transport/Logistics: paved highway infrastructure, distributed automobiles, trucks, airplanes, trains

According to Rifkin, in the First Revolution, "The coming together of steam powered printing, the telegraph and the steam powered locomotive dramatically increased the speed and dependability with which economic resources could be marshaled, transported, processed, transformed into products and distributed to customers. The newfound speed and volume of economic activity…required a complete rethinking of the business model across every industry."[3]

During the Second Industrial Revolution, the process continued and accelerated, resulting in vertically integrated corporations, "becoming the most efficient means of organizing production and distribution of mass produced goods and services…dramatically reducing transaction costs, increasing efficiencies and productivity, lowering prices to consumers and allowing the economy to flourish."[4]

Many things happened peripherally due to these two revolutions, but at least two had very important, likely unforeseen and therefore unintended consequences. The first was the creation of the middle class. Back in the 1700s, while the Guilds had already established the merchant class, it was this explosion of industry and its accompanying demand for labour that finally killed the feudal system in Europe and eventually America, drawing thousands to the cities, and restructuring the ability of the average person to earn wages without subservience to an aristocratic landlord.

Second, a far subtler and even more important result occurred: each revolution contributed to a small yet crucial shift in power from the owners of capital to the owners of labour. Now, as we've seen, unregulated capitalism resulted in the Gilded Age, with terrible exploitation of labour and the inevitable income inequality that followed. Nevertheless, these capitalist industrial revolutions still created a skilled labour pool that gained some degree of mobility; and mobility means choice which means power. Out of this system came the labour unions and periodic government regulation, all of which at least partially restrained the plutocrats, and eventually resulted in legislated minimum wages, safer working conditions, a shorter hour work week, and a higher standard of living for the new middle class.

While their disruption certainly included painful transformation for many, these industrial revolutions, with proper checks and balances enacted by responsible social, government and business leaders, have elevated society each time to a new and higher platform of existence – for example, the next generation of the average family in developed countries where the disruption took place were better off than pre-revolution.

But evidence also shows that once the dust settles and we acclimatize to the new world, human nature kicks in, we become complacent and disinterested and the frog once again starts a slow boil. Over time, exploitation, corruption and manipulation by government and business leaders can revert society to former prosperity levels or worse. Recall the purchasing power chart shown in Chapter 6 (P. 89)

As you well know by now, this book contends that we're back to 'that place' now. And yet, as this Third Industrial Revolution really begins to take off, we can make important choices that can result in an incredible world: high productivity, lower poverty, more time to pursue personal dreams and lines of work, improved health and longevity, even fewer wars, if indeed that's what we want. Here's what Rifkin says about revolution number three:

Third Industrial Revolution:

- Communication: the Internet and Internet of things, AI, VR, blockchain

- Energy: sustainable sources – solar, wind, hydro/tidal, geothermal; cheap storage

- Transport/Logistics: autonomous 'smart' integrated vehicles, roads, storage facilities, drones.

This digital revolution will result in the evolution of three separate internets (communication, energy and transport/logistics) set up atop the Internet of things platform, where all data from multiple technological devices in each internet will be shared, analyzed, and used to increase efficiencies and reduce costs across all industries. It will essentially become an external global brain. Capitalism as we know it will be radically transformed, largely by eliminating middlemen, and by reducing marginal costs to zero (marginal cost is simply an economic term for the cost of producing an additional unit). Communication is the best example to explain it: how much does it cost us to send an email? We have to pay our monthly fee to our Internet service provider (ISP) to access the Internet, but then every email we send that month drives the unit cost per email lower. (So if we pay $50/month and send 5 emails, it's $10 each. If we send 1000 emails, it drops to 5¢ each; 10,000 emails, it's half a cent each and so on. Every additional unit drives the cost per unit lower.)

These disruptive technologies are forcing the rethinking of the traditional capitalist profit model, simply because for many products and services, the cost will be zero or near zero. This phenomenon is already affecting many industries. Consider the music business, publishing, video and television, and taxis. All of them have been seriously disrupted in only the past ten years by innovative digital technology.

Consider energy. The cost of a watt of solar energy has dropped from US$78 in 1970 to 60¢ today (recall Moore's Law from the previous chapter), and is estimated to hit 21¢ by 2040. Because there is no cost to sustainable energy from source (e.g. the sun, wind, geothermal); once you've paid back the solar panels and hardware storage costs, your energy is essentially free.

For a long time, the bottleneck that prevented solar from adoption was not only cost per panel, but also storage limitations. But now, one can buy a Tesla Powerwall battery to mount on a wall, and store as much energy as necessary from sunny days, to offset cloudy times.

This is not soothsaying; it is *already happening*. In a section of Brooklyn, a <u>Brooklyn Microgrid</u> has been set up by placing solar panels on row house rooftops and inviting others in the vicinity to join. This model has amazing benefits: people become what Rifkin calls "prosumers" by producing and consuming their own electricity. And, because of another dynamic and highly disruptive technology called blockchain, they become peer-to-peer suppliers, who generate electricity, use what they need, and then sell excess to local peers and businesses who require it. They can also sell any surplus energy back to the main centralized grid, or not.

Think about that for a moment. Hurricane Sandy shuts down the main utility grid for five days, but you and your local community have no power interruption because you have a battery storage of sun energy accumulated prior to the storm. And you can sell your excess energy to others who are connected.[5]

This is an amazing opportunity. We are actually shifting energy 180°, from a significant budgeted expense, to either near-free, or even a source of income. Further, by shifting to a decentralized model (e.g. away from one huge centralized source), if a major generator goes down in a storm, the majority of the network retains power.

What about transportation? How much are you paying annually for auto insurance?

Once automated vehicles become ubiquitous, the incidence of accidents will nose dive, driving the cost of insurance towards zero. The total of your energy and insurance costs will then become additional discretionary income bettering your lifestyle.

And let's look at autos. Every day, millions of people drive their cars to work, park, go inside and work for eight hours, then drive home and park again. OK, this is simplistic, but you get the point. On average, it is said that 75% of the time, an owned vehicle sits dormant. This is grossly inefficient for a depreciating asset; an enormous waste of capital. Digital technology coupled with GPS and autonomous vehicles will soon greatly diminish personal vehicle ownership. Think about it: if you could be assured of a new, safe, clean vehicle at your door within a few minutes, anywhere you were, would you decide to still carry the financial burden of ownership? The productivity of shared vehicles will be so high that it could drive the cost to near zero as well. Imagine a world where cars, buses, subways and trains are all powered by sustainable energy and that the cost or fee is almost zero. All the funds that currently support those industries will be freed up to flow into other endeavors. Again, these things are not pipe-dreams; they are already happening. Autonomous transport trucks deliver refrigerators from Texas to California[6] regularly. 'Smart roads and trucks' have connected Austria to Switzerland for years now.

Is it starting to become apparent how a VUCA scenario also can be used to create a much better world? In the developing world, sunny climates mean sustainable energy and storage can be used to power water pumps, meaning children who normally walk miles a day to fetch water can now attend school. The positive repercussions can be enormous.

A few words about blockchain, without which much of this technology could not work together. A blockchain is like a digital accounting ledger that connects every transaction (block) to the block prior, creating a 'chain' that prevents tampering or manipulation. If someone wanted to tamper with a block entry, they'd have to adjust all the blocks registered prior; a statistically impossible task. You've no doubt heard of it mentioned in the same breath as cryptocurrencies (many think they're one and the same), but the blockchain is what allows cryptocurrencies to establish their value and integrity. Why? Earlier we talked about the importance of trust, between us and our leaders, between us and our institutions, between each of us in society. Businesses honor our currency because they trust that the government stands behind it. What true value do credit card companies provide?

They act as a middleman to vouch for us to the merchant who does not know us. Yes? A valuable service, and one worth some reasonable fee. Up until now.

Because what if you and I could find a way to conduct transactions between us where we were sure we could trust each other without a middleman? The blockchain does exactly that.

One of the original hopes for the world was that the Internet would enable peer-to-peer empowerment for all. Yet as with all tech, there are pluses and minuses. Yes, the ability to connect with billions of people globally was spectacular, but among them are spammers, identity thieves, phishers, spies, hackers, cyberbullies, data-nappers and Russian election fraudsters. How would one guard against them?

Following the 2008 financial fiasco, a person or persons known as Satoshi Nakamoto (no one knows for sure who this is) created a peer-to-peer electronic cash system using a cryptocurrency called bitcoin. Authors Don and Alex Tapscott wrote, "this (blockchain) protocol established a set of rules – in the form of distributed computations – that ensured the *integrity* of the data exchanged among these billions of devices *without going through a trusted third party.* This seemingly subtle act 'set off a spark that has excited, terrified, or otherwise captured the imagination of the computing world and has spread like wildfire to businesses, governments, privacy advocates, social development activists, media theorists, and journalists, to name a few, everywhere.'"[7]

Without getting bogged down in technological description, the greatest benefit to mankind of blockchain will be the capacity for "trusted transactions directly between two or more parties, authenticated by mass collaboration, and powered by collective self-interests rather than by large corporations motivated by profit."[8]

Take a moment to visualize a world like this. Currently, our personal data is collected, analyzed, and organized by large companies like VISA, Mastercard, Facebook, Amazon and other platforms, and often sold to other marketers and businesses. They neither own nor pay for our data, yet make money from its sale. Imagine if you owned your personal data, and could sell it directly to whomever you decided, for your own profit. Blockchain eventually will allow this. And you can instantly see the shift in power that will occur, from corporations to the public. Similarly, once the glitches inevitably experienced with a new concept like cryptocurrencies are resolved, envision a world without dependence on fiat currencies (those offered by governments). Different private markets with full transparency and solid currencies would be available to those whom the system trusts and welcomes. Another amazing feature of blockchain is its simple inclusion of the poor. People in developing countries, whom banks do not serve due to their low profitability, can use blockchain as their bank account, accessing and transferring money using only an old flip phone or smartphone. This will have a profound effect on their upward mobility and reduce their vulnerability to fiat currency and tyrannical leaders. Blockchain will heavily impact banking, finance, credit card companies, and contract law.

Artificial intelligence is already altering medicine (your new iWatch can actually read and diagnose your basic health systems; AI computers can already diagnose disease far more quickly and accurately than a panel of the most expert doctors). Virtual reality sports already see global competitions of highly skilled players, drawing millions of observers and the inevitable advertising dollars that follow. What impact will that have on professional live sports? Imagine a 'LeBron James' of virtual basketball who may be confined to a wheelchair, yet could earn a living that way? Wonderful possibilities. These are just a few trends of VUCA world that are redistributing power among us and opening doors to a much better life.

Rifkin and his colleagues are not naïve. They understand we are facing frightening challenges today, and they acknowledge that tools like blockchain and cryptocurrencies are in early stages and will require significant refining prior to going mainstream. But they have optimistic visions of the world once that happens and they maintain it is happening now. Rifkin has worked with Angela Merkel in Germany for seven years and with Xi Xinping in China for three years, building the principles of the digital revolution into their respective national growth strategies and action plans.

More important though, are the implications of technical innovations in the wrong hands. For example, AI is a perfect example to demonstrate the dire requirement for Level Five leaders as we enter VUCA world. All technological innovations are simply tools, neither good nor evil; a sharp knife can cut a steak or kill a human. It is the intention and the action that determine the utility of the tool. And this is of course, where leadership quality becomes absolutely critical. Brilliant experts like Tesla founder Elon Musk and the late Stephen Hawking were adamantly demanding that we slow down the progress of AI until proper ethical, moral and legal guidelines can be established. Their concerns are that even well-intended entrepreneurs could inadvertently 'let the genie out of the bottle' with self-learning AI, and once set 'free,' it could exceed the human capacity to control them, and endanger our very species.[9] From what I have learned so far, I agree with them. Recently, an AI-programmed computer easily beat a team of five top-skilled humans at a game called Dota 2. The game objective: for a team of super heroes to gain territory from a team of bad guys. The robot team now can play 180 years' worth of games in *a day*.[10]

Hawking drew attention directly to the necessity for quality leadership and a responsible, prudent approach: "I am an optimist and I believe that we can create AI for the good of the world. That it can work in harmony with us. We simply need to be aware of the dangers, identify them, employ the best possible practice and management, and prepare for its consequences well in advance."[11] He recognized the dangers of autonomous weapons, "new ways for the few to oppress the many", and severe economic disruption. But both he, Bill Gates and even Musk, agree that with humane and elevated leadership, AI can help raise the world to a new and better level of prosperity and progress. We need leaders who will ensure the tool is used for the right purposes.

As with earlier revolutions, some of us older ones may resist or struggle to adapt, but used correctly and wisely, these powerful technologies will reduce problems like income inequality, financial fraud, privacy violations and abuses by corporations and governments. All we must do is become aware then active; understand what is happening and lend our support to those leaders who 'get it'.

Bill Gates recently painted a picture of a world where robots created the majority of (and radically increased) gross domestic productivity (GDP), with drastic reductions in the labour force. But he said governments must levy a tax on the corporations equal to the income taxes on the previous human labor and use that tax revenue to give a Universal Basic Income to every citizen. I would go even further and tax at a rate equal to their labour expenses. The corporations' profit margins would remain the same, while preventing excess money flowing to them and further contributing to income inequality. Gates suggests using robots to make the same goods and services we have today and freeing up labour to "reach out to the elderly, have smaller class sizes, help kids with special needs."[12] Radical idea? Perhaps it sounds so now, but only in the context of our current structure, living costs and business practices.

It is all changing drastically whether we like it or not. The wave cannot be stopped, nor should it be. Just as we stopped thinking about horses and carriages and started thinking about automobiles 110 years ago, so must we embrace these technologies and their power as an entirely different and progressive scenario. We need big, courageous visions for our future.

This is definitely *not* communism; it is instead a modified form of capitalism that more efficiently distributes resources and reduces opportunities for exploitation and human abuses.

The potential for an egalitarian, prosperous and thriving global society is enormous, and a big part of that new exciting world will be created by a concept called Conscious Capitalism.

CHAPTER 9

Inspiring Vision 2 –
Conscious Capitalism

"A point may soon be reached, much sooner perhaps than we are all of us aware of, when these economic needs are satisfied in the sense that we prefer to devote further energies to non-economic purposes." John Maynard Keynes, Economic Possibilities for Our Grandchildren, 1930

SO FAR, WE'VE REVIEWED MANY OF THE SINS OF UNFETTERED capitalism that we've experienced over the past couple of centuries. It is, as Piketty showed, an inherently flawed system that, left unregulated, automatically drives wealth to the top 1%, creating a serious imbalance of money and power that eventually destroys democracies.

In Chapter 6 we looked at the societal destruction that ensued following the 2008 global financial meltdown. Capitalism run amok, by amoral and/ or corrupt leaders, who knew that if the entire house of cards resultant from their high-risk strategies failed, the governments would have no choice but to bail them out. That is what's called moral hazard: making incredibly risky bets for extreme personal gain, knowing that the full risk is transferred to taxpayers or other third parties. It's exactly what happened.

Emerging prominently in the 1980s were two other dubious inventions of the capitalist system: hedge funds and private equity funds. Neither add any significant value to the economy (my opinion), and both play important roles in fueling income inequality, primarily because they almost exclusively serve the ultra-wealthy 1%. Both merit a quick look.

Hedge funds focus on investments that offer the highest possible returns in the shortest period of time, and invest in stocks, bonds, commodity futures, derivatives, or liquid companies. Their sole objective is fast, maximum profit; get in, make as much as possible for their investors, then exit.

Private equity (PE) firms also serve the very wealthy, and lately, pension funds, but require them to lock in their funds for usually a period of several years. They invest in companies (often distressed) with a goal of improving performance and efficiency, often placing their own advisers in the company to assist current management, and then either retain ownership, or sell the revamped company privately or through an initial public offering (IPO). This approach has been favorably used in the past to eliminate complacent or incompetent management and streamline 'fat' underperforming companies. Not all PE cases have negative consequences for society, and for some – especially mid-sized companies without access to public capital markets – they can be a source of needed and welcomed expertise and funding.

While the hedge fund's goal is to simply extract financial value regardless of potential devastation, and PE firms build-up and sell distressed companies over time, both have the primary mission of simply extracting value from their investments and funnelling it to themselves and their wealthy investors. The details of how they do it are quite interesting but beyond the scope and purpose of this book. However, it is debatable what, if any, value they add to society, and easy to show examples of considerable damage.

Sears Roebuck was a legacy company that everyone in North America knows well. Started in 1892, they rose to become the largest retailer in the world (remember when the Sears Tower in Chicago was for years the tallest building on earth?) and filed for bankruptcy protection in October of 2018. In-between those events, they revolutionized retailing through their catalogue, broadened the reach and ability of everyone to purchase their goods, lowered prices through scale operations, offered good employment to millions (over their 126-year life), and created a healthy tax base for thousands of local communities in America and abroad. Sears was a proud American capitalist success story; a company that added value to individual, community and country. It was an example of capitalism at its best.

Although Sears stumbled somewhat in the 1990s, and was affected, like all in retail, by the rise of Wal-Mart and later Amazon, they were still a healthy, viable company until 2004 when Eddie Lampert and his ESL Investments hedge fund showed up. To keep it simple, Lampert used debt to buy sufficient Sears stock to become largest shareholder, and took over as Sears' CEO (though he had only limited knowledge of retailing). He then sold off Sears real estate to Seritage, a firm *he created and partially owned*, to re-develop the real estate for multi-purpose use. Next, he sold off Sears legacy brands like Kenmore *to his own hedge fund*, for $400 million, slashed operating expenses, including advertising and labour in the stores, until the business slowly died. Lampert basically hollowed out the company, and transferred its value to himself and his investors, at the expense of employees, pensioners, other shareholders, and communities.

"Lampert has been accused in lawsuits filed by pensioners and Sears shareholders of picking apart the more-than-a-century-old retailer to enrich himself. 'This is a play to wring the last drop of value from Sears until there is nothing left,' said Mark A. Cohen, a former chief executive of Sears in Canada. 'And it's working.'"[1]

Here is a sad example of both the wonders and wickedness of capitalism. Sears revolutionized retailing and raised the level of excitement (imagine rural farm kids getting the new Sears catalogue before Christmas, in the 30s and 40s. Even myself in the 60s!), accessibility to and affordability of quality products. It made their owners deservedly rich and contributed to jobs, local tax bases and supplier health across America. A strong, innovative company that weathered the Great Depression, two world wars, the sixties, and the Great Recession over 126 years, only to be hollowed out and destroyed in 14 years by greed and self-serving activity that re-distributed much of the wealth to the 1%. At the time of this writing, Sears has discontinued severance payment to regular employees, yet asked the courts to approve $19 million in bonuses for remaining executives.

One more example, this one about private equity firms. In 2005, Bain Capital, a PE firm founded by 2012 US Presidential GOP candidate, Mitt Romney, and two other firms enacted a leveraged buyout of Toys-R-Us. In a leveraged buyout, the PE firm buys the target company by taking on huge debt, using the assets of the company as collateral. This is very important to note: the buyer puts as little of their own capital as possible into the deal and is not responsible for the debt. So Bain and partners put up $1.3 billion, strapped Toys-R-Us with a whopping $5.3 billion in debt and took the company private. This added $400 million a year in interest costs to Toys-R-Us, at the exact time when their stores needed revamping; and Amazon, Wal-Mart and Target were beginning to eat away at their market share. The debt burden proved too heavy and crippling in the long-term, restricting competitive strategy options and the company finally died in September 2017. As is often the case in these events, employees are denied pensions and severance, prompting lawsuits, which are currently in play with both Sears and Toys-R-Us. The latter laid off 30,000 employees, while Sears' number is approaching 90,000, as stores close.

Think of the multiplier effect[2] of all those salaries flowing back into the economy through product purchases for homes, children, school supplies, vacations, auto insurance and the like – now that money sits in the accounts of the wealthiest, with limited circulation and contribution to the health of society. Recall the Panama and Paradise Papers.

At this point you might be thinking: *this* is an Inspiring Vision? Of course not, but it's a good way to set the stage for what *is* Inspiring Vision 2: Conscious Capitalism.

Both the Sears and Toys-R-Us stories clearly emphasize the enormous impact of leadership on our world and quality of life. In hedge and PE fund buyout situations, the 'leaders' and their objective radically shift 180 degrees:

from paid CEO and managers responsible for creating the long-term, sustainable competitive advantage and future of a company, to private owners primarily concerned with extracting as much money as possible from the organization as quickly as possible, regardless of how that action impacts the health of the company. It is *always* the leadership and their goals, in any organization, that determines outcomes. Capitalism is simply an economic system, a theory that can be interpreted and managed in different ways, by different leaders. In 1970, Nobel Prize-winning economist, Milton Friedman wrote, "businessmen who take seriously their responsibilities for providing employment, eliminating discrimination, avoiding pollution or whatever else...are preaching pure and unadulterated socialism."[3]

Although this is pure nonsense, Friedman, whom *The Economist* magazine once called "the most influential economist of the second half of the twentieth century...possibly all of it", wielded a lot of clout (for decades) in influencing government and business opinion. In 1970, it was accepted as truth. Yet many of his theories were rooted in academic models and less so on empirical observation. He had particularly strong influence on the American Reagan and British Thatcher governments, resulting in their 'trickle-down' theory[4], which has since been proven completely false. As we've seen, in real life, tax cuts flow predominantly to the 1%. Yet that was the prevailing expert thinking of the day. We saw business and companies in a Newtonian way, with decisions in one sector being disconnected from others and it justified and fueled the obsessive short-term profit maximization movement for decades.

My contention is that when our government legislative branches permit financial industry leaders – like Wall Street investment banks, private equity and hedge funds, and even to some extent, academic economists – to define capitalism, they will do so, and in ways that are at best myopic, and at worst, self-serving and questionable. Most of us will lose out.

But conversely, there is no reason to 'throw the baby out with the bathwater.' Capitalism is *why* the developed world became the developed world! Natural markets, creativity, the risk and reward of innovation, entrepreneurship; all are positive aspects of the system. In the hands of the right leaders, capitalism remains a viable and positive force. The key is that the leaders must be conscious, and when they are, an inspiring vision arises.

In 2013, an inspiring and brave little book called *Conscious Capitalism: Liberating the Heroic Spirit of Business* was published by Whole Foods Market co-founder John Mackey, and consultant and Babson College professor Raj Sisodia. They proposed not only that capitalism remains the best economic system for a democracy, but that when operated with a higher consciousness, it yields even more productive results for companies *and communities*. Since its publication, more and more research has emerged in support of their contention.

The book can be considered one of the forerunners of the momentous movement of Conscious Capitalism, a movement that acknowledges, respects and embraces the interconnectivity and interrelatedness of all aspects of society, and asserts that businesses have an obligation to take a broader view of return on investment when making decisions. This is being driven by a powerful underlying force of human consciousness, that will be further explored in Chapter 10, and reflects a broader human view of the role of business in the ecosystem, and of how the world can work more effectively for all. And it is why we can adopt a new, different and inspiring vision of capitalism to help us move progressively forward.

Following the publication of Conscious Capitalism, the authors set up a non-profit organization to explain, develop and promote the concept of running a business consciously. Look at their Mission and Vision statements, and try to imagine the societal impact if all commerce was conducted with this mindset:

Mission: "Our mission is to tell the stories and share the wisdom of those who are inspiring transformational change in the world through business."

Vision: "We imagine a world that has unleashed the heroic spirit of business, where organizations champion each of their stakeholders in leading lives of purpose and meaning, and where sharing vulnerable stories strengthens our bonds and celebrates our differences."[5]

Sound too 'Pollyanna' to you? I understand. It *does* sound far too good to be true. But there are at least two very encouraging events that support and will accelerate this movement. The first is increasing empirical academic research that confirms, with highly reliable and valid statistics, that organizations that operate with a conscious capitalist approach *actually outperform* their competitors that do not. Studies conducted by Stanford's Jim Collins (*Built to Last,* and *Good to Great)*, by Harvard's Jim Heskett (*The Culture Cycle),* and by many others, show a strong co-relation between companies that emphasize culture, purpose, emotionally intelligent leadership and an inclusive stakeholder approach, consistently generate superior results over competitors that don't. This indicates that the notion of Conscious Capitalism has shifted from an opinion or theory, to a statistically supported probability.

What does that mean? It means that in the short term, any management team can exploit and hollow out its company for fast profits. But eventually it *must* either change or

Brunello Cucinelli was born into a peasant family in Castel Rigone, a fifteenth century little hamlet near Perugia, in 1953. After witnessing his father working in an 'unwelcoming environment', in 1978 he set up a small company and captivated the market with his idea of dyeing cashmere. His dream was to promote a concept of work that ensured "being moral and economic dignity." In 1985 he created headquarters in the small town of Solomeo, offering employment and capitalizing on the high quality craftsmanship and seamstress skills of the local people. His business has since grown to become a multi-billion-dollar luxury clothing design house. He uses his successful business as a framework to develop and nurture his dream of a capitalism that enhances the human being.

die, if for no other reason than their corporate boards will be compelled by fiduciary duty to demand it. To use a simplistic example: let's say a company has resisted switching to computerized systems (ridiculous, but to just make a point). It's safe to conclude that very shortly, all of their competitors that did switch to computers would be blowing past them in speed, efficiency and profits. Part of any board's responsibility is to hire the right leadership and ensure that those leaders understand and apply the most sophisticated tools available to maximize competitiveness. At some point, the board would have to insist that the company install computers and remove any management that declined to comply. This is why as more and more companies convert to a consciously capitalist approach and generate superior results, those companies that refuse to do so will be left behind. Their boards will have to force positive change if for no other reason than to reduce their own liability exposure to shareholders.

At the 2018 Peter Drucker Forum, there was much discussion about 'the post-bureaucratic paradigm', which explored companies using this newer approach. "We need to create a new way of transforming organizations," said Professor Gary Hamel, "where we are building a coalition of the willing that starts from the bottom-up. Social systems rarely change from the top-down. They change from people who are activists. We need every single employee to become an activist rather than waiting for permission. The responsibility is on all of us. For those leading these big old organizations, the message is clear: change or die".[6]

Sustaining Growth and Performance

billgeorge.org

Former CEO of Medtronic, Bill George, now teaches at Harvard, and is credited with coining the term 'authentic leadership'. George is a strong proponent of Conscious Capitalism and has demonstrated exactly why the concept is effective (see chart). His premise is basically (and I'll add, especially in a VUCA world), that innovation and customer service always drive the bus. And to systematize those behaviours, companies must earn the loyalty, hearts and minds of their people. That's the secret sauce. But it can only be achieved when employees' personal values align with those of the organization; when there's an environment of trust and when they feel their work has meaning and fulfilment.[7]

Still not convinced? George used this business approach to take Medtronic from a market capitalization of $400 million in 1985 to $60 billion in 2000! His like-minded successor has grown it to $110 billion today. We have ample and growing proof that Conscious Capitalism works.

The second favorable event is the recent public, high profile endorsement of the concept by a globally respected capitalist. In January 2018, Blackrock Investments founder, Larry Fink, a highly regarded financial veteran who manages $6 trillion in assets, wrote what may well become one of the most important business op-ed letters in the twenty-first century. Called *A Sense of Purpose*,[8] it was directed at all CEOs in the S&P 500 and challenged them to revise their traditional approach to capitalism. He literally calls for a 'new order of corporate governance'. This, in my view, was a huge milestone in the history of capitalism; his heavyweight imprimatur essentially giving other CEOs permission to broaden their definitions of return on investment to include all stakeholders as well as shareholders. More importantly, Fink uses Blackrock's goliath investment clout to push CEOs into clarifying their purpose and values, demonstrating how those are reflected in current strategies, and how those strategies promote long-term growth and stability. Here are some of the more encouraging reasons to believe that an inspiring vision of a Conscious Capitalism will manifest:

1. "We are seeing a paradox of high returns and high anxiety. Since the financial crisis, those with capital have reaped enormous benefits. At the same time, many individuals across the world are facing a combination of low rates, low wage growth, and inadequate retirement systems. Many don't have the financial capacity, the resources, or the

tools to save effectively; those who are invested are too often over-allocated to cash. For millions, the prospect of a secure retirement is slipping further and further away – especially among workers with less education, whose job security is increasingly tenuous. I believe these trends are a major source of the anxiety and polarization that we see across the world today."

2. "We also see many governments failing to prepare for the future, on issues ranging from retirement and infrastructure to automation and worker retraining. As a result, society increasingly is turning to the private sector and asking that companies respond to broader societal challenges. Indeed, the public expectations of your company have never been greater.

    Society is demanding that companies, both public and private, serve a social purpose. To prosper over time, every company must not only deliver financial performance, but also show how it makes a positive contribution to society."

3. "The time has come for a new model of shareholder engagement – one that strengthens and deepens communication between shareholders and the companies that they own. I have written before that companies have been too focused on quarterly results; similarly, shareholder engagement has been too focused on annual meetings and proxy votes… BlackRock recognizes and embraces our responsibility to help drive this change."

4. "In order to make engagement with shareholders as productive as possible, companies must be able to describe their strategy for long-term growth. I want to reiterate our request, outlined in past letters, that *you publicly articulate your company's strategic framework for long-term value creation and explicitly affirm that it has been reviewed by your board of directors.* (Italics mine) This demonstrates to investors that your board is engaged with the strategic direction of the

company. When we meet with directors, we also expect them to describe the Board process for overseeing your strategy."

5. "Furthermore, the board is essential to helping a company articulate and pursue its purpose, as well as respond to the questions that are increasingly important to its investors, its consumers, and the communities in which it operates. In the current environment, these stakeholders are demanding that companies exercise leadership on a broader range of issues. And they are right to: A company's ability to manage environmental, social, and governance matters demonstrates the leadership and good governance that is so essential to sustainable growth, which is why we are increasingly integrating these issues into our investment process. Companies must ask themselves: What role do we play in the community? How are we managing our impact on the environment? Are we working to create a diverse workforce? Are we adapting to technological change? Are we providing the retraining and opportunities that our employees and our business will need to adjust to an increasingly automated world? Are we using behavioral finance and other tools to prepare workers for retirement, so that they invest in a way that will help them achieve their goals?"[8]

Note the no-nonsense tone of items 4 and 5. This is unprecedented and very powerful language. Fink is not only counselling senior management of top companies to get their acts together and change their status quos, but also serving notice to the boards of those companies that BlackRock will hold them accountable for their own governance performance. Those companies refusing to change risk Blackrock divesting their shares. This is really important and encouraging news! When someone as respected, influential and powerful as Larry Fink concludes that we must change capitalism for the betterment of all, the probability of that vision happening increases significantly.

Now of course, it is very possible that at least part of Fink's motivation is to protect BlackRock, and hedge against possible BlackRock shareholder lawsuits, given that it is somewhat exposed for investing in the companies he's criticizing. But I suggest that regardless of motive, any action that moves capitalism to a more responsible and transparent plane is a positive development. Altruistic, self-serving, or both, in this case the end result is what matters.

Should you agree by now that to resolve our serious global problems, business practices must drastically change, you will be encouraged and heartened by Fink's letter and advice to his peers, so I encourage you to read it (see link above).

I found the language (recall 'vivid descriptions') in the Conscious Capitalism organization to be uplifting, bold and inspiring; so much so that it merits quoting select parts here:

- "Conscious Capitalism is a way of thinking about capitalism and business that better reflects where we are in the human journey, the state of our world today, and the innate potential of business to make a positive impact on the world. Conscious businesses are galvanized by higher purposes that serve, align, and integrate the interests of all their major stakeholders."

- "Pioneering naturalist John Muir observed that 'when you tug at a single thing in nature, you find it attached to the rest of the world.' Such is the case with business, which is an intricate and interconnected web of relationships.

  Unlike some businesses that believe they only exist to maximize return on investment for their shareholders, Conscious Businesses focus on their whole business ecosystem, creating and optimizing value for all of their stakeholders, understanding that strong and engaged stakeholders lead to a healthy, sustainable, resilient business. They recognize that, without employees, customers, suppliers, funders, supportive communities and a life-sustaining ecosystem, there is no business. Conscious Business is a win-win-win proposition, which includes a healthy return to shareholders."

- On Conscious Culture: "'Culture eats strategy for lunch.' Famed management guru Peter Drucker didn't mince words and knew how to identify and articulate the keys to success in business.

  Culture is the embodied values, principles and practices underlying the social fabric of a business connecting the stakeholders to each other and to the company's purpose, people and processes.

  A Conscious Culture fosters love and care and builds trust between a company's team members and its other stakeholders. Conscious Culture is an energizing and unifying force, that truly brings a Conscious Business to life."

This is a strongly positive development for global business. Right now, there are 1320 companies formally committed to the practice; and from 1998 to 2013, they have earned cumulative returns of 1641%, compared to 118% for the S&P 500, and 263% for the famous Good-to-Great companies. Members include Whole Foods, Southwest Airlines, Costco, Home Depot, Panera Bread, Nordstrom and Hyatt Hotels, all formidable competitors in their fields. As mentioned, the more these companies continue to dominate their markets, the higher the likelihood that their competitors will have to follow suit.

It is becoming increasingly apparent that capitalism as we have known it is definitely transforming, and a conscious model will play some part in the new format. But no one has a crystal ball. There are other elements that are exerting disruptive, unpredictable forces on the system. Blockchain and cryptocurrencies we've already touched upon. Recently, two restaurant chains in Canada and the US announced they will no longer accept cash payments. How would a cashless society impact commerce? And capitalism, even when conscious, is still based upon the tenets of scarcity of resources, private property ownership, and the behaviour required to function in such a system.

But what if Jeremy Rifkin is right about zero marginal cost, when things like electricity, publishing and music are almost free? What happens when millennials have no desire to own a car; they just want low cost, instantly accessible means of transportation? He is not even certain that capitalism will survive: "Admittedly, the very idea that an economic system that is organized around scarcity and profit could lead to an economy of nearly free goods and services and abundance is so counterintuitive that it is difficult to accept. Nonetheless, this is exactly what is enfolding."[9]

Like Piketty, but for different reasons, Rifkin contends that the very nature of capitalism (striving for ever increasing efficiency and productivity and driving costs as low as possible) ensures its very demise. And he says the new market paradigm will be the Collaborative Commons, where we will all exchange goods and services through sharing, and that we are already witnessing the emergence of a hybrid economy, part capitalist market and part sharing economy, on the Collaborative Commons. This is only possible because of the Internet of Things (IoT) "which will capture Big Data in real time and feed it to countless nodes where it will be analyzed, used to create algorithms, which will dramatically increase efficiencies and productivity and drive costs towards zero."[10] This thinking is not new: even back in the 1930s legendary economist John Maynard Keynes, in a paper entitled *Economic Possibilities for Our Grandchildren* wrote, "a point may soon be reached, much sooner perhaps than we are all of us aware of, when these economic needs are satisfied in the sense that we prefer to devote further energies to non-economic purposes."[11] Rifkin continues on to add: "He looked expectantly to a future in which machines would produce an abundance of nearly free goods and services, liberating the human race from toil and hardships, and freeing the human mind from a preoccupation with pecuniary interest to focus more on the 'arts for life' and the quest for transcendence."[12] We are fast approaching that possibility, if we want it.

We should be pressing our leaders to explore and embrace this inspiring vision. Regardless of whether we move immediately into conscious capitalism first, and then ease gradually into a collaborative commons system, or end up with some hybrid form of capitalism in goods and services exchange, one thing is certain: the new system *will be* more egalitarian, compassionate, efficient, encompassing and beneficial to all stakeholders, and it will be far less vulnerable to manipulation and exploitation than our current system. The opportunity for us now is to envision the possibilities of a conscious capitalist system and other options and resolve to make it manifest. We have great reason for hope and optimism. This vision alone can help us deal in a powerful way, with each of the three burning platform issues: climate change, income inequality and the VUCA world.

As an avid student of business for forty years, I have shifted over the years from a strong capitalist, to a confused and disillusioned businessman, to pessimism and disgust over the 2008 financial fiasco and finally to renewed optimism and energy today. As I researched many of the reasons why our society has seemed to struggle and decline of late, I discovered also some of the opportunities for transformation that these inspiring visions offer us. And the journey will be exciting and fulfilling for all of us, if we agree to collaborate for positive change. Part of my personal and professional objective for this book is to share these facts and encourage you to be enthusiastic and optimistic too.

CHAPTER 10

Inspiring Vision 3 – Conscious Awareness

"The mind, once stretched by a new idea, never returns to its original dimensions."

Ralph Waldo Emerson

"The best way to predict your future is to create it. Abraham Lincoln

THE THIRD SUGGESTED INSPIRING VISION FOR POSITIVE transformation (in my view the most promising and exciting), is human conscious awareness. It is a collective acknowledgement that we can use intention to make manifest the world we want to experience. This may cause some to raise an eyebrow and may seem quite 'out there' at times, but please don't throw the book across the room. Science is beginning to support the claim.

We have known for some time that the vast majority of cognitive activity occurs in the subconscious mind, which has been programmed by our earliest experiences and handles the bulk of decision-making in our lives. It's why we can simultaneously drive and sing a song, or eat pizza and watch TV. The downside is that many of our decisions are made from the 'triggered' subconscious (an environmental event awakens a hardwired memory of our past). "The subconscious mind...observes both the surrounding world and the body's internal awareness, reads the environmental cues and immediately engages previously acquired (learned) behaviours – all without help, supervision, or even awareness of the conscious mind."[1]

These decisions, reactions actually, involve the ego, and it's with ego-driven, emotional decisions that we often run into trouble.

Conscious awareness is a state in which we pause and witness our subconscious reactions as they occur and decide whether they truly reflect our values and desires. If we decide they do not, we can then consciously change them. This is incredibly powerful because it eventually dispels ignorance, and ignorance has played a large role in creating the world we are currently experiencing.

For example, let's assume my parents were often overly critical about my task performance. At work in an annual performance review, my boss is quite critical of my work on certain projects or tasks. My initial reaction will likely be defensive, and even angry, because her approach triggered my subconscious, reviving the feelings I had when my parents criticized me as a child. Conscious awareness means I first notice the rising emotions, ask myself if the boss could possibly be right in her observations, remind myself that failing at a task does not make me a failure, and then *choose* a non-defensive response to the situation. I can ask for specific details, more clarification, explain what happened and why. If I remain unconscious I simply go away angry and resentful, setting up for further conflict and tension between my boss and me. I forfeit an opportunity to actually improve my relationship with my boss by seeking support and guidance, dispelling ignorance and improving understanding. "By becoming conscious choice-makers, (we) begin to generate actions that are evolutionary for us and for those around us."[2]

When we are consciously aware, it is impossible for the frog to boil.

Most of us are aware of the terms conscious and subconscious mind. As scientists and psychologists learn more about them, definitions shift, debates continue and the insights add up. But for our purposes, a simpler definition will suffice, along with a few other details. Wikipedia says consciousness is the state or quality of awareness or of being aware of an external object, or something within oneself. Experts generally agree that a) it is "a cognitive process accompanied by basic perceptual, sensory and emotional experience, and b) that a 'higher-order consciousness' is a more elaborate self-awareness – a concept of self – held by a thinking and reflecting subject."[3]

It is also agreed by most scientists and psychologists that the conscious and subconscious mind work in tandem to allow us to process experiences and function in the world. Not as well accepted by Western scientists are the Eastern notions of a universal consciousness and of a collective unconscious, yet there are phenomena that indicate they do exist. Similar to a computer that connects to the cloud to access a much larger body of information, mystics have long professed that individuals can access, through yoga, meditation or prayer, a state that connects them to God or a higher collective wisdom. It's kind of like that flash thought, instinct or gut feel that you receive at the very moment you need it, but that seems to come out of nowhere.

Where I'm going with all of this is to the concept of *manifestation*, which purports that through focused attention, and intention, we *can* actually and consciously create the future we want. So far, my research has not discovered any science that *proves* this, yet scientists do not rule it out, and are now approaching the subject with greater curiosity and open-mindedness. The systemic approach to science indicates that there *is* an interrelatedness of each line in the web of life, and that *fields of energy can be influenced by thought*.

Time and more research will tell if this is true, but one thing is certain: we have a higher probability of solving our current problems if we are more, rather than less, conscious.

Earlier I mentioned that in researching such diverse topics of interest as neuroscience, ancient sages and mystics, faith, metaphysics, quantum physics, leadership development, organizational culture, and social trends, there came a point when I noticed a convergence of certain aspects in each of the fields of study; in some cases, even conflation. To some this may sound bizarre, but the truth is, our recent technological scientific discoveries have enabled us to unlock doors previously closed tight and provided many answers while raising even more new questions about life, human behaviour, the interconnectedness of our universe and finally, consciousness.

Science is beginning to validate the ideas of ancient scriptures from India, China, Jerusalem and the Middle East and other civilizations. The notion of 'oneness' or what is often called non-duality.[4] The latter refers to an awareness that there is no real separation of matter; "a mature state of consciousness, in which the dichotomy of 'I and other' is 'transcended', and awareness is described as 'centerless' and 'without dichotomies.'"[4] Highly conscious people are keenly aware of the interdependence and interrelatedness of all things, and the resulting potential impact of their decisions.

This is where it can get really challenging for most of us to grasp. Quantum mechanics reveals that at the subatomic level, all things are the same (and mostly space), with the only difference being in the energy and information of objects. At the quantum level, everything is just the movement of energy and information. "Einstein revealed that we do not live in a universe with discrete, physical objects separated by dead space. The Universe is *one indivisible, dynamic whole* in which energy and matter are so deeply entangled it is impossible to consider them as independent elements."[5]

Western educated doctor and Eastern philosopher Deepak Chopra writes: "Your body is not separate from the body of the universe, because at quantum mechanical levels there are no well-defined edges. You are like a wiggle, a wave, a fluctuation...a localized disturbance in the larger quantum field. The larger quantum field – the universe – is your extended body. It is why the ancient seers exclaimed 'I am that, you are that, all this is that, and that's all there is'."[6]

And here's where it gets really interesting: Science is revealing that "we are able to consciously change the informational content that gives rise to our physical bodies and because of that we can also influence, through focused thought, the energy and information of our extended body, – our environment, our world – and cause things to manifest in it."[7]

As Lincoln suggested, we can predict our future by creating it. Sounds incredible, but it reflects the same need for open-mindedness and adaptability as did the acceptance of the sun as the center of the universe in Copernicus' time, or the belief in 1902 (pre-Kitty Hawk) that man would fly. We need to humbly remember that our temporary inability to scientifically prove something does not mean it is not true.

Just as Conscious Capitalism advocates an inclusive, systems approach to business, so is the world of science now viewing the world with what they call a systemic view. It is a recognition that *all things* are interconnected; that our Newtonian approach to solving problems treats the world as a machine of separate parts, and in many cases, no longer reflects what we're now learning to be true. For any skeptics, a beautiful video[8] chronicling the impact of the re-introduction of wolves into Yellowstone Park, shows the astounding inter-relatedness of nature.

As another example, within the past two decades, scientists have reversed their 400-year-old conclusions that problems in the brain were incurable or irreversible. It was thought to be incapable of healing itself. Once again, the Newtonian world view influenced the thinking, with doctors and scientists looking at the brain as a discrete machine, a computer with hardware and software and thus incapable of repairing itself or growing new parts. With new technology, most notably the fMRI developed in 2011, the field of neuroplasticity has quickly developed and is showing that the opposite is actually true. An MRI takes a snap shot of one's brain at a given point of time. An fMRI allows doctors to watch activity in the brain in real time by following the blood that flows to active areas of the brain. This procedure has accelerated scientific learning about the brain because it is safe and non-invasive to the patient and allows observation of the brain while it performs different functions. We have now learned that, among other things, the brain is plastic; that is, it can be reprogrammed. Psychiatrist Norman Doidge writes, "Neuroplasticity is the property of the brain that enables it to change its own structure and functioning in response to activity and mental experience"[9] Even more exciting, he writes, "it is remarkable the extent to which almost all the neuro-plasticians I visited were deepening their understanding of how to use neuroplasticity by insights from Western neuroscience to insights from Eastern health practices, including traditional Chinese medicine, *ancient Buddhist meditation and visualization,* [italics mine] martial arts such as tai chi and judo, yoga and energy medicine."[10]

The Western medical community is finally beginning to accept that interconnectedness of mind and body: "Thus cognition became associated with all levels of life. This means that mind and body are not separate entities, as Descartes believed, but are two complementary aspects of life – its process and its structure."[11]

Doctors are safe to now describe, without risk to their careers, the near death experiences (NDE) that their patients have had, which has deepened professional interest in consciousness. In 1999, an American orthopedic surgeon, Dr Mary Neal, herself experienced an NDE while kayaking in Chile. Her descriptions,[12] (See video) coupled with her scientific understanding and creditability as a doctor, helped add insight to the phenomenon. While science has yet to establish what is really happening with NDEs, at least they are now being openly acknowledged, discussed, and formally researched.

Many best-selling books, including *Think and Grow Rich* by Napoleon Hill, Rhonda Byrne's *The Secret, The Power of Intention* by Wayne Dyer, and Tony Robbins's work, and others have been traditionally relegated by critics to the 'self-help' category, implying that they are interesting theories and opinions, but not rooted in science. Yet Hill's book has sold over 100 million copies since its 1937 publication, as has *The Power of Positive Thinking* by Norman Vincent Peale. Robbins has helped millions to heal and succeed for decades; unlikely, were his methods false and ineffective. Something about their message, while not provable by science at the time, deeply resonated with the public. It was an intuitive knowing that something very powerful yet undefined exists: *the ability to make manifest one's desires.*

Today, we are coming to know that 'something' as consciousness. While Sigmund Freud and Carl Jung pioneered early Western notions of consciousness, it was helped to spread more widely in America with the 1946 book *Autobiography of a Yogi*, by Paramahansa Yogananda. It exploded further in popularity when The Beatles' 1968 trip to India to visit the Maharishi turned a klieg light on the subject, and perhaps made it cool to explore. It is also likely that the 60s drug culture raised curiosity about consciousness. Since then, authors like Deepak Chopra and Eckhart Tolle and technological advances have spurred new interest and research to attempt to define it and explore the effects of conscious awareness on virtually every aspect of our lives. A whole new field, Positive Psychology, has emerged, that is challenging the traditional assumptions, theories, and therapies. Other evolving fields include cognitive behavioural therapy (CBT), anthropology, mindfulness, neuropsychology and neuroscience, epigenetics and the study of emotional intelligence.

A collaboration between scientists at the Mind and Life Institute and the Dalai Lama, since 1987, has brought together scientists and monks to compare notes and discuss the many similarities between what science, particularly quantum mechanics, is discovering, and what ancient teachings like Buddhism have long held. In 2005, the Dalai Lama was invited to open the international meeting of the Society for Neuroscience in Washington, DC. Interestingly, quantum physicists have just recently discovered the potential human ability to *directly* perceive, through the five senses, the quantum nature of phenomena. The study has been delayed due to the realization that participants need to possess the perceptual abilities of highly advanced, long-term, adept practitioners of special forms of observational meditation; in other words meditation experts, and not the average Joe. Scientists are now approaching practitioners of the ancient meditative traditions and cultures of Tibet, India, and East Asia.[13] Yet another example of cutting edge science catching up with the millennia-old scripture and practices of ancient cultures.

Every year in Cortona, Italy, scientists, philosophers, graduate students in the sciences and arts, artists, musicians, religious leaders, and professors gather for a week of living together and exploring ideas, trends and ways the different disciplines interrelate. One objective is to create young conscious leaders with a broad understanding and appreciation for the complexity and interconnectedness of life. There is even an annual conference for science and consciousness.[14]

These are unprecedented and most encouraging developments, as they are efforts to better understand and relate to our VUCA world and to influence events from chaos into order.

Why am I telling you all this? Because there is a growing body of evidence that any increases in human consciousness raise our level of existence and enable manifestation of desired results. Science is confirming that conscious awareness, long espoused by ancient sages of Eastern religions, enables us to see the bigger picture, understand the unity and interrelatedness of all things, generate more diverse solutions and connect to a deeper wisdom. Consider the Arab Spring. By using the Internet to communicate shared values, clarify desired goals, and co-ordinate flash meetings and protests, a relatively conscious young generation taught us that transformation *is* possible when we energize and act consciously and collectively. They sought to manifest a new Egyptian society. Of course, the initial effort failed for now, but why? Because leader of the army, Fattah El-Sisi, motivated by greed and lust for power, used force to restrain the movement. Now think for a moment what might have happened in a more conscious world, if all other countries said, 'we will impose global sanctions if you repress this movement'; if we globally accepted principles of freedom and human rights, and transcended national boundaries in the name of humanity? The UN is supposed to do this today, but we are not truly committed to it. Yet we are moving in the right direction. As oppressed people reach the point where death is preferable to the status quo of their lives, change will happen. It always has. Hopefully, the rest of the world will help them so that the change will not cost them their lives.

Inspiring Vision 3 is to recognize and harness the power and possibilities of collective conscious awareness and to seek highly conscious leaders to lead us toward a mutually envisioned future.

And the power of elevated consciousness is why we should take heart and be hopeful about our ability to resolve our serious problems.

Conscious leaders, by definition are more tolerant, more empathetic, clearer about priorities, comfortable with diversity and ambiguity, committed, honest and more keenly aware of the interrelatedness of all things. This allows them to make better decisions, take more effective action and generate stellar results.

Some examples of conscious leaders include: German Chancellor Angela Merkel, Canadian Green Party leaders Elizabeth May (National) and Mike Schreiner (Ontario), US Senators Bernie Sanders and Elizabeth Warren, Professor Robert Reich at UC Berkeley, Tony Hsieh at Zappos, A.G. Lafley (former CEO of P&G), Malala Yousafzai for girls education, social icons Martin Luther King Jr, Nelson Mandela, Mahatma Gandhi, Albert Einstein, several of the leaders mentioned in Chapter 2 (you'll know which ones), and of course, John Mackey and Raj Sisodia, who are leading the conscious capitalism movement. If you benchmark the behaviours of these leaders against the research based, quality leadership characteristics in Chapter 2, you'll instantly see the co-relations.

Two other fields, both related to consciousness, have recently emerged, that further support the argument that it can help us generate better results: those of epigenetics, and emotional intelligence (EI).

Epigenetics is "the science of how environmental signals select, modify and regulate gene activity. It's the single cell's 'awareness' of the environment, not its genes, that sets into motion the mechanisms of life."[15] Professor of molecular biology Bruce Lipton is credited with this radical discovery. Prior to his 2005 work, there was what academics called the Central Dogma, a belief that DNA controlled all biological life: physical, emotional and behavioural. This theory basically supported pre-determinism, and Darwin's theory of survival of the fittest. Lipton's discovery challenged those beliefs, because he proved that the cell's environment (nature) influences its behaviour without changing the genetic code. He, and others, have determined that the membrane of a cell is like a computer chip that can be programmed, and actually is programmed, *by the outside environmental stimuli*. Concisely, he states that our hardwiring in our subconscious drives much of our behaviour, but if we consciously evaluate our response to environmental stimuli, we can change responses anytime we like. "Beliefs control biology."[16] As with all new science, there are peers who rightly challenge the theories, and there are those who disagree with Lipton. It should also be noted that his journey has taken him, while still a practicing scientist, into the spiritual realm, espousing beliefs that cannot as yet be scientifically proven. But having read *The Biology of Belief* and carefully searched for serious 'debunkers', I was unable to find any who completely dismissed his theories, especially those related to the impact of beliefs on cellular development, and consciousness. And the recent science of epigenetics continues to make new discoveries as better technology permits. For our purposes, we can now assume that we are not predetermined by DNA and can use consciousness to not only positively affect our biology, but also our thoughts and beliefs, and creation of our ideal world. This is free will.

> Your beliefs become your thoughts
>
> Your thoughts become your words
>
> Your words become your actions
>
> Your actions become your habits
>
> Your habits become your values
>
> Your values become your destiny
>
> **MAHATMA GANDHI**

The other relatively new field of study, emotional intelligence, is also yielding outstanding results, particularly within the business world. Popularized in his book *Emotional Intelligence*, science journalist Daniel Goleman posits that, in addition to our IQ, we need to develop social skills: An emotional quotient or EQ.

Emotional Intelligence (EI) is defined as "the ability to monitor one's own and other people's emotions, to discriminate between different emotions and label them appropriately, and to use emotional information to guide thinking and behavior."[17]

The concept has been increasingly used for training and leadership development in organizations, largely because it results in improved human interaction and corporate culture. It starts with self-awareness, helping the leader to reflect and clarify who they really are and what they stand for and believe in. It teaches how to self-manage: to recognize in advance when our limbic brain (the 'fight, flight or hide' driver) is beginning to take charge, and to override it by switching back to the rational prefrontal cortex. Once we begin to master self-awareness and self-management, we can extend the learning to social awareness and relationship management, the most important requirement of which is empathy. Recall back in Chapter 2 we saw that for decades the primary hiring criterion for management is often the IQ, but for leadership, where those Soft S's are so critical, the EQ becomes more important.

Perhaps the best side effect of the explosion of EI training is the general effect it's having on the conscious awareness of the general population. People trained at work, for work purposes, nevertheless grow in general conscious awareness and this new knowledge and practice transfers to their relationships with spouses, children, neighbors and communities. Once we learn the techniques, we cannot 'un-know' them. Consciousness does not become unconscious. So as we all increase our own consciousness, we can insist on leaders who are more conscious too, and start to set the vision of overcoming our major challenges and creating sustainable prosperity

To end this chapter, I want to share with you a few random facts and quotes I encountered in my research, to illustrate how quantum physics, metaphysics and other scientific discoveries are reflecting an entirely new paradigm of reality, one where the notion of consciousness is deeply entangled:

- Everything in the vast universe (including our bodies) is 99.9999% space. When you touch someone, you aren't actually touching their atoms; you're feeling the electromagnetic force of your electrons pushing away theirs.[18]

- French physicist Alain Aspect proved that elementary particles are *affected by connections that exist invisibly across time and space.* Einstein called this "spooky action at a distance."[19] Imagine a pair of protons, split and sent thousands of miles apart (don't ask me how they do that!), and then any operation you perform on one proton, causes an equal but opposite reaction in the other proton, at exactly the same time. While we don't yet know why, this is exactly what happens.

- Neurons that fire together wire together – repeated mental experience leads to structural changes in the brain neurons that process that experience.[20] With repeated concentrated thoughts we can alter our brains to respond differently.

- "unobserved quantum phenomena are radically different from observed ones…an electron is *both* a wave and a particle until our observation causes it to collapse as *either* a particle or a wave." (Wheatley) This means "when we change the way we look at things, the things we look at change."[21]

- The subconscious mind processes some 20 million environmental stimuli per second, versus 40 environmental stimuli interpreted by the conscious mind in the same time.[22]

- "the biggest impediments to realizing the successes of which we dream are the limitations programmed into the subconscious. These limitations not only influence our behaviour, they can also play a major role in determining our physiology and health."[23]

- "When my left language centers were silenced and my left (brain) orientation association area was interrupted from its normal sensory input, my consciousness shifted away from feeling like a solid, to a perception of myself as a fluid – at *one* with the universe."[24] (Neuroanatomist Dr. Jill Bolte Taylor, observations from her own stroke) (See video in Endnote)

- "A University of Wisconsin study of meditating monks produced gamma waves that were extremely high in amplitude and had long-range gamma synchrony—the waves from disparate brain regions were in near lockstep...the synchrony was sustained for remarkably long periods. New theory is showing that gamma synchrony helps bind the brain's many sensory and cognitive operations into the miracle of consciousness."[22]

- "When we quit thinking primarily about ourselves and our own self-preservation, we undergo a truly heroic transformation of consciousness." (Joseph Campbell)

One last point about conscious awareness: it results in our looking inside and outside of ourselves, living in and paying closer attention to the here and now, and thinking critically about what is happening. This practice causes us to look through others' eyes, to stand in their shoes, to consider all the potential consequences of our decisions on all stakeholders. By doing so, we quickly come to realize that we are, in essence, all the same. As we saw in conscious capitalism, that mindset prevents corporations from polluting the environment, from raiding employees' pension funds, from exploiting suppliers. Conscious business leaders 'get' the reality of systems and interrelationships.

Similarly, conscious leaders do not send drones to kill, nor shrug off civilian deaths as 'collateral damage.' They do not sit by as 14 million Yemeni civilians starve, because of some power-base strategy in the region. At the quantum level, everything is energy and information; it is one, and we are starting to realize, that even at our Newtonian level, so are we also one. We all bleed when cut, cry and suffer when our loved ones die, need clean water and air and fresh food to survive. The vast majority of our 'differences' are culturally programmed into our subconscious and we come to see them as reality. It's why Tutsis kill Hutus, Croats kill Serbs, Northern Irish and the IRA blew each other up for centuries. Yet those differences are *not* real. Thoughts, beliefs, values all arising from the subconscious led to our current predicament, driven by fear, greed, power and money. Higher consciousness transcends those vices, and we will need to pursue it if we wish to survive. The good news is that when we do this, it is like awakening, and the frog jumps out of the pot before it boils us to permanent sleep!

Part II of this book asked 'So What?'

Why should you or any of us care about the implications and consequences of where we are now in our global human situation? Hopefully, the suggestion of what went wrong, and the descriptions of the three Burning Platforms have raised awareness of the facts behind them and caused you to feel something of a '*yikes!*' experience; a sense of urgency.

Even more hopefully, the three Inspiring Visions have accomplished just that: raised an enthusiasm and curiosity within you that will inspire you to further clarify and define what kind of world *you* want. What vision will move you to commit to, and participate in, the manifestation of a better world? What, if any, personal changes might you have to make, and will you be willing to make them?

To answer those questions, let's move to the final part of the book: Now What?

There we will take a look at who can do what to help us individually and collectively make the transformations that will deliver on our visions. For those who do decide to get more deeply involved, to step up and become a leader themselves (and by the way, it's quite OK if you don't; just decide what you want your own role to be), I offer some research-grounded actions you can take to help in your own leadership development.

PART III: NOW WHAT?

"Each time a man stands up for an ideal, or acts to improve the lot of others, or strikes out against injustice, he sends forth a tiny ripple of hope, and crossing each other from a million different centers of energy and daring, those ripples build a current which can sweep down the mightiest walls of oppression and resistance." Robert F. Kennedy

CHAPTER 11

A Challenge to Current Leaders

"For unto whomsoever much has been given, of him shall much be required." Luke 12:48

MANY, PERHAPS A MAJORITY, OF OUR CURRENT LEADERS WILL likely have no interest in reading this book. That is because they are either ignorant of, or simply don't care about, the true definition and responsibilities of leadership, and are thus part of, if not the cause of, our current problematic situation. They would likely see this as a criticism of their performance and would not be completely mistaken. This *is* a personal and professional judgement on my part, but one which I think, as we've seen in earlier chapters, this book can defend given the available evidence.

And yet, these leaders are also human beings, with strengths and flaws like all of us. Until one has stood in their shoes, faced the decisions they faced, understood the information and mindsets they had upon which to make the decisions, and experienced the pressure from lobbyists and stakeholders, it is not entirely fair to judge them from afar.

But Luke 12:48 still stands.

We *do* have a right to expect our leaders, especially at the highest levels, to execute their duties with the highest level of integrity and that means, at the very least, placing the wellbeing and common good of their followers ahead of that of themselves and a small group of similar colleagues. It is altogether fair that much be required, and therefore, demanded of them.

That means when George W. Bush invades Iraq, illegally and under false pretenses, and in the following fifteen years flows $5.3 trillion of taxpayer dollars to defense manufacturers and contractors, while education, homelessness, income inequality, healthcare, and veterans' affairs all worsen, it is at best poor leadership; at worst, criminal activity.[1] He and his administration should be held accountable.

Then there are our lauded business leaders. Following the Trump administrations 2018 tax cuts, General Motors used their $514 million tax rebate to buy back $100 million of stock (increasing the wealth of remaining shareholders) and shutter five plants, terminating 14,700 employees, all in a year of high profitability, and a salary increase for CEO Mary Barra to $22 million.[2]

Ford Motor Co. also lost $1 billion due to Trump's trade war with China, and will lay off thousands. Monsanto continues to lobby governments around the world to allow its Round-Up product, which uses highly carcinogenic glyphosate, to be sold, despite losing lawsuits and irrefutable science that shows its product is deadly.[3] Leadership failures, all.

And then there is Wall Street, the royalty of which we've looked at earlier, whose reckless and shady investments caused the financial meltdown of 2008, and the foreclosure of nearly 10 million American homes between 2006 and 2014. How are those guys doing? Richard Fuld (former CEO Lehman Bros.), Jimmy Cayne (former CEO Bear Stearns), Chuck Prince (former CEO Citibank), Stanley O'Neal (former CEO Merrill Lynch), and Ken Lewis (former CEO Bank of America) *each have a net worth in the high nine figure range, and at least three residential properties.* Jamie Dimon, Chairman and CEO of J.P. Morgan Chase, retained his job and now has a net worth of $1.5 billion. Perhaps the least admirable culprit, former Goldman Sachs CEO Lloyd Blancfein, (who interestingly stepped down just as the 1MDB scandal investigation heats up) is approaching the $1 billion mark.[4] All the remaining banks that were judged 'too big to fail' in 2009, (Bear Stearns and Lehman

Bros. are gone) are now, as we've already seen, 80% larger today. (See p. 59) That millions of citizens continue to struggle back to liquidity a decade after this event, while the perpetrators live in luxury, is reprehensible. This was undeniably an example of failed leadership:

"...the Financial Crisis Inquiry Report, said the financial collapse was avoidable. 'The captains of finance and the public stewards of our financial system ignored warnings and failed to question, understand, and manage evolving risks within a system essential to the well-being of the American public. Theirs was a big miss, not a stumble,' the report said."[5]

Now it certainly needs to be emphasized that many, most likely the majority, of our leaders in business and politics deserve their positions of trust, and are toiling daily to do the best they can with the resources they have. They are to be valued and commended for their work and, while it is hoped that some of the ideas in this chapter may still be of use to them, they are not the primary audience, because they do not cause or exacerbate our leadership crisis.

Instead, a challenge is in order for those very senior leaders in business and governments who have been negligent, yet still hold their positions. This includes, during the past three decades, leaders in Big Pharma, Big Oil and the fossil fuel industry, investment and commercial banks, pesticide manufacturers like Bayer and Monsanto, lobbying firms, and government agencies around the world charged with monitoring and regulating those industries that failed in their duties. It is meant for those leaders who have pursued narrow, self-serving strategies of personal enrichment and power, at the expense of the general public.

The challenge to our current leaders is simple: either step up, or step down and leave.

To use General George Patton's phrase: 'Lead, follow, or get out of the way.' For the remainder of your time in a leadership capacity you owe it to your followers and to society, to reflect on your ideal leadership mission, evaluate where you have fallen short to date, and take action to remedy the situation. If you have yet to adapt to the radical changes the world is experiencing, *now* is the time to do so. This is the responsibility that comes with a leadership relationship and in case you fail to see the reasoning behind why you should change your tack, there are at least three good arguments.

You Didn't Do That

First, you didn't do that. In a campaign speech in Virginia in 2012, Barack Obama was recounting the historical opportunities that American society had traditionally offered citizens. He was lamenting how in the past decade things had changed for the worse. In comments that were taken out of context (and for which he was criticized by many on the right), he mentioned successful people who had built companies, risen to places of leadership and acquired great wealth, and challenged them by saying, "you didn't do that." Within context, he was *not* denigrating their accomplishments. But as we've examined the interrelatedness of our ecosystem world, Obama was calling on those people to recognize that even if they had worked incredibly hard, were diligent in studies and ingenious in creativity, their success also grew out of a supportive system of rule of law, high quality education, a capable labour force and a modern, efficient infrastructure. And especially if they were financially successful, it was within the context of a prosperous, democratic, capitalist society that their customers arose; that is, a healthy middle class. How would they have fared had they been born in Armenia, Republic of Congo, or Russia? The truth is, *you didn't do that alone.*

"So we say to ourselves, ever since the founding of this country, you know what, there are some things we do better together. That's how we funded the GI Bill. That's how we created the middle class. That's how we built the Golden Gate Bridge or the Hoover Dam. That's how we invented the Internet. That's how we sent a man to the moon. We rise or fall together as one nation and as one people, and that's the reason I'm running for President – because I still believe in that idea. You're not on your own, we're in this together."[6]

Aside from highlighting the fact that most leaders benefitted from the ecosystem and infrastructure of a highly developed, democratic nation, this argument also revisits Warren Buffett's 'ovarian lottery' analogy. If you recall, his suggestion was that we are each born really as the drawing of a lottery: our genes, nationality, health, social status, level of intelligence and the like are random probabilities. We had no control over it, so how can we justify an ego-centric arrogance about our abilities and achievements? How would any of us have fared if born into the 'untouchable' caste in India? Do you really think you could bootstrap yourself out of that kind of systemic prejudice?

And did you ever consider that it could very well take the same determination, concentration, energy, courage and persistence for a Multiple Sclerosis (MS) patient to tie their shoes each day, as it does for a star athlete to score a goal in a highly competitive game? Both deserve possibly the exact same credit for effort and accomplishment, but what force determined their respective reality? Similarly, if you are one of Tom Wolfe's 'masters of the universe' with a giant IQ, how did you get that? You get credit for developing and leveraging it, but you simply lucked out if you have it.

So if you are among those highly successful people who have risen through your own hardy initiative to a place of great leadership and responsibility, congratulations! You deserve to enjoy the fruits of your labours, just not at the expense of neglecting the leadership duties that go with the position. And one of those duties is to review the current realities, and decide if changes have rendered old ideas and methods invalid.

What would happen, Mr. Jamie Dimon, if you used your considerable business and political clout to broaden the definition of ROI at J.P. Morgan Chase to reflect that of Conscious Capitalism? Who would stand in your way? What would be the ripple effect in the banks' ecosystem and beyond? At the very least, your tabling such a discussion would permit others who may agree with it also to speak up without fear. That discussion could lead to amazing opportunities. Your power, ability and station in life, and those of every senior leader today, give you the pulpit and potential for greater impact on our future than was the case fifty years ago. Your talents, ideas, networks and skills can yield far more benefit to society if you embrace a broader, eco-system view of the world and acknowledge that your accomplishments were partially achieved within a larger system from which you benefitted. If you or I were to make a phone call to any political leader, to spark action on any world problem, whose call would be accepted? Whose call carries a higher probability of achieving positive action? Find the humility to acknowledge that you didn't do that alone, and therefore need to contribute back on a scale commensurate with your ability and the benefits you've enjoyed. You have an extraordinary opportunity to create the future for mankind.

Re-read Luke 12:48.

Self-Preservation

A second motivation for our current leaders to change their leadership hab-its is self-preservation. As we've seen in earlier chapters, the disruptive forces at work today are powerfully changing the business and political landscape. Power is shifting towards the workforce. The talented employee so criti-cal to success knows he or she has many more options than in the past. This is beginning to cripple any company that stubbornly adheres to the mechanistic approach to management; one that uses hierarchical, com-mand and control methods. Should this be your approach, coupled with a short-term shareholder maximization mindset, your tenure as a leader is becoming increasingly jeopardized, and your company will experience increasing difficulty in remaining competitive. Why? Because companies are not merely formal structures with charts, policies, manuals and rules; they are living social systems, self-generating systems of informal commu-nication. It is largely the informal systems that accomplish the results. Have you ever experienced a company that worked to rule? Everything slows to a crawl, yet management cannot bring action against the employees because they're following the rules to the letter. It is the informal structure, what Capra and Luisi call "communities of practice," that creates the culture, interprets the meaning of things and drives results in an organization. "In order to maximize a company's creative potential and learning capabilities, it is crucial for business leaders to understand the interplay between the organization's formal, designed structures and its informal self-generating networks…the formal structures are the sets of rule and regulations that define relationships between people and tasks, and determine the distribution of power… Informal structures, by contrast, are fluid and fluctuating networks of communication."[7]

Here is where fluidity, resilience and agility (all critical capabilities for thriving in VUCA world) reside, and the informal structure draws its energy from the mission and meaning of the organizations' work.

Simply put, if your organization doesn't make a difference, neither will the work of your employees and if their work has no meaning for them, you'll never achieve the innovation and productivity that is paramount to success today. It is the leader's job to identify and instill this sense of purpose. Contrary to common belief, people do not resist change, they resist having change imposed on them. It's why re-engineering rarely succeeds; it fails to include the living aspect of the organization. But as Capra continues, "There is no need to push and pull, or bully to make it change. Force, or energy, is not the issue; the issue is meaning."[8]

It is the leader's job to clarify and communicate purpose and meaning.

And so, even from a purely rational perspective of self-interest, if you as a leader have applied a myopic and self-serving approach to the job, with a narrow agenda, competitive market forces will likely result in your eventual removal. Because as those leaders who embrace the changes, and restructure their organizations to better respond, become more skilled in new leadership techniques, they will sail past your organization with superior results. Your board will then call you to task, and demand a new approach. In short, even to maintain your status quo, for self-preservation, you will need to change.

Self-Actualization and Fulfillment

Finally, and particularly in the intended positive spirit of this book, you should consider changing and stepping up, for your own happiness and fulfillment. We are all keenly aware that we only get one run around the track (at least in this incarnation!). What we choose to do between cradle and coffin has a deep impact on the quality of our lives. Back in 1943, social scientist Abraham Maslow gave us his now widely- known hierarchy of human needs. His theory was that we move through phases of needs, rising to the next level once we have satisfied those of the one below. It is quite logical: a starving person likely does not sit around contemplating the philosophy of life. The objective is food, and fast. Similarly, we

Maslow's Hierarchy of Needs

Self-actualization — The need for development, creativity, growth.

Ego — The need for self-esteem, power, control, recognition.

Social — The need for love, belonging, inclusion.

Safety — The need for safety, shelter, stability.

Physiological — The need for air, food, water, health.

move up the pyramid. When we feel safe and fed, we seek to branch out and encounter other people, to socialize. If you are a senior leader, you are probably ensconced at the ego stage. This is the level of higher achievement, competition, and as you can see in the chart, power, control and recognition. While the levels do tend to follow an order, modern research shows that there can be overlap, and even contradiction; for example, some people can be in ego stage, with little or no regard for the social stage (the Koch brothers come to mind). But basically it represents an upward journey towards greater consciousness. Source: Commons.wikimedia.org

And there *is* a higher level to which humans can aspire, that of self-actualization, and it is at this level where the earlier reviewed concepts of conscious awareness and fulfillment are experienced. As living creatures, when growth and learning stop, we stagnate. Entropy sets in. To find fulfillment, we need to adopt an attitude of life-long learning and it is people who do so whom research finds to be the happiest.[9]

In his famous book *The Prince*, even Machiavelli insists that it is not constancy that brings success in a leader, but adaptability: "the successful ruler is the one who adapts to changing times."[10]

The dichotomy is that as we age, if we get to the 'ego needs' stage, we acquire more, get comfy, can get stuck in our warm cocoons and routines and often also develop a fear-based inertia to further change. Why take on any additional risk? This is not ideal, but not necessarily problematic, for many people. For some, ignorance can be bliss. But if your desire is to lead others, especially at a high level, then to remain effective, a life-long learning attitude is a must.

"It's not any one set of skills — rather, it's the ability to acquire them. The pace of change — of technology, of our economy — continues to increase. In any environment, it's not necessarily the strongest or smartest that are best able to survive. It's who is best suited to the changing conditions. In today's world, that means always being willing to learn."[11]

Recall in Chapter 2 the INSEAD leadership development program, where many of the world's top business and government leaders apply to be accepted, only to be put through a rigorous, stressful and often anxiety-filled psychological and peer-reviewed program. The program centers around each participant writing a life story and using it to learn about themselves, their subconscious behaviors, fears, insecurities and blind spots. The peer reviews can be stinging and painful. And yet, graduates report deep and meaningful life changes upon completing the program. Some even concluded that their high leadership positions were not what they truly sought in life, or that their current company did not fit their values, and decided to leave.

Pretty intense stuff. But once they embarked upon that path, they no longer saw things as a destination; self-actualization as a place or thing. They began to realize that the more they learned, the more they came to realize that they really knew nothing.

One of the most highly regarded experts on corporate culture and leadership is Richard Barrett, who has dedicated his entire life to raising awareness and knowledge of leadership practices.

Reprinted with permission from Barrett Values Center

His Seven Levels of Leadership (above) are aimed at helping leaders map out their growth plans to increase their own effectiveness, based upon their current level. Worthy of note is that as one moves up to Levels five, six and seven, the focus moves away from the ego and internal personal concern, to one of external and 'other'. (Note the Vision for Future Generations at Level 7)

Barrett says, "the culture of an organization is a reflection of the consciousness of its leaders. Thus, cultural transformation begins with the *personal transformation* [italics mine] of its leaders."[12]

Although it sounds terribly patronizing, this is not meant to be so. Nor is it meant to scold or preach; it is more of a combined challenge and plea. If you have risen to a place of power, influence and wealth it is because, among other things, you have remarkable skills and talents; attributes that, if applied to larger issues facing humanity, could yield truly significant results. Step out of your insulated world, of your comfort zone. Spend time among people in other walks of society. Be curious about how that person became homeless: medical bankruptcy? Mental illness with no recourse to treatment? Realize that if you had to hold a starving Syrian or Yemeni child, your heart would be moved just as would everyone else's and you just might intervene to help fix that horrific situation. I have no idea if Bill Gates is happier in his role with their Foundation than he was at Microsoft, but I would bet he is. He has continued to grow and learn as a leader. He has applied his considerable intellect, influence and status to solving problems that deal in human lives, and I would suggest that while his money facilitates important change, it is his and Melinda's involvement that makes the biggest difference; for their causes, and for them. That must give him more satisfaction than any profit and loss (P&L) statement, or even the incredible feat of putting a PC on every desk back in the 1980s.

Similarly, people may think Elon Musk is quite deluded, given some of his super-ambitious projects and dreams; but I believe he is precisely the type of leader we need many more of. Money and status and security do not drive his ideas and actions. He fears for humanity due to climate change and our abuse of the planet and of unmanaged AI. He has moved past ego stage to self-actualization and Level 7 leadership, initiating projects that may earn profit too, but are primarily concerned with the greater good. I suggest that so far his greatest accomplishment is not Tesla as a company; it is that he forced all automakers to convert to sustainable electric far sooner than they otherwise would have. That just may have saved us precious time in defeating climate change, if in fact we do succeed.

And so this is a challenge to all senior leaders, in government and in business: review your organization's mission and values. Why does it exist, and whom does it serve? Is it a liability to the planet? To humanity? Do you truly understand its interrelatedness and responsibility to the larger ecosystem of the world today? Who is it harming? Can any of the Inspiring Visions be integrated into your organization? Do you have even better ones? If you conclude you could be doing better, this is a challenge to take up the torch.

Enjoy your home(s), enjoy your car(s) and any other assets you have earned, but then have the courage and wisdom to move past them to a higher level of awareness and service. Use your considerable talents in the best way possible. You will be happier by helping make the world a better place.

Lead, follow, or get out of the way. It remains as appropriate and urgent today, perhaps even more so, as it was in Patton's time.

Note: Harvard professor Clayton Christensen wrote a marvelous article called How Will You Measure Your Life. It is a <u>highly recommended read.:</u> <u>ais.ku.edu.tr/course/20319/how-will-you-measure-your-life-by-clayon-chris-tensen.pdf</u>

CHAPTER 12

A Message to
Would-Be Leaders

"… Your playing small does not serve the world. There is nothing enlightened about shrinking so other people will not feel insecure around you. You are meant to shine, as children do. We were born to make manifest the glory of God that is within us. It is not just in some of us; it is in everyone and as we let our own light shine, we unconsciously give others permission to do the same. As we are liberated from our own fear, our presence automatically liberates others." Marianne Williamson

"What needs to be done? What can, and should, I do about it?" Peter Drucker

You Can Do it

IN 1984, IRISH ROCK STAR BOB GELDOF WATCHED A CBC documentary on the Ethiopian famine. He became first disgusted, then enraged and after calls to British politicians left him convinced that nothing was being done, he organized some friends and raised $14 million in aid money through a music project called Band Aid. Had any of us stepped forward and accomplished that, we would feel very proud, especially since that wasn't even our calling in life. But Geldof didn't stop there; he went to Ethiopia to experience first-hand what was happening, and to oversee the distribution of funds. He soon realized that $14 million was "a spit in the ocean" and so went back and organized the Live Aid mega-concerts, to raise global awareness of the crisis and inspire massive action resulting in over $300 million in aid funding. He then returned to Ethiopia to again supervise relief efforts. Imagine all this from a foreign musician with no authority or experience in either government, non-governmental organizations (NGOs), or charitable organizations. He saw a situation that deeply affected him, tried to influence those responsible to act, and when they resisted, himself acted with ownership, accountability, responsibility, persistence, and passion. All attributes of excellent leadership.

You may say, 'well, he was an international rock star with a network of very famous, wealthy people.' Quite true, but that is not the point. The famine was not *his* responsibility, nor had he in any way contributed to it happening. But he asked himself two important questions:

What needs to be done? and *What can and should I do to make a difference?*

Those are two questions that management guru Peter Drucker suggested every leader needs to constantly be asking.[1] Anyone has the ability to ask and then act upon those questions, but how many of us habitually do so: in society, schools, corporations, or public service? In an organizational context, leadership development is about creating an environment that supports and motivates everyone to constantly ask those questions; to identify and take ownership of their own role in the work, regardless of size or importance. It's about fostering that Geldof attitude ('if no one responsible for this will take action, then I will'), and involves a mindset shift from cynicism, apathy and helplessness, to one of passion, ownership and contribution.

Leadership is about effecting positive *change;* if there is no need for change in a situation, there's no need for leadership. It is about identifying the gap between a current situation and a much better future outcome and then creating and executing a plan to get there. In short: if you want something changed, *you* can do something about it! A growing body of research shows that leadership is a learnable set of skills,[2] as opposed to an attribute that someone is born with. More importantly, the same research shows that effective leadership *always* starts at the personal level. It is about becoming aware of our own gaps between who we are now and who we ultimately want to become, or what you're dissatisfied with and want to improve upon, and then taking appropriate action to improve.

After the December 14, 2012 shooting at Sandy Hook Elementary School in Newtown Connecticut left 20 six- and seven-year-old children and 6 adults dead, many thought, 'that *does* it! Enough!' and that gun control action would finally begin in the US. It did not.

Just over five years later, 17 students and staff were shot and seventeen more wounded at Marjory Stoneman Douglas High school in Parkland, Florida. Following the massacre, several students including David Hogg, Emma Gonzalez, Cameron Kasky, Sarah Chadwick and Alphonso Calderon (apologies to any others I have failed to acknowledge), became deeply dissatisfied with the lack of response from the National Rifle Association (NRA), and especially from state and national governments, and formed the anti-NRA advocacy group Never Again MSD. These eighteen-year-olds clarified their requests and demands, eloquently and concisely articulated them on television, radio, social media and in print and began to rally public support for their cause. They raised funds and travelled across the country advocating for changes to gun legislation, such as raising the minimum age to purchase guns, instituting criminal background checks and eliminating 'bump' stocks for semi-automatic weapons, to name a few of the most important.

Only weeks prior, these were normal teens pre-occupied with the things of all eighteen-year-olds: "will I go to college? Where? Who loves whom? Will I go to the prom and with whom? What's the coolest music?" Yet an experience of death and loss coupled with anger and disgust over inaction by responsible agencies, caused them to gather together, plan, set a vision and take action to make it happen. And with much of their objectives, they succeeded. Florida state yielded to pressure and raised the legal age to purchase rifles, instituted background checks and eliminated bump stocks. Several popular TV personalities criticized and mocked them, only to be met with calls from the kids for boycotts of the advertisers' products. Show ratings dropped, resignations happened and apologies were publicly issued. They would doubtless say their work is not yet finished, because the gun issue in the US remains out of control and the NRA far too powerful. But they have definitely succeeded in raising the issue to the top of the list for politicians (who fear voter retribution for inaction) and the public. Despite threats, criticism and lawsuits, they continue to plug away at their mission and have already done much to advance their cause. This is yet another example of conscious leadership in action.

The important lesson here is to understand that ordinary people can become emotionally and intellectually passionate about something and *become leaders through taking action.* Anyone who wants to, can become a leader. Yes, we do have our traditional leadership structures in business, government, non-profits and other organizations that entail formal authority that comes with responsibility. This still follows the hero-leader model, and though prevalent, is waning in popularity for reasons cited in earlier chapters. Yet more and more people, especially in the dissatisfied younger demographics, are deciding to effect positive change themselves. Let's look at two more examples of conscious leadership.

Boyan Slat is a twenty-four-year-old Dutch citizen who, while diving in Greece in 2011, was alarmed to notice more garbage in the water than fish. It caused him to investigate the situation, and he discovered The Great Pacific Garbage Patch, an accumulation of plastic corralled by ocean currents, that at the time was the size of France. Curious and inventive, and upon learning that no major effort was being made elsewhere to deal with the problem, Slat asked himself (consciously or unconsciously) those same Drucker questions. He decided that his education and inclination towards technology could make a huge difference in crafting a solution. He also felt a passionate sense of urgency that the plastic must be removed. So in 2013, he started up The Ocean Cleanup Project. The idea was to use floating corrals and utilize the ocean currents to drive the plastic into the corrals, where it could be scooped up by boats and returned to the mainland for recycling. During the next five years, he encountered many setbacks, disappointments and failed experiments; but in October 2018, the first working system went into service, and began collecting plastic from the ocean. This is an incredible act of leadership, requiring Slat to persuade many others in manufacturing, finance, engineering and government to bring his dream to fruition. He had to drop out of university in order to devote sufficient time to the project. He may not have perceived himself as a leader, but he rose to the occasion because of an issue about which he was passionate, saying, "if you're not truly obsessed (with your idea) it's not going to happen." Slat also realized that his technological background and skill meant he was the right person to tackle this problem: *"Technology is the most potent agent of change. It is an amplifier of our human capabilities, whereas other change-agents rely on reshuffling the existing building blocks of society, technological innovation creates entirely new ones, expanding our problem-solving toolbox."* [3]

While he has enjoyed, and acknowledges, help from many sources, it was he who drove the idea and the process.

It is remarkable that a twenty-four-year-old can make such an enormous impact on the well-being of the entire planet, yet he has done so. We can all take inspiration from his example and realize that we too can take leadership action to manifest better outcomes for issues we are passionate about.

A final example that you, too, can do it. Let's revisit the story of Alexandria Ocasio-Cortez, last seen in Chapter 2 (See p. 32), because what she accomplished is truly astounding, and demonstrates convincingly how excellent leadership ability can defy enormous odds.

In the 2018 US mid-term elections, at twenty-nine years of age, Alexandria Ocasio-Cortez (now known as AOC) was elected the youngest female member of Congress.

Raised in a working-class family in the Bronx, New York, AOC was an accomplished student in high school and university and active in social issues of interest to her. Her degree in International Relations and Economics reflects an inclination towards public service, as did internships for Senator Ted Kennedy, and later, Bernie Sanders' 2016 presidential campaign; but she did not see herself as qualifying for a leadership role.

"In an interview she recalled her visit to Standing Rock as a tipping point, saying that before that, she had felt that the only way to effectively run for office was if you had access to wealth, social influence, and power. But her visit to North Dakota, where she saw others 'putting their whole lives and everything that they had on the line for the protection of their community,' inspired her to begin to work for her own community."[4]

This young woman, who worked as a bartender and waitress during college, unseated Joe Crowley, a multi-term, powerful Democratic Representative in her district, despite his $4 million spend versus her own $300,000, all raised from small donations. Since then she has created, with other newly elected progressive House Representatives, a movement for a Green New Deal. Shortly after her win, she showed up to support protestors outside Speaker Nancy Pelosi's office, publicly berated fellow Congressmen for using unpaid interns and paying staffers less than a livable wage, and openly questioned why the Koch brothers and Goldman Sachs were invited to address the newly-elected Representatives at orientation, yet no one from labour or the social sector. And she did all this *before* officially starting her job in January 2019. In that same month, the global 'elite' at the World Economic Forum in Davos, Switzerland, discussed her call for a 70% marginal tax rate on the wealthy. She has really shaken the tree. AOC is pulling no punches; pressing for strong and immediate action on the issues of climate change, income inequality, racial injustice and more. She is an excellent example of courageous leadership, and another example of one who did not initially see themselves as a leader.

It's also worth mentioning that many leaders remain unsung heroes. The people at Standing Rock who so inspired AOC are leaders too. They were there before she was, risked arrest and physical danger, yet remain anonymous to us. They sparked action from a formidable person who will now rattle the status quo in Congress. Conscious leadership.

Each of these leaders – a musician, a group of high school kids, a Dutch university student, and a working-class college graduate – encountered issues that touched their hearts and minds and decided to step up and do something about it themselves. You can do it too, if you choose to.

What Are You Passionate About?

It should not be surprising to learn that none of those mentioned above had considered themselves to be leaders and especially leaders in the fields where they eventually made a difference. They simply discovered, by encountering situations, something that deeply resonated with them; that they were passionate about.

Why is it so important to be passionate?

Change under any circumstances, is usually difficult to achieve. In any leadership journey, there are always times when resistance and obstacles seem overwhelming, when hope waivers or disappears, when roadblocks seem insurmountable. It is during those times that passion drives persistence, and helps a leader break through the walls of opposition and discouragement. If we don't care passionately, it is extremely difficult to bear the failures, criticism, even threats that inevitably arise.

Before we can determine what we're passionate about, it is very important to clarify three things in our lives: our identity, our values, and our purpose (our IVPs)*. As well, the relatively new and exploding field of personal, professional and life coaching is proving highly beneficial to many. Many business and government leaders at the highest levels have gained excellent results from working with a coach and coaching has also helped accelerate leadership development at all levels of management.

Our identity deals with our uniqueness and is a combination of our personality, beliefs and˙ talents. It is very often misconstrued as our work, our marital status, our need to feel part of a clan, religion, group, or political party. While these factors contribute to our *sense* of identity, they are changeable and ephemeral; not really who we are. We are, at a deeper level, meant

---

* There are several excellent books that help in this exercise, including *What Colour is Your Parachute?* by Richard Bolles, *Unlimited Power* by Tony Robbins, Stephen Covey's *7 Habits of Highly Effective People*, *The Leadership Challenge*, by Jim Kouzes and Barry Posner.

to contribute something that may be initially unknown to us. Italian singer Andrea Bocelli graduated as a lawyer, but at thirty-four years old decided to follow his passion for singing instead. Lucky us!

There are many psychometric assessments that will help you discern your traits, personality type, strengths, motives and values. It is very helpful to understand these prior to embarking on a leadership project, simply because it will give you a solid foundation of confidence when the waters get rough. We have predispositions and temperaments that are hardwired, and if we identify and leverage them, we can be more effective in whatever we do.

As an example author Malcolm Gladwell tells of three predispositions of people. The first are Connectors, who are skilled at introducing us to our social circles; "people with a special gift for bringing the world together."[5] Then there are Mavens, who accumulate knowledge and enjoy sharing it with everyone else. With this book, I realized that I am likely one of those. Finally, he speaks of Salesmen, people naturally skilled in persuasion. Of course, these are just several examples of roles, but if we are predisposed to any one of them, it will guide us to our ideal purpose in life; and if we fail to leverage them, as natural tendencies and strengths, we will be less effective as leaders.

Clearly understanding our values and purpose are equally important for leadership for the same reason. Leaders drive change, and change involves varying degrees of uncertainty, ambiguity, and risk. That VUCA world. Even the most rock-solid leaders can be rattled by the challenges they face and only deep self-knowledge will provide the stable foundation and the confidence to make difficult decisions. Your values, and eventually, your discovered purpose or mission will serve as your compass when you feel lost.

Values are simply things you hold dear; things you believe are important in life. It could be the welfare of animals, the thrill of sport, children, freedom, justice, quality; anything at all. They're really important to a leader for at least two reasons: 1) to get things done, a group must hold *shared* values, and 2) they must be aligned. It will be difficult to instill the values of conscious capitalism in the investment banking industry, because the values of the two groups, far from being shared, are actually at odds. Shared values in a group or organization serve as a common language, and even a type of control mechanism. Rather than ask my boss, I can ask myself, 'does what I want to do fit with our values?' and the answer is usually there.

Alignment means that, as a follower or leader, I see accomplishing the organizations goals as also serving my own personal ambitions. When that alignment is present, actions are swift, clear and effective. The leaders mentioned above sought out others who shared their values, and then aligned with them for efficient action, to create Live-Aid concerts, design and build ocean clean-up equipment, organize a national bus tour for gun control, and create a plan for a Green New Deal.

Finally, our purpose or mission is sometimes the most difficult to determine, simply because most of us have many options and this can lead to 'fear of missing out' (FOMO) and confusion about which one is truly the most important to you. Business authors started writing about the power of having a mission back in the 1980s, and now most organizations have some sort of formally-stated mission that hangs in a prominent place and is carried in the annual report. But actually keeping it alive is much harder. The mission, similar to the vision we looked at in Chapter 8, is the reason *why* a person or organization exists; what they are here to accomplish. It usually does not change over time. Henry Ford said his mission was to "enable a large number of people to afford and enjoy the use of a car, (and) give a larger number of men employment at good wages."[6]

At its founding, leaders at Sony decided its mission was "to experience the sheer joy of innovation and the application of technology for the benefit and pleasure of the general public."[7] It's fair to say that both companies, particularly in their earlier years, remained faithful to their missions, at least partially fulfilling them.

Identity, values and mission serve as a beacon in the storm. Every decision that we take, for ourselves and our organizations should be compared to the IVP to ensure it supports and aligns. If it does not, it should be re-thought or even scrapped. During the past fifty years, many companies, consciously or unconsciously, replaced their formal missions with one of profit maximization and caused significant damage to the world in the process. When our sole purpose for work is not the creation of quality products and services, but rather to earn the absolute highest amount of money for management and shareholders, it breeds a myopic view of life and the world that justifies and rationalizes greed.

Determining our IVPs requires effort, reflection, humility and honesty. It benefits from learning, reading the works of experts, using coaches, psychologists, friends and family as advisers and sounding boards. It is not for anyone else to judge or say, because it is about *you*, at your deepest, most intimate and personal level. Also it can be a very difficult process because it can be very elusive. As we grow up, our subconscious is programmed primarily by our parents, siblings, other family, teachers, and things we see on TV, social media, and in magazines. Often it is our desire to please and/or emulate these others that helps set our early self-impressions and ambitions. Do we want to be a doctor because our parents were, or desired it? Do we see ourselves as businesspeople because that is 'where the money is'? We are complex creatures, with many influencing variables at play in our lives and it is thus very easy to inadvertently fool ourselves into becoming something that we are not.

Perhaps sharing my own story might illustrate just how elusive it can be.

Ever since I was a twelve-year-old kid with a large newspaper route, I knew I would be a 'captain of industry.' I wasn't sure if I had the chops to be a CEO or President, but I was determined to climb as high up the management ladder as possible, given my skill set. As a teen, I would read books like *The Canadian Establishment*, about titans of Canadian business. Not from a wealthy family, throughout high school and university, I worked sixteen hours on weekends at a warehouse of the largest grocer in Canada and on Friday nights my job was to clean the office of the EVP of Distribution. After vacuuming his floor, I'd sit in his chair and imagine myself as belonging there. In university, I started out to get a chartered accountant degree, then switched to marketing and finance, because I thought it would provide a faster track to the top. After a couple of years in the workforce, I realized that those moving fastest had MBA degrees, so I left my job at twenty-eight, with a wife and new baby, to go back to school to get one. Throughout all this time, I voraciously gobbled up the works of every prominent author on business 'best-practices' and leadership. After graduating I went into management in the hotel industry and rose to a hotel manager's position with a prominent luxury hotel company. I became a workaholic.

Can you see how deeply rooted my self-identity was? I was raised to reflect on the higher values of life (honesty, integrity, compassion, etc.), and I did so. Yet I also came to identify myself with status as a business leader, wealth, material things and authority. As I inevitably burned out, the 'little voice' we all have started whispering, 'this is not it; it's not what you're meant to do.' Of course, this made me angry and actually quite frightened and I stuffed that voice down for years, until finally, in what I later realized was a state of depression, I left the hotel business. Dejected and confused about why I was so unhappy, I wondered what to do next. A failed marriage, my young son – who lived with me – feeling alone, concerned about my health, and not getting my full attention that he deserved, and the premature deaths of my mother and two other people very close to me, left me feeling very hurt and alone. It was extremely frightening because, at mid-life, and after being so self-identified as a businessman, I was completely lost. But as is often the case, tragedy and suffering can cause us finally to face tough issues, to develop clarity and learn valuable information about ourselves, about our IVPs.

After working with various professionals (psychologists, coaches), taking several psychometric assessments, and conducting my own research, I concluded the following:

- Identity: a catalyst for awareness, growth, hope, and inspiration
- Values (top ten ranked): fairness/justice, integrity, creativity, freedom, humor, learning and growth, humility, compassion, recognition of others and excellence.

- Personal Purpose/Mission: to move people to positive action that enriches their lives

- Professional Purpose/Mission: to help companies bridge their performance gap between actual and desired results

- Vision: to help elevate society by inspiring leadership development in organizations everywhere.

Once I had gained this clarity, it became apparent that becoming a leadership development consultant and coach would allow me to better fulfill my mission and vision, be true to my values and provide a higher level of work fulfillment, than would a career in management for any single company. So I set up my own shop in 2006 and began seeking clients to do leadership development consulting and executive coaching.

After researching the 2008 financial crisis, I realized that I also had a deep belief in (i.e. valued) equality, fairness, justice and the greatest good for the greatest number. Witnessing the vast global ruin that the crisis caused and the lack of proper remedial action by governmental authorities left me angry and frustrated. And yet, because I did not identify myself as a writer, other than writing a couple of related leadership articles to post on LinkedIn, I simply tried to do my best by consulting in the small world of my clients and continued to rant about the state of global leadership to anyone who would listen.

It was only in June of 2018 that I decided I could not achieve my vision by working with only a relatively small number of clients. 'Help elevate society…' is a pretty ambitious dream. I would either have to scale down the vision, or shift the strategy and approach to reach a much broader audience. That's when the flash thought of writing a book occurred. Note how the project of writing a book aligns with and satisfies each of identity, mission and values.

Obviously I hope the book reaches and resonates with a large audience, but regardless, writing it has been a most cathartic, healing and consciousness-raising experience. Knowing our IVPs is also a process that grows over time: As we age and experience more of life, it is quite normal for some of our values to sometimes shift, or even drop away. Once achieved, we can change our vision to the next challenge we feel strongly about. Although our mission changes much less frequently, at times it too can change. I don't know if Bill Gates' original mission consciously involved spreading personal computing around the globe, but it's safe to say he succeeded; and regardless, he has a much different mission now through his work with the Bill and Melinda Gates Foundation. So don't be too concerned about getting your mission perfect the first time around, or about carving it in stone. Allow for yourself to grow and change as your life experiences indicate. But the key takeaway here is to ensure you have some form of IVPs. Without them you will simply drift along and waste precious time and energy.

Obviously, I hope you will be persuaded by the arguments and facts presented here and take steps to enrich your own life by answering these important questions for yourself and considering stepping up as a leader yourself. But most important is for you to not sell yourself short; if you do want to lead change about your passions, you have every reason to believe that you *can* do it!

That said, for those of you who feel either the timing, or the notion of leading, is not quite right for you (and remember, it's quite alright if not – most of us are followers in the majority of situations in our lives), you may want to skip the next chapter. For those of you who wish to do a 'deeper dive,' chapter 13 offers five research supported leadership practices that you can learn and use immediately to get results, as you seek to engage others in issues important to you.

CHAPTER 13

Five Simple (But Not Easy) 'How-To' Steps

"Being a great leader is like being a parent. Just as we provide our children opportunity — to build self-confidence, education and discipline when necessary all so that they can achieve more than we can imagine."
Simon Sinek

THOSE OF US CONVINCED OF THE IMPORTANCE OF STRONG leadership for a thriving society are fortunate that there is now a large and growing body of research on the subject. During the past thirty years in particular, academic and private sector research have resulted in many diverse leadership development models, replete with traits, qualities, practices and styles, all of which add to the quality of leadership in some way or another, when followed. Most of the models deal with business, government, or organizational leadership, and my approach here will be the same; but bear in mind that you can apply these steps effectively in community service, churches, or volunteer groups.

In reviewing the more successful models, I attempted to learn whether there were a few powerful practices common to all and have determined that at a minimum, five specific actions are embedded in some form in all of the models I examined.

If you simply wish to get started as a leader with some simple steps, and inspire action among others for your cause, these five will give you a great start:

1) Be the Change, 2) Light a Fire, 3) Ask What If? 4) Clear a Path, 5) Dare to Care.

Each action is explained below, and if you simply begin with the first one, and work your way through in sequence (or in parallel if you wish), you will find that followers begin to respond to your call to action.

To become a high level leader, it helps to ask the question, 'why should anyone be led by me?' The answer can go as deep and into as fine detail as one wants, but if you ask that question for each of the five practices, you'll discover your own authentic answer. Try writing out your answers in a journal; journaling is a proven method for gaining clarity and valuable reflection.

It is true, as in all things related to people, that some have greater innate skills at certain tasks than do others. There are definitely the Wayne Gretzkys, Michael Jordans, Serena Williams's in the world; but just as any athlete can study and implement the best practices of those athletes and improve their own performance, so too can leaders at every level in their organization.

1. Be the Change

"A good example is the best sermon." Benjamin Franklin.

A long-time colleague of mine – let's call him Conor – and the first boss I had who fits Collins' definition of a Level 5 leader, left a senior position in a restaurant chain to open his own restaurant. It was highly successful and twenty-eight years after opening, it was time to sell and move on to the next chapter of his life. At his farewell gathering were some of us who had worked for him and stayed in touch for decades; former managers, bartenders, waiters, many of whom, like myself, had gone on to do many different things in different walks of life. Our presence was testament to something much more than friendship or respect. It was an acknowledgment of how this person had in some way influenced or touched our lives.

One of the speakers was a former worker we'll call Luis. He recounted a tale of how, many years ago as a new immigrant to Canada escaping the violence in Nicaragua that had killed his brother, he was hired by Conor as a dishwasher. One busy evening, Conor came to him and said, "there's a big spill in the kitchen. Could you do me a favour? Leave the dishes for now, and go mop it up?" Luis defiantly answered, "that's not my job!" Instead of making an issue of it, Conor found a mop and began cleaning the spill himself, only to find Luis quickly snatching the mop from his hands, saying, "it is not the owners job either. And before you will do it, it is for me to do it!" and he cleaned it up. In the coming years, he became the most loyal and spirited employee, moving through a succession of increasingly responsible positions. He was even invited by the chef to advise on how to spice certain Latino recipes. After learning as much as possible about the business and after many years of service, he ventured out to start his own successful restaurant, specializing in Nicaraguan ethnic cuisine.

Great leaders never lose sight of the other person's reality or of their dignity, and don't ask their followers to do what they would not do themselves. They walk their own talk. Historian and business guru Peter Drucker said that the main reason there was so much mass slaughter during WWI was that "not enough generals were killed; they stayed way behind the lines and let others do the fighting and dying."[1] At that time, the arrogant practice of high-level military officers was to witness key battles from afar, with no personal risk. This led to an attitude of human dispensability, and impersonal decisions to send men to fight in suicidal situations, often for a stretch of land that was not even strategically important. The tragedy at Gallipoli in WWI is a perfect example. Had the generals been required to lead from the front, many of those decisions would not have been taken.

Gandhi said, "you must be the change you wish to see in the world," and if you do this, you will succeed as a leader, because your actions will attract like-minded people who will follow and assist you. This is why you must first get clear on what you believe and stand for; on your own non-negotiables and then check to ensure you live according to those principles. I remember reading an article about Pope Benedict, who was supposed to be Christ's Vicar on earth, espousing the attributes of Christ such as humility, charity and care for the poor. There was a picture of the Pope exiting a Mercedes limousine, wearing what were described as $3000 red Prada slippers. While there is nothing inherently wrong with an old Pope using a Mercedes, or wearing expensive slippers, it risked causing a large snicker factor among his followers and especially his critics. It sent a powerful and confusing message, and it certainly does not reinforce the message of poverty preached from the Vatican for centuries. Contrast that with the act and symbolism of Pope Francis, who upon being elected, washed the feet of twelve prison inmates including Muslims and women. Within the Church Curia, many were horrified about that, yet Francis knew the message he wanted to send and powerfully acted it out himself.

If the CEO of a tobacco company told employees that health and wellness was a core value of the company and people were expected to uphold that value, what impact would that have? If the Weinstein companies had sexual harassment policies, how seriously would they have been taken by employees? We watch our leaders for clues about acceptable behavior, and what they do has far greater impact on us than what they say. Credibility matters. To be an effective leader, we must first become very clear about our own personal and professional values. If we do not happen to be the leader and our IVPs are not highly aligned with those of the organization, department, or team we work for and we are unable to change their values, it's often best to leave. It is simply unreasonable to expect followers to do what we ourselves are not willing to do, particularly in this age where the young seem far more savvy than in previous generations.

Here are some simple steps you can follow in your efforts to 'be the change':

- To determine your IVPs: Journal or write a story about an event in your life that deeply moved you, something that caused intellectual *and* emotional responses from you. Ask yourself what values that event represented. Ask, 'how important is this to me in my life?' Ask, 'why do I want to do this, and at what point would I walk away from this issue? What are my non-negotiables?' Hint: if you actually *have* non-negotiables about an issue, chances are you could be a leader for or against that issue.

- Once you have clarified your IVPs, ask yourself, 'how do I display the behaviors I believe in? How do my values show up at work, with family, at my place of worship, in sport, etc.? How do I let people know what I believe to be important?'

- Assess how others *perceive* your honesty, credibility and authenticity. These character traits build trust and when we trust our leaders we engage and commit more strongly to the task at hand. How do your peers, friends or business direct reports see you? Whether or not one agrees with Bernie Sander's politics, he cannot be accused of hypocrisy or inconsistency. For forty years, he has espoused the same values, called for the same policies, and lived according to his beliefs, despite being cast as an outsider. He is authentic in what he does and in what he asks of others. If you find there's a gap between what you believe and how others perceive you, select actions that can close the gap.

- Select one or two key messages of importance and actually *schedule small events or actions in your calendar* to reinforce your message. Is your company supposed to be customer obsessed? Go visit a few customers. Does your organization serve the homeless? Leave your office and serve for a spell on the front lines with your employees. Do you claim to care about what your employees think? Check to see what policies solicit their input. Walk the factory floor and chat with them or ask to join them for lunch in the staff cafeteria. And of course, do it with joy and sincere intent, not out of a calculated motive; people can always tell the difference.

If we seek to inspire behavioral change in others, we must first ensure that our actions embody those desired behaviors. We must be the change.

2. Light a Fire

"Vision refers to a picture of the future with some implicit or explicit commentary on why people should strive to create that future." John Kotter

Lighting a fire refers to setting a vision that gets people excited and engaged about your vision of the future. In the VUCA world, change is now a permanent force, and can be intimidating and frightening. This is where vision becomes an indispensable and powerful concept. People follow leaders who can answer their questions and alleviate their anxiety: 'where are we currently, and what are our challenges? What are we all about? Where are we heading, and what could we potentially become in the future? And why do we want to bother doing this?' In discussing and answering these questions, leaders discover and set a vision that everyone can embrace, with intellectual understanding and emotional connection.

This step in becoming a leader is to engage potential followers and supporters in your cause. In many cases, the initial vision comes from a leader, often as a new and unusual idea. But in an organizational context, the most powerful effect emerges when a team or group create the vision together. We all connect much more deeply with something we help create, than to something that is foisted upon us. Sometimes this is impractical, so the trick in setting the vision as the leader is to understand and connect with the shared values of your people.

When Sam Palmisano became CEO of IBM, he knew that radical change would impact the company and that a rejuvenated set of mutually agreed values was critical to success. Here's what he did: "Enterprises built to endure stand on a foundation of core values. In 2003, we undertook the first disciplined re-examination of our Values in nearly 100 years. Through Values-Jam – an unprecedented 72-hour discussion on the global intranet – IBMers came together to define the essence of the company. The result? A set of core Values – defined by IBMers for IBMers – that shape everything we do and every choice we make on behalf of the company. This shared set of Values helps guide our decisions, actions and behaviors and is at the core of our collective aspiration to be recognized as a great company."[2]

Writer Marcus Buckingham says the leader's job is to rally people toward a better future. It's actually not as easy as it sounds; rallying people can be complex. But the odds for success increase significantly when we help people get clear about what needs to be done and why, and invite them to embrace their roles in bringing the vision to life. This is the second step in becoming an effective leader.

The vision of a Nazi-free world galvanized Allied troops to make huge personal sacrifices until victory was achieved. Conversely, with no clear, plausible vision for why the US troops were in Vietnam, both troops and citizens eventually turned against the war effort and it subsequently and understandably failed.

In business, we've seen the early visions of Ford and Sony and their remarkable achievements that followed. Today, Elon Musk has endured many trials and obstacles in getting Tesla to succeed, to fulfill his vision of a sustainable clean energy transportation system. Reusable rocket systems for space travel, large-scale battery storage and solar panel roof tiles are all results of his broader vision for a sustainably healthier planet and he has won over many former skeptics as converts because of his passion and expressive descriptions of the future. We are fortunate that today the motivation of many entrepreneurs is not profit-driven, but rather visionary, treating profits as the necessary and deserved result of things done well for their own sake.

Here are some practical steps you can take in order to set a vision that lights a fire in your people:

- **What's most important?**

Assuming you've done the exercise in Be the Change, you will have determined what is most important to you. Searching for recurring themes in your life where you felt capable, effective and happy often gives a clue. What was the common experience in all of them? Visions of the future are more often intuitive than logical, so don't discount your gut feelings; pay attention to them. When you hear that little voice saying, 'You gotta be kidding! You can't do that! What makes you think you can do that?' shut it down quickly. In coaching, this negative self-chatter is referred to as 'The Gremlin'. Don't be intimidated by your mental pre-programming. Allow every possibility to arise, because often you cannot know in advance which one will be perfect for you. As Alexandria Ocasio-Cortez said, her experience at Standing Rock with the Dakota Indians led her to the conclusion that public service was something she just had to do. It was unexpected but the feeling was powerful and she found her calling.

In your company or organization, you must do a similar exercise for the organization's history too. Why did it start in the first place? What was important back then and what accomplishments are we most proud of? What has changed since then? Have we – and if so, how – drifted of course; have we betrayed our values? What future opportunities can we select that preserve our core values and purpose while letting us build a brand new future?

- **Establish the vision gap**

'Here's where we're at, and here's where we have to go.' Once you've determined an issue about which you care deeply, explore, with others if you're able to, the present situation and possibilities for the future. How are things right now and how much better could they be? What would be required to manifest that? What additional information would you need? Who would you need to help you and how? How would the world, community, town, people benefit if the situation was improved? What would be different?

The difference between current reality and your idealized future is your leadership 'gap', and your task becomes one of mobilizing like-minded people to eliminate that gap. My business tag line as a consultant is 'helping you bridge your performance gap'. As you become clearer about what will be required, take stock of your own skills and talents and identify areas where they will not suffice. This will help you determine who else will be needed to achieve the vision. A sports team needs strength in each of many positions. Seek those people.

Try not to censor yourself during this exercise. Ignore how grandiose or ridiculous your vision may sound. There are countless stories where people have set outrageous visions and pulled them off beautifully and against all odds (e.g. the moon shot). Science has yet to prove conscious manifestation, but those who have achieved it believe in its power. Conceive, believe, achieve. If you are somewhat more pragmatic, remember that if we aim for the stars, we will definitely clear the trees.

If a vision is not sufficiently ambitious (it should ideally have a 'stretch factor' with 20-30% chance of failure), it is difficult for people to get excited and engaged about it. Who cares about 'ho hum'? This is why companies that set a 'vision' (that's not really one) that deals with revenue goals or capital asset values, usually fail to inspire. Yet so many are solely driven by those mundane goals. There is nothing inherently wrong with a vision for growth; all organizations need to grow. But when growth for growth's sake is the objective, it is empty for most people involved. In 1992, Sam Walton, founder of Wal-Mart, set a vision to become the world's first retail company to hit $125 billion in annual sales by the year 2000. They were at $32 billion at the time.[3] They achieved it ahead of schedule, but mostly through technological advances, and questionable treatment of suppliers and employees. And so what? What former employee sits and tells that story to their grandchildren children? Wal-Mart is not known for its employee engagement or morale, and instead has been widely criticized for its treatment of them and for damage to local retail communities wherever they build.

•   **Clarify and energize with powerful language**

Write out your vision and condense it into a short powerful statement; the shorter the better. A strong vision, as John Kotter defines it, should be imaginable, desirable, feasible, focused, flexible and communicable.[4] Keeping these six simple characteristics in mind as you express your dream will result in a powerful, effective message. Most importantly, try to include intellectual logic in the *content*, but emotional language in the *description* of your vision.

Below are some good examples of missions and visions that capture intellect *and* emotion. What do you think and feel when you read them?

•   "Build the best product, cause no unnecessary harm, use business to inspire and implement solutions to the environmental crisis." Patagonia

•   "To bring inspiration and innovation to every athlete* in the world (*if you have a body, you are an athlete.)" Nike

•   "To create the most compelling car company of the 21st century by driving the world's transition to electric vehicles." Tesla

Actually, the first two are really mission statements, because they are not time-dated. Missions are the reason an organization exists, the Why of existence, and are rarely if ever achieved because a mission is ongoing (e.g. 'to reduce global hunger').

The vision might be 'to ensure no child goes to school hungry in the city of Chicago.' Patagonia and Nike can continue doing those stated activities forever and never achieve the end. They are laudable missions, but not exactly visions.

A good vision usually has an end date; that is, once achieved, we move onto the next vision.

McDonald's recently changed its vision statement to reflect the changing competitive environment. From the previous: "*Our overall vision is for*

McDonald's to become a modern, progressive burger company delivering a contemporary customer experience", the vision was modified in 2017: "to move with velocity to drive profitable growth and become an even better McDonald's serving more customer's delicious food each day around the world."[5]

It is worth noting a couple of things here, especially the absence of "burger company" in the new vision. This reflects McDonald's flexibility and response to the public trend toward healthier foods, and allows them to change their menus accordingly. Next, their mission ("to be our customer's favorite place and way to eat and drink") has not changed, nor have they dropped their famous sixty-year-old values of QSCV (quality, service, cleanliness and value).

Tesla, once most cars and trucks are electric, intends to be making all homes and businesses energy self-sufficient, alleviating traffic jams with underground tunnels, and eventually flying to Mars. Talk about ambitious! Don't let your vision settle for mediocrity. Be bold, and put your heart and soul into the description to energize others.

(Note: Panmore.com is an excellent source for examples of actual corporate mission and vision statements)

- **Anticipate the future and possible consequences**

When Martin Luther King Jr was creating his vision, he knew that violence would eventually come into play, from both sides. Being non-violent, he ensured that his vision statements, his speeches and his own actions, sent a strong signal of passive resistance. Once you feel you have ignited your own passion about your issue, consider potential adverse or negative future scenarios and set a plan for how to avert or deal with them prior to their arising. As a leader, you assume responsibility for your own actions and in many ways, also for those of your followers. So it's helpful at the beginning stages to ask, 'How might this go wrong for us? What could sabotage or blow up our good intentions? What steps and caveats can we include now to prevent those things from happening?' One can never anticipate all the possibilities (Facebook is a perfect example of this); indeed, good leadership adapts to inevitable surprises, but the exercise can often prevent damage to people and reputations, and also protect your own credibility against those who might seek to undermine your vision.

- **Communicate powerfully and endlessly**

Once your vision is clear to you, it is time to share with others; to spark engagement, inspire faith, courage and commitment to overcome the inevitable obstacles that will arise on the journey and, most importantly, to keep everyone focused on the big picture. Do not be discouraged if you are not the most eloquent speaker. When anyone speaks deeply from their heart, we sense it and respect it. Even if they disagree, most people admire those who speak from a place of honest vulnerability. And those who share your values will be attracted to your cause.

I recently read online that a man in the US outfitted his pick-up truck with a portable shower. He would drive it on weekends to a town square and encourage homeless people to use it, free of charge. He treated them with dignity and respect and the program took off. Soon he added a section in his truck with used clothing, and made that available to the people too. Eventually, it became a community event, with people bringing food, music, clothing and simply gathering to connect with the homeless and offer encouragement and support. This fellow simply got the idea and took action. When I googled to find his story again, I was unable to find him, but I did notice that there are now similar programs in Australia, Canada, and several US cities. It is testament to how one person taking action can spark awareness, compassion, energy and action in others. He did not have to speak. His presence every weekend was the consistent message, and spoke much louder than words.

Two of your most critical jobs as a leader is to keep people a) inspired and b) focused on the task at hand. To do this, you will need to paint a vivid and compelling picture of the future, and repeat it, perhaps ad nauseam, in all aspects of your operation. Listen to speeches by great orators, Churchill,

King Jr, and JFK. Read Lincoln's Gettysburg address. These will give you ideas for colorful and emotional language that will touch people's hearts and add meaning and purpose to their lives. That may be the most important contribution of any leader. We are desperately hungry for meaning in our lives and can find it in our work, when our personal values align with those of our employer. As the leader, try to always tie back your interactions with followers to the overriding vision. When you praise someone for an excellent job, refer to how that action advances the vision. Massage the message until people start to internalize it.

Use slogans (one I saw that I really liked was 'Stay Hungry') that embody the spirit and speak volumes about the vision and values. And build certain phrases into your messaging. This is not new; PR people have been embedding 'talking points' into the speeches of CEOs and politicians for decades for a reason. It works. Repetition works. There is so much noise out there with email, texting, tweets, blogs, RSS feeds, and advertising, that it is incredibly easy to get distracted and veer off track. You cannot let this happen to yourself, or to your people. Stay focused, stay on message and repeat endlessly. When they're sick of hearing you, you've almost made it! Remember that it is one thing to light a fire, but quite another to keep it blazing throughout all types of weather. Tend to the fire with diligence, care and consistency once lit. (For an excellent talk on lighting the fire watch Simon Sinek's TED talk ; 37 million views https://www.ted.com/talks/ simon_sinek_how_great_leaders_inspire_action)

3. Ask "What if?"

"Good is the enemy of great." Jim Collins

Leadership is a dynamic relationship between those who wish to lead, and those who choose to follow. Implicit in that agreement is that something is going to change; we're going somewhere else literally, or we're reshaping something, or we're creating something completely new. Whatever is happening, the one certainty is change. Things are not going to be the same when we're through.

Among the duties of the leader, being a catalyst for change ranks among the most critical. In a business or organizational context, those who accept the status quo, even while generating excellent *current* results, are merely excellent managers. Leaders are change agents, seeking to disrupt the proverbial 'that's always how we've done it around here' routines internally and constantly scanning (and prompting others to scan) horizons for new opportunities and threats externally – seeking 'kaizen' (continuous improvement) internally and the next best idea externally.

The best leaders don't accept 'good enough', and continuously ask 'why' and 'what if'. What if it could be better? What if we could be number one? Best in class? Make a bigger impact on the world? It's not so much a state of permanent dissatisfaction as it is the act of pulling people towards extraordinary achievements, pausing awhile to let everyone catch their breath and celebrate what they've accomplished, then moving on to the next adventure. Embedding a change mindset as part of the culture.

The following activities can be applied when crafting a vision, and equally importantly, when leading an organization. If you deploy these as tactics, you'll see progress in moving along toward the envisioned state.

- **Embed a 'Change' Mindset**

We've already seen how the VUCA world has removed the luxury of choice for companies (and governments) to learn how to change and adapt. It really is do or die. That means to protect their organization and its people, leaders need to retrain them to think of change as simply the new norm. There is widespread existence of something known as 'cultural entropy.' It is defined as "the proportion of energy in a human system (organization) that is consumed by non-productive activity,"[6] and includes bureaucracy, negative politics, empire building, silo maintenance and similar detrimental activities that distract mental focus from the mission and vision. Cultural entropy drastically reduces speed of response, agility and resilience, and is prevalent, to some degree, in many, if not most, large corporations.

Assuming your vision is already clearly articulated and communicated, the next step is to begin examining your company's current practices, asking *why* you perform them, and *what if* you didn't, or did them differently. While extremely time-consuming, zero-based budgeting is a powerful way to do this. No funds are allocated to any program until the department manager can justify how it contributes to the overall mission and vision. But you don't need this extreme exercise to send the message that constant change for the better is the new norm.

Instead, challenge your people to look at their areas of responsibility with fresh eyes, asking, 'Why? and What if?' Then ask them to select just one item that they believe could be improved upon. Or one that might be eliminated without negative effect. Encourage this to be done with a sense of urgency and tell them not to worry if they don't get it right the first time. The point is to demonstrate through activity that change is not something to be feared, but will rather be part of ongoing operating procedure.

Asking What if? and Why? creates opportunities for what John Kotter calls, "short-term wins," which he also claims are paramount to your leadership success. The reason is that while the macro vision can inspire and excite, over time, people's attention and emotion naturally wane. Short-term wins keep people engaged and excited, and prove in incremental steps that the vision is working. They are projects that are rather easily achievable and demonstrate that change is a good thing when approached intelligently. A good short-term win has at least three characteristics:[7]

1. It's visible; large numbers of people can see for themselves whether the result is real or just hype

2. It's unambiguous; there can be little argument over the call

3. It's clearly related to the change effort, vision and mission

You can strategically decide which short-term projects have a high probability of success, and set several in motion at once in different departments, or one small project across a broader group. The key is to get small change activities happening quickly and positive results supporting the change. Gradually, your people will become comfortable with it.

- **Know What Your People Can Handle**

One crucial factor that will crystallize as you evolve your vision, and discuss ideal changes, is the efficacy of your people. Your employees or followers will have a varying and diverse skill set among them, leaving them well equipped to handle certain tasks and ill-equipped for others.

You as the leader need to be constantly mindful that a) change always causes stress, b) that some stress is negative and detrimental to performance, and c) that part of your role is to manage their stress by knowing them well and creating an environment that will make them feel safe.

Consultant and coach Dr. David Rock developed a model (SCARF) that is based in neuroscience, and reflects domains in the brain area that drive threat and reward responses.

1. **Status** – our relative importance to others

2. **Certainty** – our ability to predict the future

3. **Autonomy** – our sense of control over events

4. **Relatedness** – how safe we feel with others

5. **Fairness** – how fair we perceive the exchanges between people to be.[8]

These are all pretty straight forward, yet the leader must be consciously aware that they are primal forces, often unconscious, that can be easily triggered by the unsafe feeling that change often brings. By keeping the acronym in mind, you can assess how your decisions and changes will impact your people and take corrective or supportive steps in advance.

The other aspect of efficacy relates to skill sets and culture. The former can be addressed with training or perhaps bringing on board new people who have the required skills. The other is a bit trickier. When reviewing this, good leaders "make a distinction between the need for knowledge, which training can address, and the need for adaptation, which is more complex. What's known as an adaptive challenge is a gap between the shared values people hold and the reality of their lives."[9] Adaptive change is much scarier than simple skills-driven change, because it triggers all the SCARF elements. As you can imagine, the majority of companies globally are deep into adaptive challenges caused by VUCA world. And they're not generally coping too well, largely because their leaders do not know how to cope.

In adaptive change situations, you need to spend time with people to find out what they're afraid of, determine whether the fears are real (90% are said to be all in our heads), and persuade them that the vision will lead them to a better place.

As an example, let's say you're a new leader in a legacy organization in a tier three (slower moving industry). You hold the patent on widgets for fifty years, are the clear market leader and have chugged along profitably for that half century. Now, there are Chinese and Indian widget makers, with labor costs 10% of yours, that are deeply pressuring your prices; and worse, some kid in a garage has developed a 3D printed widget that doesn't require any labor force, has lower materials costs and faster production times.

See the challenge? Your people are good people. But long-term success and supremacy have embedded a slow-moving, resistant mindset into the culture. Retraining will only be a small part of the solution. The major challenge will be an adaptive one: changing the deeply entrenched values and perceptions of the culture and alleviating fears. Setting up short-term win projects will definitely be required and helpful, but human interaction will be even more important at the outset.

Were it me, as one step, I would identify the most loyal and influential employees (and not just in management), break them into small groups, and host informal luncheons to discuss the vision casually. Here, I would explain the Burning Platform we're facing, get the fears and anxieties out in the open, and face them honestly and then enlist their input and support in re-invent-ing Widget Co. for the next fifty year run. A big part of the task is to gain buy-in, and work to establish new habits.

So as a leader, it cannot be overstated that the more effort you make to intimately understand your people (or followers) the more successful you'll be. It is largely your job to determine what skills and culture gaps exist and to close them, with the help of your people.

- **Constantly seek new information and knowledge**

The process of systematically challenging the status quo by asking 'what if?' and 'why?' will inevitably result in ideas and questions for which new info is needed.

This seems like a no-brainer, but it is quite surprising how easily organi-zations can become insular and internally focussed on the day-to-day busi-ness. Sometimes it's deliberate: Steve Jobs of Apple never cared about what competition was doing because he was so intense about staying so far ahead in innovation. For a long time, he was right, but it would be interesting to see if Tim Cook can still afford that luxury today. So often companies get so engrossed in their own affairs that they not only fail to systematically look outside of their company, but even create silos within their own organiza-tions, resulting in information being stored instead of shared. Both flaws are risky and forfeit opportunities.

So, very simply, you as the leader need to keep yourself and your people abreast of not only what's happening now, but more importantly of what's coming down the pike. There are numerous useful models for assessing the external environment – notably the SWOT analysis,[10] and also Porter's Five Competitive Forces [11]– and you can assign the task to a group (if you're in a larger organization), or to an employee who has an affinity for research and trends in your industry. I guarantee you have one somewhere.

For internal information, it's the same process. Systematize the 'What if?' process to occur regularly and when questions and ideas arise, assign responsibility to people for acquiring and reporting back the information. Evaluate what you learn internally against what the external analysis uncovers, and then compare both to the mission and vision, in order to come up with new action plans that are tightly aligned with both.

Eventually you will find that the constant practice of asking 'what if?' and 'why?' will infiltrate the culture and become part of the new normal. People will eventually be asking you, 'What's Next?'

- **Communicate, Communicate, Communicate**

Your actions will speak the loudest of all, but effective leaders recognize that communication is a multi-pronged tool, and seek to *systematically and consistently,* leverage all of them. It is OK if you're not the most comfortable speaker; it just means you need to take bolder or more visible

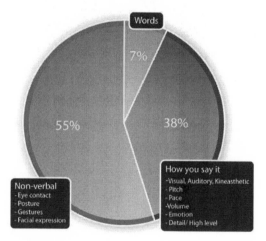

actions to express yourself. But speaking *does* have its merits, simply because when spoken from the heart, people are moved. So perhaps consider a Dale Carnegie or other course to help you sharpen your speaking skills. Other than that, the most important tactic is to set up a structured communication system with a clear and inspiring message and then stick to it. Use the tools shown above to maximize the impact of your message and deliver it through print, social media, video, corporate interior signage and any other creative and highly visible methods you can find. Again, repetition is the key. There is a *lot* of noise out there, and there is a good reason why excellent companies, militaries, sports teams, emergency response teams and the like drill and drill and drill. Repetition shifts mindsets. Ask 'What if?' and 'Why?' until it becomes second nature in everyone.

4. Clear a Path

"None of us is as smart as all of us" Kenneth Blanchard

The traditional notion of the 'hero-leader' is fast fading. Why? Because the pace and breadth of change in a VUCA world is far too much for even the genius leader to manage alone. Effective leaders today use feedback and collaboration to arrive at the right vision and strategies, align the best people with the right skills into the right teams, clear the path of bureaucracy, stifling policies and internal politics, and then get out of the way to let their people shine. It should be apparent that the last part requires a highly conscious leader whose ego is under control and who trusts his or her people. They understand that things get done through others.

Perhaps most important to becoming an effective leader is our attitude towards leadership itself. Do we see ourselves as traditional, top-down, command and control leaders who possess most of the answers? Or are we more inclined to create an environment of trust and collaboration, where people feel safe to speak truthfully and candidly, to stretch and grow as professionals and as people, to challenge the 'elephants in the room'? Do we perceive our role as helping our people to become their 'best selves' and then removing obstacles and barriers to excellent performance, or simply telling them what to do? As management guru Tom Peters says, "Leaders don't create followers; they create more leaders."

Outstanding leaders subordinate their own egos to the task of clearing a path: to help followers 'get out of their own ways' (both individually and as a team), and to then clear the path of structural and policy obstacles that hinder the speed and agility of the team to achieve.

They trust that if they and their team don't yet have the answers, they do have the capacity to find them when they collaborate and honor and leverage each other's skills, knowledge and attitudes.

Prior to clearing the path, leaders must first ensure that their people can handle the tasks that will be required. Below are a few actions you can take to do that.

- **Know and Grow Your People**

We saw earlier that when Lou Gerstner Jr took over at ailing IBM in 1993 it had lost $8 billion the prior year and its stock was down 75% from earlier highs. It is perhaps the greatest corporate turnaround in modern history and most notable was that in his first month, he had personally interviewed his top 200 people in five countries. After six months in office, he'd spoken to thousands of customers and 20,000 employees. He said he mostly asked questions, and listened intently.

Once he knew his people and their skills, experience and capabilities, he was able to craft the change strategy that eventually saved IBM. (See p.38) Great leaders take time to know their people professionally and personally. If their company invests in psychometric assessments (DISC, Myers-Briggs, 360 Reviews), a good leader will familiarize him or herself with that information for as many key employees as is practical. This allows the leader to identify any skill gaps that may need to be addressed. Setting up personalized leadership development and growth plans will add structure and consistency to your organization and will allow you to assign 'stretch' projects to your best people, keeping them engaged and growing as people and as leaders. Knowing where our people are at developmentally and encouraging and enabling them to grow to the next level, builds trust and loyalty, two major ingredients necessary for change initiatives to succeed.

But he or she also needs to gain employees' engagement and commitment to the company vision, and that comes from taking a *personal* interest in people. Kids? Pets? Hobbies? Causes? If we believe leaders genuinely care about us as people, we tend to form personal allegiances to the leader and enthusiastically do our part to support the vision.

- **Build Trust**

Before you can begin to clear the path for your people to run and flourish, you first need to trust that they're capable of handling their responsibilities. Remedying skills gaps (as shown above) is a must-do, but only appeals to the intellect. To capture hearts and energy requires strong trust. Earlier we looked at the effect of 'Be the Change' on followers. It engenders trust when people witness leaders consistently walking their talk.

Next is to nudge your people out into unfamiliar territory, and always 'have their back' when they inevitably stumble during the learning process. Research on expectations indicates that we perform better when we believe that others – particularly parents, coaches and bosses – believe in us. By assigning projects that are slightly beyond a person's current comfort zone, we permit them to grow to the next level of competence. This builds our trust in them as they succeed, and their trust in us for having faith that they would succeed. You will soon find that as trust builds throughout the organization, you will be able to remove barriers like approval steps, tight job descriptions, low signing authority limits, restricted resource policies. Trust creates an environment of ownership and accountability and a culture that places organizational goals and vision ahead of personal agendas. While it is difficult in the beginning to generate, the results of a high-trust culture are phenomenal.

- **Drive Collaboration**

As you continue to deepen trust among your followers, it will become easier to focus on collaboration. Without a collaborative mindset, organizations fall prey to internal politics, sabotage, unfair competition for resources and resource hoarding, and overall cultural entropy and stagnation. Collaborative organizations utilize teams to accomplish work and there is a wide body of literature on the effectiveness of teams. As well, you can find an excellent Collaboration Audit to conduct with your people in *The Leadership Challenge*, by Jim Kouzes and Barry Posner.[12] It will help you determine a quantifiable score which can then be targeted for clear improvement.

One strong method of fostering collaboration is to set team goals. Team goals tie bonuses and performance ratings to collective results. The team either achieves its objectives or not, together. Whereas a group is also comprised of people working on a project, their individual performance is usually treated separately. If the group misses a deadline, I can still collect my bonus for my own work. True teams are powerful because they value a common mission, vision or even goal, and cover for each other when necessary. As a leader, you need to spend time clarifying individual accountabilities and then discussing how people will collaborate to support each other. There is now a rich body of research on all aspects of teams and their effectiveness for you to access when you're ready. One of my absolute favorites is *The Five Dysfunctions of a Team* by Patrick Lencioni

- **Educate and Expand Responsibilities**

Clearing the path means getting rid of policies, procedures and rules that slow your people down in their pursuit of results. We can only do that when a) our people are qualified, competent and confident and b) engaged, trusting and committed. The first part comes from establishing an atmosphere of constant education – formal and informal. Hallway and cafeteria conversations can be the most effective method of education; about customer issues, innovations, corporate history and culture. Expanding responsibilities as people become ready provides opportunity for growth, which in turn increases engagement, trust and commitment.

Seek to establish a mindset of never-ending learning. It will become a source of new ideas and excitement in the workplace.

The notion of a leader as path-clearer may be foreign to you. It takes a deep level of self-confidence to see a leader's role as one of facilitator, enabler,

teacher, coach and cheerleader; but particularly for the younger generations
(X, Millennials, Y) it is proving to be the most effective.

5. Dare to Care

"Vulnerability is engaging in life, being all in, dedicating yourself to something."

Brene Brown

Remember the Gallup statistic quoted earlier, that 85% of employees
are either "not engaged" or "actively disengaged" in their work? (See p.104)
While there are several contributing factors to this, one of the strongest is
the perception that leaders don't care. No matter how sophisticated our technology and corporate processes become, human factors will always dictate
human responses.

Traditionally, the most difficult issues for most managers to talk about are
the 'soft stuff' – passion and the heart issues. Caring in business has traditionally been considered a sign of weakness. Ironically, it's exactly the opposite:
leaders who dare to care achieve superior results. The fact that companies have
been rushing to educate their employees in <u>emotional intelligence</u> reflects the
proven co-relation between advanced human interaction skills and performance results.

We've looked at Jim Collins' <u>Level 5 leaders</u>, those rare characters who
are defined as possessing intense professional will and deep personal humility. Intense will means they care deeply about results and set high expectations for themselves and their teams. Personal humility means they also care
deeply about their people, constantly recognizing and celebrating the efforts
of their employees.

The key idea here is that they subordinate their egos to the service of
their cause (results) and the service of their people (encouragement). Great
leaders set high expectations to stretch people to achieve their very best. They
then give their people full credit for victories, yet shoulder full responsibility
for failures. They coach more than command. They recognize contributions,

celebrate victories and constantly encourage their teams, especially during difficult times.

Because they dare to care, they implicitly signal everyone that not only is it OK to care, but it's required in the effort to achieve our vision.

- **Set the Bar High**

Good leaders know that setting high expectations is a sure way to show they care about results. A good sports coach senses the current capability of her athletes and then sets the achievement bar just high enough to reach, if they make their best effort. Business is no different. Research clearly shows that when leaders expect their people to fail, they usually do. If we expect them to succeed, they usually do that too. Setting high expectations implicitly says, 'I have full faith in your ability!'

Setting high performance standards means we care enough to work a bit harder to achieve a better result. It is safe to say that those companies that settle for average simply don't care as much. Customer service, product quality, environmental conscientiousness and stakeholder relations are examples of where setting high expectations means daring to care. It is *not* in setting overly aggressive sales and financial goals. Those are the *result* of caring about the high quality of operations.

- **Be Vulnerable**

At one point in my career, I was Hotel Manager of the very first luxury hotel that our founder Isadore Sharp had built with his father. The Four Seasons Inn on the Park hotel in Toronto was a marvelous innovation at the time (early 1960's) and its profits helped build many other hotels in the company. Its service levels set the standard for future Four Seasons Hotels and Resorts, as Four Seasons became synonymous with the pinnacle of luxury hotel service. But for a variety of uncontrollable factors, by the early 90's, the hotel had to be sold. It was put up for sale, and it took two years to find the right buyer. Running a hotel that was for sale with all the inherent uncertainty, was a major challenge; one of the most difficult things I've been involved in. Once the deal was closed, Chairman and CEO Sharp visited the hotel and asked me to go for a walk outside in the courtyard. He explained how much the hotel meant to him, how frustrated he was that despite countless financial scenarios and analyses we could not find a way to redevelop and keep it and mostly, how much he loved the employees. Then he said that while many said they knew what I had gone through and accomplished, no one knew like he did, just what a task it had been. He thanked me for my efforts and the way I had tried to look after the employees during such a prolonged, stressful time.

Aside from being stunned and excited by a personal visit from Mr. Sharp, I learned two important leadership lessons: 1) how a personal gesture like that left me, though 39 at the time, walking on air, feeling deeply appreciated, and that all the struggles had been worth it, and 2) the power of vulnerability. This highly accomplished man displayed no hubris or machismo. He allowed his humanity to show through, telling me stories of his experiences with several of the employees, (one bellman had been with him for 36 years, even though the company was 34 years old!), and how letting them go was hurting him deeply. By expressing these sentiments, my already high opinion of him grew even higher. He was being human, vulnerable, and that, especially at high business leadership levels, takes courage. I realized how vulnerability can evoke intense loyalty in followers.

Research in the leadership field is confirming my personal conclusions:

"Brené Brown, an expert on social connection, conducted thousands of interviews to discover what lies at the root of social connection. A thorough analysis of the data revealed what it was: vulnerability. Vulnerability here does not mean being weak or submissive. To the contrary, it implies the courage to be yourself. It means replacing 'professional distance and cool' with uncertainty, risk, and emotional exposure. Opportunities for vulnerability present themselves to us at work every day. Examples she gives of vulnerability include calling an employee or colleague whose child is not well, reaching out to someone who has just had a loss in their family, asking someone for help, taking responsibility for something that went wrong at work, or sitting by the bedside of a colleague or employee with a terminal illness."[13]

Think of the best boss you ever had. How did you feel when you saw him or her walking towards you at work? Recall the same situation for your worst ever boss. For whom did you make the extra effort. The second component of daring to care, vulnerability, deals with that simple notion.

- **Recognize Achievement**

In my hotel sale example, at thirty-nine with an MBA and responsibility for 450 employees and a multi-million dollar budget, I felt I had long outgrown the positive motivational effects of a 'pat-on-the-head' acknowledgement, and yet my short time with the chairman was like shot of adrenaline, because it was sincere. The fact that he came in person still impresses – though doesn't surprise, knowing the person he is.

Formal and informal recognition should be given regularly. Formal is usually systematic, and includes programs like recognition for best performance, with prizes, celebratory events, bonuses, status (parking spots, posted pictures, etc.). Informal, while less comfortable for some leaders, *can be far more powerful*: personalized hand-written thank-you notes, walking around and stopping to chat with employees in their cubicles, shop floor, cafeteria. Yes, these take a little more time but it is anything but wasted. These short moments, when done with sincerity, puts deposits in the relationship bank, showing people that you genuinely care about how they feel at work. When the inevitable change and challenges arrive, leaders can then ask more of their people, because they will have earned their trust and loyalty. And often, you won't even have to ask. People will recognize the situation and step up on their own.

For decades, the implicit assumption in business has been 'leave your problems at the door when you come to work.' The phrase 'it's not personal; it's just business' prevailed and was used to excuse all manner of abuses. These days, the leaders who dare to care, about the mission, the work and the people, achieve superior results in all areas that matter. Taking a sincere interest in the lives of our employees recognizes the fact that as corporate as we wish to be, in the end, we are first human. Humans respond best to an inclusive, challenging and caring environment. The best leaders understand and leverage that fact.

Beginning Your Leadership Journey

As mentioned at the beginning of this chapter, this has been a *very* cursory review of some of the most basic leadership steps one can take for quick results. Remember that it's part science, part art, and the best leaders will tell you they never stop learning more about it. Fortunately, many of them have shared their knowledge in books, case studies and white papers, creating a wide and rich body of research into which you can dive for details. The bibliography for this book includes works I have read, (some many times), and continue to draw from for wisdom and ideas. I hope you will find them useful to your leadership journey too.

CHAPTER 14

Conclusion – A New Zeitgeist of Conscious Awareness

"We shall not cease exploration, and the end of all our exploring will be to return where we began, and know the place for the first time."
T.S. Eliot

HOPEFULLY, THIS BOOK HAS HELPED PERSUADE YOU THAT society in general has been lulled to sleep over the past few decades and is, in most cases, ignorant of what is really going on in business, government and media. Those among us who are not asleep are often indifferent and dangerously tolerant. We have permitted and thus fallen victim, to a lower quality of leadership that has failed us in lieu of advancing their own agendas.

It is long overdue that we wake up.

We must recognize that the frog has been slowly coming to a boil and ensure it jumps out, *now!*

Zeitgeist is defined as "the spirit of the time; a general trend of thought or feeling characteristic of a particular period of time." (Dictionary.com) We must create a new zeitgeist, one of conscious awareness, that includes critical thinking, and a much wiser understanding of how life works best when we make decisions that benefit the entire ecosystem.

In December 2018, a movement known as *'gilets jaunes'* ('yellow vests') began in France. The main instigator, Ghislain Coutard [1], is very much like the other people in this book who did not in any way consider themselves leaders, yet became dissatisfied with a situation or condition and resolved to take action themselves. As a machine repairman who was required to drive between 200 and 500 kilometres daily, and upset by yet another raise in diesel fuel prices, he created and posted a video expressing his anger and disgust. It went quickly viral, indicating that his sentiments were very broadly shared.

"I did this video to complain like everyone else and I got the idea to use the yellow vest because I use every day at work. When I placed it on my car's dashboard I realised how visible it was. It's an idea that came all alone. I was very surprised at how many views my video got and how fast I got them. Because I see everything going up (in price) without any real reason. I don't know where the money goes so it got me angry. Life is becoming more and more expensive. We work and we do extra hours but we're taxed for everything so at the end I ask myself why I work just to survive. We only have one life and to have to give it all away…it's not possible. So I just sleep, work, sleep, work and pay, pay, and pay. If any sort of problem comes along, we can't deal with it because we can't save any money."[2]

Some of the protests became violent at times, with destruction of private and public property, yet Coutard and the majority of yellow vests oppose and condemn that behaviour. They simply want their message to be heard, after years of being ignored by government and business.

Coutard again: The government "needs to be less arrogant because they don't have the same lives we do. They don't even know what the minimum wage is, they don't know how much diesel currently costs, they don't have to pay for diesel to go to work, they don't pay for restaurants. They're in another world, they can't compare. Unless we have someone who knows what life is really like, we'll never get through this. Somebody needs to know what it is not to have enough money in their bank accounts once in their life. Not to confuse the *gilets jaunes* with the people breaking things and being violent, the movement is really specific and started from a very good reason. It's not jealousy against the rich like some say. The government does everything so that rich stay rich and the poor stay poor. Everyone needs to know that the rich do everything to stay rich and try to divide. If everyone was richer everyone would be happier."[3]

The movement has had enormous impact: following a week of massive protests in many cities across France, President Emmanuel Macron reversed the diesel tax, accepted partial responsibility for the poor economic status of many in the country and even apologized for his arrogant tone. He then pressured large companies to raise wages and pay bonuses to their employees. Many, including energy company Total, Michelin, Publicis and Altice have complied.[4] A recent Harris International poll showed that 72% of French citizens approve of the yellow vests movement, while condemning the few fringe actors who are destructive. It should be mentioned that, as in cases in many countries of the world, false flag protesters are planted among the crowd and incite and cause the violence, to influence public sentiment *against* the protesters. Many suspect this activity of the French police with the yellow vest movement.

Here we have yet another encouraging example of how one person, with no formal authority and no position of power or fame, can use their own opinions and passion to leverage our interconnectedness and ignite a movement for positive change. *That,* as we have seen many times now, is leadership. However, it is a two-edged sword, because the quality and conscious awareness of the leaders can have either favourable or unfavourable effects. Recent awakenings of the alternative-right, neo-Nazi and anti-Semitic constituencies also have been caused by demagogue 'leaders' who understand the power of leadership and manipulate it for their own purposes. These are dangerous movements, led by unconscious people and need to be constantly countered by all of us.

But the takeaway here is that you too may have strong feelings and opinions about an issue, yet feel like you're completely isolated and alone in your views. These examples show that you may be quite surprised to learn that there are in fact many, many others who share them. All that is needed is for you to clarify your personal IVPs and your message and send it out there. This book is my own simple effort to do just that. Rather than continue to rant about what I saw as a major leadership crisis and our looming high-risk problems, it suddenly occurred to me that perhaps others in the world, once fully aware of what is happening, might care just as much as I do. You can do the same with your passionate issues. Test to see if your issue or cause might reflect a zeitgeist of the general public, or even a smaller group. If it does, it will give you guidance as to which audience you can approach and how to craft your message.

Zeitgeist is very often unspoken and felt without conscious awareness. Sometimes there is a generally accepted assumption that even if we don't quite agree, there's no point in speaking up because 'that it is just the way things are'. Yet a zeitgeist can shift, sometimes quickly and even violently. It can be said that the 1950s in the western world reflected a zeitgeist like this. Post-war attitudes of young and old tended towards automatic respect for authority, trust in business and in government. Societal values and mores seemed quietly conservative. But at least partially triggered by a new thing called rock 'n' roll music, a different zeitgeist awakened in the young and manifested uncontrollably in the 1960s. It appears that today, after protests in at least twelve major cities, much of France feels as equally dissatisfied as does Ghislain Coutard. The zeitgeist was already there running deep and only needed a spark to bring people forward in support.

Similarly, the #MeToo movement that exploded in the US in October 2017 revealed a long silent zeitgeist. Prior to the movement, famous award-winning movie Hollywood producer Harvey Weinstein was widely considered to be one of, if not the, most powerful men in the industry. Within days of one person coming forward with charges of sexual harassment, Weinstein had stepped down from the CEO role of his company, which eventually filed for bankruptcy. The Me Too phrase, coined by women's rights activist Tarana Burke in 2006, went viral after it was tweeted to a large audience by well-known actress and activist Alyssa Milano as #MeToo, and swept rapidly across seventeen countries from Afghanistan to Nigeria.[5]

It seems that millions of women around the world, in all walks of life, had been silently suffering and tolerating unacceptable male behaviour, likely due to fears regarding safety, job security, and/or cultural backlash. But once an opportunity to speak up safely was provided, they responded with vigor, anger and in huge numbers of support for each other, fomenting powerful change. Even in countries where the culture treated women as lesser citizens with fewer rights, this explosive and pervasive movement has driven new discussion and debate about whether cultural norms need to change.

By now it should be apparent how genuine leadership, including yours, can affect our quality of life in so many ways. It should also be apparent how critical to our well-being is a free, reasonably regulated, and easily accessible Internet. This marvelous technology permits instant, grassfire, viral transmission of important and innovative ideas, and likely harbours many more silent zeitgeist groups simply waiting to be awakened. It is the global neural network that connects us as nodes to each other, accelerating learning and the diffusion of knowledge.

The stories of these movements are also an important reminder of how critical it is to be clear about our own values, purpose and message, prior to stepping up as a new leader. The #MeToo movement resulted in immediate dismissals of many in the entertainment (and other industries) and in governments; and many believe, as is often the case with swift and emotional change, that some cases were not dealt with fairly, resulting in some men being convicted without fair hearings. In the previous chapter we explored steps involved in Lighting a Fire to inspire your potential followers, including thinking through potential consequences of your message, decisions, and calls to action.

A pendulum released after being held to one extreme side *never stops immediately in the middle.* It always first swings almost as far to the other side, swinging back and forth with decreasing energy, before eventually coming to rest at the center. Because of this, disruptive change can result in unintended consequences, including violence, in the short term. Conditions can swing from one extreme – say long-time, cruel oppression – to the other – bloody revolution. It is wise to anticipate this and make appropriate allowances and strategies, so you will be prepared for any surprises. The French Revolution of 1789 resulted in the murder of many in the aristocracy who were likely innocent, because the pendulum of public anger over years of severe injustice swung hard to the other extreme: a blanket verdict delivered by the enraged, newly-freed public to everyone considered an aristocrat. Similarly, the unplanned aftermath of the invasion of Iraq, as we've seen, has been a complete disaster by every measure, as opposed to the Bush Administrations naively assumed greetings of American 'liberators' by the Iraqi people.

For the many reasons outlined in this book, I suggest we are shifting, or perhaps awakening, to a new zeitgeist. Just as a difficult or painful experience can often push us out of our comfort zone, expose us to new knowledge and learning and re-shape us as stronger people, so do our serious challenges ahead offer opportunity to recognize and throw off the old zeitgeist in favour of a new and better one. They offer the chance to awaken the frog and have it leap out of the hot water before it's too late.

We may soon discover that the biggest oversight by our boiling frog society was the acceptance of the official government and media version of 9/11, and once again, ordinary citizens have stepped up to fill a leadership role in pursuing truth in service to society.

Since 2001, an organization, founded by architect Richard Gage, formed under the name Architects and Engineers for 9/11 Truth[6]. Its members number around 1500 professional people from many fields: architecture, structural, mechanical, forensic and civil engineering, chemistry, aeronautics, demolition, law and academia. They have one thing in common: their professional expertise and experience in their respective fields left them completely convinced that the official government explanations of what happened to the buildings [7] (particularly WTC Building 7) on 9/11 are not true. For seventeen years they have collaborated, researched, investigated and shared available information provided by 'official' sources, and concluded that what was claimed to be the cause of building collapse was scientifically impossible. Because of their professionalism and insistence on dealing only with evidence, they do not speculate as to who or what was involved; there are no conspiracy theories. They simply challenge, with scientific proof and eyewitness evidence, the officially-stated causes of building collapse and have demanded a legal investigation of the momentous event. In December 2018, their law committee successfully achieved that: US Attorney for Manhattan advised he would comply with 18 USC Section 3332 and present their evidence to a Federal Grand jury for review and investigation. They have also filed a suit against the FBI for withholding evidence from their Congressional Report in 2015.

These ordinary, yet passionately concerned citizens, reflect the new zeitgeist, and have stepped up collectively and courageously to provide a valuable service for the world. The repercussions of 9/11 have been far reaching all around the globe, from thousands of deaths, to trillions of wasted dollars, to seriously restricted human freedoms, to a nebulous, perpetual 'War on Terror,' to creating refugees and instability in the Middle East and more. It has deeply impacted all of our lives and we have a right to know the truth. These architects and engineers are examples of unsung leaders who have quietly and persistently worked away on our behalf for a long time. They are refusing to ignore what they know to be scientific truth, despite perhaps personal and professional risk, and are acting on behalf of the general public by insisting that the government provide credible answers to their scientific questions.

We have examined how age-old assumptions about capitalism fostered a zeitgeist of individualism, consumerism and, accelerating in the 1980s, unchecked materialism. Corporations gained power, operated in ways that polluted the planet, betrayed the public, and influenced our governments to carry out their agendas. Throughout the world, in varying degrees, each class sought to rise to the next level of material prosperity. This was not, in itself, a negative thing, except that it grew into the Me Generation, with a 'keep up with (or exceed) the Jones's' mentality. That zeitgeist remains prevalent in much of the world today, perhaps nowhere more evident than in the changing

Chinese economy. As we continue, and burgeoning middle classes in China, India and elsewhere begin to acquire material possessions, the strain on the planet is becoming unsustainable. In many important ways, we are already at that point.

We are now standing at the most critical cross-roads of human existence.

In twenty-five years the world will be unrecognizable to us, but in either a marvelous, or a disastrous way. Which one we make manifest will depend on the choices we *collectively* make right now.

The result of those choices will be either disastrous (possibly fatal), or an exhilarating renaissance. Never before have we faced the possible complete annihilation of our species as a likely result of making the wrong decisions. And perhaps the most dangerous threat is that the choice that will prove disastrous is the easiest and most tempting to make: *the choice to do nothing.* Maintain the status quo. Remain on fossil fuels, addicted to unfettered capitalism and its inevitable income inequality, allow AI to explode without careful, advance consideration of the potential negative consequences, do nothing to mitigate wide-scale corruption, continue to perpetuate the myth of rugged individualism, while ignoring all the science pointing to our ecosystem existence and interdependence. As we've seen, change can be scary and intimidating, particularly when there are significant unknowns. Doing nothing will be easy, yet in addition to doing nothing in many areas, we seem to be moving in an even more troubling direction: populism and protectionism on the rise globally and the continuation of the materialist consumption mentality that has created unprecedented personal debt, and foot-dragging on sustainable clean energy and reducing CO_2 emissions.

However, we face also another choice, one that is more difficult but full of excitement and promise; one that will stretch and test us, yet forge the bonds of community that come from joint problem solving. We face the opportunity to adapt to the powerful forces at play and create a better world that benefits all of us. We can consciously create a zeitgeist of shared values, of tolerance and respect for each other and of the planet.

Fortunately, there is a palpable change underway in the collective psyche that gives hope and encouragement that we will opt for the better choice.

In a *Huffpost* article in September 2016, writer Patrick Streubi shared his experiences at that year's World Economic Forum of New Champions.:

"There has never been so much potential in so many hands. There have never been so many people who have wanted to turn that potential into positive impact for the sake of our world. That is how I would describe our historical moment, and I think it's truer by the day.

It's not just a question of the technology at our fingertips, though that of course is fundamental to our new reality. It's a question of something deeper: a new value system that has inspired a new zeitgeist.

A desire for purpose and mission. An emphasis on positive impact over material gain. A preference for sharing and giving over owning and taking. A willingness to break down silos and connecting the dots in new ways. An urgent, enthusiastic desire to find new solutions to the world's most pressing problems."[8]

Sounds familiar, yes? 'Purpose, mission, system of values, connecting the dots...' – all of this is the language of the new zeitgeist and it is from this mindset that will emerge the correct solutions to our looming issues. From this mindset will emerge our new leaders.

More from Streubi, who captures it so well:

"And no longer are they the values of young idealists only. They are the values held by growing legions of people in all generations in all parts of the world. They are the dominant values of the generation that is coming of age right now. *And the people who hold these values dear have the means to effect real change on a massive scale. This has never been the case before. Never. Think about that.* [italics mine] "[9]

Clearly the new zeitgeist reflects a deepening awareness of what's at stake. It would appear that we, the boiling frogs, are finally awakening and preparing to take charge once again of our own destiny, rather than place it inadvertently in the hands of the wrong people.

The three Inspiring Visions are already well underway, yet remain only three of the many that we can collectively explore and co-create. We can adopt what Jim Collins calls the Stockdale paradox: "accept the brutal facts of reality while maintaining an unwavering faith in the endgame and a commitment to prevail."[10]

Try to envision a world where these realities prevail:

- The success of Conscious Capitalism companies forces others globally to adopt the same operating strategy, creating additional value for shareholders, employees, suppliers, their communities and their environment. Business fulfills its true mission as an engine of broad prosperity, creating and satisfying customers, and raising living standards in the process.

- Three-dimensional printing allows cost-effective manufacture of prosthetic limbs for disabled children as they grow, and prints exact heart replicas from images of in-utero babies with heart defects. Exoskeletons restore mobility to paraplegics and war veterans. Printed tiny homes can be afforded by even those with the lowest incomes, giving shelter and dignity. Homelessness disappears.

- Autonomous electric vehicles and various forms of public transportation, with low or no cost, cause a rise in discretionary income, alleviating financial stress and poverty.

- Homes and businesses, equipped with solar panel roofs and wall-mounted battery storage panels capture clean, near-free solar energy, powering the structures for miniscule cost, and guaranteeing power even in the worst storms.

- Intelligent and *wise* management of the Internet of Things frees humans to pursue their passions and interests, because basic survival needs are provided for by robotic unprecedented productivity gains, and universal basic incomes.

- A world renowned expert surgeon in Atlanta walks a Doctors Without Borders surgeon in Uganda through a procedure in real time using Internet audio video, saving a patient in a rural area.

- Burgeoning middle classes emerging in China, India and African nations leap-frog old infrastructures of energy and commerce, using mobile smart phones for everything from communication to banking. Local WIFI from fiber and even floating balloons gives them access to the Internet for minimum costs.

- Our planet gradually heals as we shift away from fossil fuels to sustainable clean energy sources. Rain forests flourish and glaciers return as global temperatures drop back to natural levels. Species of all animals are treasured and preserved as part of our interdependent ecosystem. A Green New Deal sets us on this path to a safer and more fulfilling existence.

These are but a few examples of positive possibilities we can make manifest, and several are already happening. As before in our history, focus, clarity, determination, and above all, collaboration can carry us through events that seem daunting and overwhelming. We have proven before that we can conquer adversity and in the process, create an even better future.

Old economy jobs are already disappearing, and despite the fact that our governments and businesses have not begun to accept the reality of the need to retrain and re-educate existing vulnerable workforces, we have been here before. Just as those working in disrupted industries in 1899 eventually adjusted, so will it happen again. Blacksmiths became tool and die makers, horse carriage makers became automobile coach manufacturers. The new industries absorbed those released from the old ones. A transformation to sustainable energy through a Green New Deal will re-employ many displaced workers of the fossil fuel industry.

Many in my own family, most now departed, recounted the grim hopelessness they and their parents experienced during the Great Depression. It was perhaps one of the darkest times in modern global economic history, with widespread hunger and a prevailing deep feeling of helplessness. Enter Franklin Delano Roosevelt (FDR) with his proposed New Deal and his indefatigable spirit and fireside chat encouragement that helped lift those of Americans, and indirectly others, in the world. Although WW II also contributed to their emergence from the economic disaster, it was the collaborative mindset, the *conscious* effort to face the brutal facts and forge ahead with courage and creativity that was the real driving force that created the American business juggernaut, pulling the rest of the world, through trade, along with it.

When in WWII, a German pincer movement closed in on British Expeditionary Forces (BEF) stranded with their back to the Channel in Dunkirk, military leaders feared the capture or death of 75% of the soldiers. It was one of the bleakest moments of the war, with slim chance of rescue. Yet ingenuity, collaboration, and selfless action combined to create what many call the 'Miracle of Dunkirk.' Appealing to the loyalty and compassion of the people, the military requested that every seaworthy vessel mobilize to sail the Channel and retrieve the trapped men. The zeitgeist of the time was one of strong patriotism and fierce resolve against the enemy, and the turnout was astounding, despite German aircraft patrolling the skies. In the words of US Field Officer George Fielding Eliot:

"No purely military study of the major aspects of the war could do justice to the skill and the heroism of the evacuation from Dunkirk. Suffice it to say only that, when it began, members of the British imperial general staff doubted that 25% of the B.E.F. could be saved. When it was completed, some 330,000 French and British troops, together with some Belgian and Dutch forces who refused to surrender, had reached haven in England.

... One of the most motley fleets of history — ships, transports, merchantmen, fishing boats, pleasure craft — took men off from the very few ports left, from the open beaches themselves, for German air attacks had virtually destroyed most port facilities."[11]

Those crises, while most serious for the players involved, were not nearly as dangerous as what we face today, for never before have we faced a situation that would equally and negatively impact our entire race. Climate change is that challenge, and we cannot overcome the threat without a consciously clear, focused and co-ordinated strategy, agreed, embraced and executed collectively. The Union of Concerned Scientists estimates we have about eleven more years to get it right.

And yet we also have a more powerful and quickly growing arsenal of tools than ever before, with which to not only avoid disaster, but radically and wonderfully transform our society and standard of life.

If something in this book resonated with you, struck a positive nerve, or even angered you, dig deeper. Learn about it and ask yourself those two questions: 'what needs to be done?' and 'what can and should I do about it?' Ask how what you've learned here will affect your children and grandchildren, and what you think about that. Decide if your preferred role is as a follower, and if so, which causes and their leaders inspire you to support them, with donations, volunteering, presence at local chapter meetings, protest marches, or with your special skills and talents in other ways.

If you choose to step up as a new leader, congratulations! And working through the steps in chapter 13 should prove useful in helping you to clarify your IVPs, and your vision for the issue that touches you the deepest.

Most importantly, if by reading this book you have become dissatisfied with any or all aspects of our global status quo, find your own non-violent way to push back. Conscious awareness is the critical Step One, and after that, crystallizing your opinions and sharing them with your network to galvanize agreement and inspire remedial action.

Our strength lies in our numbers, as does our genius and our ultimate happiness, and always has. Let us integrate that fact into the new zeitgeist.

ENDNOTES

Part I: What?

INTRODUCTION: WHY THIS BOOK?

1. "The Paris Climate Agreement: Deliverance or Disappointment?" Huffington Post, last modified December 15 2016, https://www.huffingtonpost. com/alliance-for-research-on-corporate-sustainability-/the-paris-clmate-agreemen_b_8812466.html.

2. https://www.theguardian.com/business/2019/jan/21/ world-26-richest-people-own-as-much-as-poorest-50-per-cent-oxfam-report

3. Laloux, Frederic, Reinventing Organizations: A Guide t Creating Organizations Inspired by the Next Stage of Human Consciousness. 2014 Nelson Parker, Belgium

4. Pew Research Center, https://www.people-press.org/2017/12/14/public-trust-in-government-1958-2017/"Do You Approve or Disapprove of the Way the Congress is Handling its Job?" Statista, February 2019, https://www.statista. com/statistics/207579/public-approval-rating-of-the-us-congress/.

5. "U.S. Trails Most Developed Countries in Voter Turnout,' Pew Research, May 21 2018, http://www.pewresearch.org/ fact-tank/2018/05/21/u-s-voter-turnout-trails-most-developed-countries/

CHAPTER 1: HOW WE GOT HERE

1. Moore's Law is a computing term originating around 1970; the simplified version of this law states that processor speeds, or overall processing power for computers will double every two years. It has done so.

2. ALEC: American Legislative Exchange Council. Through ALEC, corporations hand state legislators their wish lists to benefit their bottom line. Corporations fund almost all of ALEC's operations. They pay for a seat on ALEC task

forces where corporate lobbyists and special interest reps vote with elected officials to approve 'model' bills. Learn more at the Center for Media and Democracy's ALECexposed.org, and check out breaking news on our PRWatch.org site

3. Pinker, Steven, *The Better Angels of Our Nature: Why Violence Has Declined.* (Penguin Books, 2012), 43.

4. Pinker, *The Better Angels of Our Nature*, 74

5. 5.Aristotle, Book Three, Chapter Sixteen of *Politics.*

6. 6."Frederick Douglas," Wikipedia, https://en.wikipedia.org/wiki/ Frederick_Douglass.

7. Pinker, *The Better Angels of Our Nature*, 35.

8. Rifkin, Jeremy, *The Zero Marginal Cost Society: The Internet of Things, the Collaborative Commons and the Eclipse of Capitalism,* (Palgrave MacMillan, 2014), 39.

9. Haidt, Jonathan, *The Righteous Mind: Why good people are divided on politics and religion*, (Vintage Books, 2013), 150.

10. Haidt, *The Righteous Mind*, 183.

11. Pinker, *The Better Angels of Our Nature,* 181.

12. Margaret Wheatley, *Leadership and the New Science: Discovering Order in a Chaotic World,* (San Fransicso, Berrett-Koehler, 1999), 29.

13. Pinker, *The Better Angels of Our Nature,* 190.

14. Haidt, *The Righteous Mind,* 367.

15. Wheatley, *Leadership and the New Science: Discovering Order in a Chaotic World,* 10.

16. Goldsmith, Marshall, *Whatever* Luigi, *The Got You Here Won't Get You There,* Roundtable Companies, Mundelein, IL Oct 2011

17. Capra, Fritjof, and Luisi, Pier Luigi, *The Systems View of Life: A Unifying Vision,* (Cambridge University Press, 2014), xi.

CHAPTER 2: OUR LEADERSHIP CRISIS

1. https://www.researchgate.net/publication/284689712_The_War_for_Talent/

2. Monbiot, George, The Guardian, March 31, 2016 https://www.theguardian. com/politics/audio/2016/mar/31/george-monbiot-and-ed-miliband-discuss-climate-change-politics-weekly-podcast

3. Kouzes, James, and Posner, Barry, *The Leadership Challenge*, (J. Wiley & Sons, 2010)

4. *HBR's 10 Must Reads On Leadership*, Kotter, John P., "What Leaders Really Do," (Harvard Business Review, 2011), 33.

5. *HBR's 10 Must Reads On Leadership*, George, Bill, "Discovering Your Authentic Leadership," (Harvard Business review, 2011), 129.

6. *HBR's 10 Must Reads On Leadership*, Heifetz Ronald, "The Work of Leadership," (Harvard Business Review, 2011), 51.

7. Fairholm, Matthew, "The Themes and Theory of Leadership: James MacGregor Burns and the Theory of Leadership," *George Washington University, Centre for Excellence in Municipal Management*, Working Paper No. CR01-01, (2001).

8. Bass, Bernard, M.,

9. Kouzes and Posner, *The Leadership Challenge*, 25.

10. Goleman, Daniel., Boyatzis, Richard., and McKee, Annie., *Primal Leadership: Unleashing the Power of Emotional Intelligence*, (Harvard Business School Press, 2010).

11. Kets De Vries, Manfred, F, R., and Korotov, Konstantin, "Transformational Leadership Development Programs: Creating Long-Term Sustainable Change," In *The Handbook for Teaching Leadership Knowing, Doing and Being*, Snook, Scott., Nohria, Nitin., Khurana, Rakesh (Sage Publications, Inc., 2012), 263-282.

12. Harrington, Matthew., "Survey: People's Trust Has Declined in Business, Media, Government and NGOs," *Harvard Business Review*, January 16, 2017.

13. Reichheld, Fred., *Loyalty Rules: How today's leaders build lasting relationships*, (Boston:Harvard Business School Press, 2001).

14. Kouzes and Posner, *The Leadership Challenge*, 37.

15. George, "Discovering Your Authentic Leadership," in *HBR's 10 Must Reads On Leadership*, 131.

16. *Barrett, Richard., Building a Values Driven Organization: A Whole System Approach to Cultural Transformation,* (Elsevier Inc., 2006), 170.

17. Heskett, James., *The Culture Cycle: How to Shape the Unseen Force that Transforms Performance,* (Financial Times Press, 2012), 28, 158.

18. Collins, Jim., *Good-To-Great: Why Some Companies Make the Leap…and Others Don't,* (Harper Collins Publishers, 2001), 22.

19. Collins, *Good-To-Great,* 30.

20. Wheatley, *Leadership and the New Science,* 55.

21. https://www.ted.com/talks/ dean_kamen_previews_a_new_prosthetic_arm?language=en

22. "Tommy Douglas," Wikipedia, https://en.wikipedia.org/wiki/ Tommy_Douglas.

23. Senate Report on Pre-war Intelligence on Iraq

24. https://www.forbes.com/sites/kotlikoff/2018/07/21/is-our-government-intentionally-hiding-21-trillion-in-spending/#796fd1594a73

25. *Wall Street Journal,* November 8, 2017.

26. Chuck Lucier, "Herb Kelleher- the Thought Leader Interview", *Strategy & Business Journal,* June 2004, Issue 35, https://www.strategy-business.com/ article/04212

27. Quoted in "National Leader of the month for September 2007: Herb Kelleher", Leadernetwork.org, September 2007 Available at http:// leadernetwork.org/herb_kelleher_september_07.htm

28. *Forbes Magazine,* May 2018 https://www.forbes.com/sites/ joannmuller/2018/05/03/vws-former-ceo-martin-winterkorn-charged-with-fraud-and-conspiracy-in-diesel-cheating-case/#331622b34e90

29. "Ex-Volkswagen CEO Winterkorn Charged in US Over Diesel Scandal," Reuters.com, May 3, 2018.

30. *Time Magazine,* Person of the Year 1940 and 1949

31. History.com, May 21, 2014.

32. *Time Magazine*

33. Bruce Livesey, "Is Harper Canada's Worst Prime Minister?", quote from Professor McKay, Ian., Queen's University in *Canada's National Observer*, June 7, 2015. https://www.nationalobserver.com/2015/06/07/news/harper-worst-prime-minister-history-part-two

34. Mckay,

35. Gerstner, Louis, V., *Who Says Elephants Can't Dance? Leading a Great Enterprise Through Dramatic Change*, (Harper-Collins, 2003), 181-182.

36. Gerstner, *Who Says Elephants Can't Dance?* 78.

37. Gerstner, *Who Says Elephants Can't Dance?*

38. Collins, *Good-To-Great*, 44.

39. Hedges, Christopher., *America: The Farewell Tour*, (Simon and Schuster, 2018).

CHAPTER 3: WHAT WENT WRONG?

1. Covey, Stephen, M, R., *The Speed of Trust*, Free Press, imprint of Simon & Schuster, 2006, 2018.

2. Rifkin, Jeremy, *The Zero Marginal Cost Society: The Internet of Things, the Collaborative Commons and the Eclipse of Capitalism*. (Palgrave MacMillan, 2014), 40.

3. Rifkin, *The Zero Marginal Cost to Society*, 65.

4. Rifkin, *The Zero Marginal Cost to Society*, 57.

5. "The Gilded Age," History.com, https://www.history.com/topics/19th-century/gilded-age.

6. "The Gilded Age," History.com.

7. Macmillan, Margaret., *Paris 1919: Six Months That Changed the World*, (New York: Random House Trade, 2001), 415.

8. Chomsky, Noam., *Hegemony or Survival: America's Quest for Global Dominance*, (Metropolitan Books, 2003).

9. Zakaria, Fareed., *From Wealth to Power: The Unusual Origins of American Power*, (Princeton University Press, 1998).

10. Eisenhower, Dwight, https://www.youtube.com/watch?v=8y06NSBBRtY

11. See National Security Memorandum #263, US Archives

12. Note: see *JFK and the Unspeakable* by James W. Douglass, *Family of Secrets* by Russell Baker, and *Best Evidence*, by David S. Lifton

13. "The Iran Contra Affair 30 Years Later: A Milestone in Post-Truth Politics," National Security Archive, https://nsarchive.gwu.edu/briefing-book/iran/2016-11-25/iran-contra-affair-30-years-later-milestone-post-truth-politics.

14. Twentieth Century Fox, American Entertainment Partners L.P., Amercent Films, 1987

15. Greenwood, Robin., and Scharfstein, David., "The Growth of Finance," *Journal of Economic Perspectives*, 27, no.2 (Spring 2013), 3-28.

16. "Under the Microscope: Convergence in the U.S. Television Market between 2000-2014," Steiner, Tobias., from Wikipedia.

17. Leibovich, Mark., *This Town: Two Parties and a Funeral in America's Gilded Capital*, (New York: Penguin Group (USA) Inc., 2013).

18. . Jeff Stein, "Many Lawmakers Who Crafted Financial Regulations Work for Wall Street",Washington Post, September 7, 2018, https://www.washingtonpost.com/

19. Drutman, Lee., , "How Corporate Lobbyists Conquered American Democracy," *Atlantic* Monthly, April 20, 2015.

20. 99.7% of Unique FCC Comments Favoured Net Neutrality, See Motherboard. Vice.com

21. Architects & Engineers for 9/11 Truth, www.ae911Truth.org

22. Sorkin, Andrew, Ross., *Too Big to Fail: this Inside Story about how Wall Street and Washington Fought to Save the Financial System and Themselves*, (Viking Press, 2009).

23. Taibbi, Matt., "Ten Years After the Crash, We've Learned Nothing," *Rolling Stone*, September 13, 2018 https://www.rollingstone.com/politics/politics-features/financial-crisis-ten-year-anniversary-723798/.

24. Vox, "It's Time for Liberals to Get Over Citizen's United," May 7, 2018.

25. Legal Information Institute, Cornell Law School, "Opinion of J.P. Stevens, J., Supreme Court of United States, Citizen's United appellant vs. Federal Election Commission," January 21, 2010.

26. International Consortium of Investigative Journalists; Wikipedia Paradise Papers, Panama Papers. https://www.icij.org/investigations/panama-papers/

27. Aguay, John., "Deus Vult: The Geopolitics of the Catholic Church," *Geopolitics* 15, no. 1, (February 12, 2010) 39-61.

28. "Church attendance among Catholics resumes downward slide," News.Gallup. com,

29. "Journalists Killed," Committee to Protect Journalists, cpj.org/data/killed www.euronews.com/2018/10/08/ six-journalists-killed-in-europe-since-the-start-of-2017

Part II: So What?

CHAPTER 4: WHY CHANGE? BURNING PLATFORMS AND INSPIRING VISIONS

CHAPTER 5: BURNING PLATFORM 1 – CLIMATE CHANGE

1. See msn.com/en-ca/video-news-Elizabeth-May-delivers-impassioned-speech-during-climate-debate/ vi-bbosvwl

2. Garfield, Leanna., "China's latest energy mega-project shows that coal really *is* on the way out," *The Independent,* January 29, 2018.

3. "One Simple Chart," Business Insider, May 8, 2018.

4. Wikipedia

5. https://www.climate.gov/news-features/ understanding-climate/2014-state-climate-ocean-heat-content

6. https://www.livescience.com/40206-as-ocean-warms-impacts-multiply.html

7. "Ten Signs of Global Warming," Union of Concerned Scientists, https://www.ucsusa.org/global-warming/science-and-impacts/science/ ten-signs-global-warming-and-climate-change-are-happening.

8. "Fire, Fire Everywhere: the 2018 Global Wildfire Seasons is Already Disastrous," *Huffpost,* July 28,2018.

9.	"Hurricanes and Climate Change," Union of Concerned Scientists, https://www.ucsusa.org/global-warming/science-and-impacts/impacts/hurricanes-and-climate-change.html#.XDAHj1xKjIU

CHAPTER 6: BURNING PLATFORM 2 – INCOME INEQUALITY

1.	Pimentel, D, A, V., Aymar, I, M. and Lawson, M., "Reward Work, Not Wealth," *Oxfam International,* Januray 22, 2018. https://www.oxfam.org/en/research/reward-work-not-wealth

2.	Chris Hedges, America-the Farewell Tour, Toronto, Alfred A. Knopf, 2018

3.	World Bank Group, data.worldbank.org/indicator.

4.	https://www.cnbc.com/2018/09/05/bernie-sanders-introduces-the-bezos-act-slamming-amazon-low-wages.html

5.	Pimentel, Aymar, and Lawson., *Oxfam International.*

6.	Minton Beddoes, Zanny, For Richer or Poorer, The Economist, October 13, 2012 https://www.economist.com/special-report/2012/10/11/for-richer-for-poorer

7.	"CEO Pay Skyrockets to 361 Times That of Average Worker," *Forbes Magazine,* May 22, 2018. Diana Hembree, https://www.forbes.com/sites/dianahembree/2018/05/22/ceo-pay-skyrockets-to-361-times-that-of-the-average-worker/#60582eb5776d

8.	Piketty, Thomas., *Capital in the 21ˢᵗ Century*, (Bellknap Press of Harvard University Press, 2014).

9.	Piketty, *Capital in the 21ˢᵗ Century*, p.26 See also piketty.pse

10.	Piketty, *Capital in the 21ˢᵗ Century*, p.571.

11.	Ibid, p. 529

12.	Smith, Adam, "An Inquiry into the Nature and Causes of the Wealth of Nations," Boston, MA, 1776,

13.	Mayer, Jane., *Dark Money: the Hidden History of the Billionaires Behind the Rise of the Radical Right*, (Doubleday, 2016), 147.

14.	Hartmann, Thomas., "Billionaire Fascists Are Coming for Your Social Security and Medicare," October 18, 2018, Salon.com.

15.	Hartmann, Salon.com.

16. Aristotle, *Politics*, as quoted in Salon, October 18, 2018.

17. Taibbi, Matt., "Ten Years After the Crash, We've Learned Nothing," *Rolling Stone,* September 13, 2018, https://www.rollingstone.com/politics/politics-features/financial-crisis-ten-year-anniversary-723798/.

18. Ibid, Taibbi, M.

19. Ibid, Taibbi, M.

20. Buffett, Warren, https://www.youtube.com/watch?v=zeD8NOPyatw

CHAPTER 7: BURNING PLATFORM 3 – CHAOS IN THE VUCA WORLD

1. Collins, Jim, Good to Great: Why Some Companies Make the Leap and Others Don't, Harper Business, 2001, p8

2. Friedman, Thomas, L., *The World is Flat: A brief History of the Twenty-First Century*, (New York: Farrar, Straus, Giroux,2005), 4.

3. Denning, Steve, "How to Launch a Global Management Movement," *Forbes Magazine*, December 2,2018.

4. "Dismal Employee Engagement is a Sign of Global Mismanagement," Gallup. com. https://www.gallup.com/workplace/238079/state-global-workplace-2017. aspx?utm_source=link_wwwv9&utm_campaign=item_231668&utm_medium=copy

5. Pontrefact, Dan., "If Culture Comes First, Performance Will Follow," *Forbes Magazine*, May 25, 2017.

6. Canadian Manufacturing magazine, February 6, 2017 "40% of Canadian Jobs Could Be Lost to Automation, McKinsey Chief Says."

7. Laloux, Frederic., *Reinventing Organizations: A Guide t Creating Organizations Inspired by the Next Stage of Human Consciousness*, (Belgium: Nelson Parker, 2014), 100.

8. Laloux, *Reinventing Organizations*, 113.

9. Peterson, Jordan, B., *12 Rules for Life: An Antidote to Chaos*, (Random House Canada, 2018), 27.

10. Wheatley, *Leadership and the New Science*, xvi.

11. Wheatley, *Leadership and the New Science*, 105.

CHAPTER 8: INSPIRING VISION 1 – THE THIRD INDUSTRIAL REVOLUTION

1. Collins, Jim., and Porras, Jerry., *Built to Last: Successful Habits of Visionary Companies*, (Harper Collins, 1994), 224.

2. Collins and Porras, *Built to Last*, 52, 239.

3. Rifkin, *The Zero Marginal Cost Society*, 55.

4. Rifkin, *The Zero Marginal Cost Society*, 57.

5. Cardwell, Diane., "Brooklyn Solar Grid Energy Trading," on NYTimes.com, March 13,2017. www.nytimes.com/2017/03/13/business/energy-environment/brooklyn-solar-grid-energy-trading.htm

6. www.Wired.com/story/embark-self-driving-truck-deliveries

7. Tapscott, Don., and Tapscott, Alexander., *Blockchain Revolution: How the Tech Behind Bitcoin is Changing Money, Business, and the World*, (Penguin Random House, 2014), 5.

8. Tapscott and Tapscott, *Blockchain Revolution*, 5.

9. www.vanityfair.com/news/2017/03/elon-musk-billion-dollar-crusade-to-stop-ai-space-x machines

10. Gates, Bill., "Open AI Robots Beating Humans at Dota2 is a Milestone," CNBC.com, June 28, 2018. www.cnbc.com/2018/06/27/bill-gates-openai-robots-beating-humans-at-dota-2-is-ai-milestone.html

11. Hawking, Stephen., "AI Could be the Worst Event in Human History," CNBC.com, November 6, 2017. https://www.cnbc.com/2017/11/06/stephen-hawking-ai-could-be-worst-event-in-civilization.html

12. Gates, Bill., "Job Stealing Robots Should Pay Income Tax," CNBC.com, February 17, 2017. https://www.cnbc.com/2017/02/17/bill-gates-job-stealing-robots-should-pay-income-taxes.html

CHAPTER 9: INSPIRING VISION 2 – CONSCIOUS CAPITALISM

1. Corkery, Michael., "How Sears Dying Stores Are Fueling a New Fortune in Real Estate," *New York Times*, August 28, 2018.

2. asp www.investopedia.com/terms/m/multipliereffect

3.   Koehn, Nancy., *Harvard Business Review*, November 2013. https://hbr. org/2013/11/the-brain-and-soul-of-capitalism

4.   Trickle-down theory, started in the Reagan administration, claimed that tax cuts to corporations and the wealthy would result in investment, innovation and job creation, boosting the economy and standard of living for society. It has *never worked.*

5.   Mackey, J. and Sisodia, R., Conscious Capitalism.org, Resources, https://www. consciouscapitalism.org/

6.   Denning, Steve., "How to Launch a Global Management Movement," *Forbes Magazine*, December 2, 2018.

7.   George, Bill., "Op. Ed: 'Why Blackrock CEO Larry Fink is not a Socialist,'"*Harvard Business Review,* March 12, 2018.

8.   "Corporate Investor Relations," Blackrock.com. https://www.blackrock.com/ corporate/investor-relations/larry-fink-ceo-letter

9.   Rifkin, *The Zero Marginal Cost Society*, 11,12.

10. Rifkin, *The Zero Marginal Cost Society*, 14.

11. Rifkin, *The Zero Marginal Cost Society*, p.8.

12. Rifkin, *The Zero Marginal Cost Society,* p.8.

CHAPTER 10: INSPIRING VISION 3 – CONSCIOUS AWARENESS

1.   Lipton, Bruce, PhD., *The Biology of Belief: Unleashing the Power of Consciousness, Matter and Miracles*, (Hay House, Inc., 2008), 136.

2.   Chopra, Deepak, M.D., *The Seven Spiritual Laws of Success*, (Amber Allen Publishing, 1994), 48.

3.   Capra, and Luisi, *The Systems View of Life*, 260.

4.   "Non-dualism," Wikipedia, https://en.wikipedia.org/wiki/Nondualism.

5.   Lipton, *The Biology of Belief,* 71.

6.   Chopra, *The Seven Spiritual Laws of Success,* 69.

7.   Chopra, *The Seven Spiritual Laws of Success,* 70.

8.   https://www.youtube.com/ results?search_query=yellowstone+wolves+reintroduction

9. Doidge, Norman, PhD., *The Brain's Way of Healing: Remarkable Discoveries and Recoveries from the Frontiers of Neuroplasty*, (New York: Viking Books, 2015), 8.

10. Doidge, *The Brain's Way of Healing*, p.xix.

11. Capra, and Luisi, *The Systems View of Life*, 256.

12. Dr. Mary Neal, https://www.youtube.com/watch?v=9-QjMRF1gkI

13. Bushell, William, C., Seaberg, Maureen "Experiments Suggest Humans Can Directly Observe the Quantum," *Psychology Today*, December 5, 2018.

14. https://www.youtube.com/watch?v=BZ0YFoUcY0s

15. Lipton, *The Biology of Belief*, p.xxiv, 38.

16. Lipton, *The Biology of Belief*, 105.

17. Salovey and Meyer, Emotional Intelligence, Imagination, Cognition and Personality, 1989 http//positivepsychology.org.uk/emotional-intelligence-mayer-salovey-theory/

18. Sundermier, Ali., "99.9999999% of Your Body is Empty Space" *Business Insider*, September 23, 2016. https://www.sciencealert.com/99-9999999-of-your-body-is-empty-space.

19. Wheatley, *Leadership and the New Science*, 41.

20. Doidge, *The Brain's Way of Healing*, 7.

21. Dyer, Wayne, PhD., *The Power of Intention*, (Hay House, Inc., 2004), 256.

22. Norretanders, T., *The User Illusion: Cutting Consciousness Down to Size*. (New York: Penguin Books, 1998), Taken from Lipton, *The Biology of Belief*.

23. Lipton, *The Biology of Belief*, 112.

24. Bolte-Taylor, Jill, PhD., *My Stroke of Insight: A Brain Scientists Personal Journey*, (Viking Press, 2006), 68. https://www.ted.com/talks/jill_bolte_taylor_s_powerful_stroke_of_insight?language=en

25. Dobbs, David., "Zen Gamma," *Scientific American*, April 2005

Part III Now What?

CHAPTER 11: A CHALLENGE TO CURRENT LEADERS

1. News.Brown.edu/articles/costs summary https://watson.brown.edu/costsofwar/costs/economic

2. Kitman, Jamie, Lincoln., "Don't Blame Trump for GM's Layoffs – Blame GM," Politico, November 29, 2018, Politico.com/magazine/story/2018/11/29.

3. Business Insider, BusinessInsider.com/What-is–glyphosate-Monsanto-cancer-roundup-lawsuit.

4. The Center for Public Integrity, Publicintegrity.org/2013/09/10/Ex-Wall-Street-Chieftains-living-large-post-meltdown

5. The Center for Public Integrity,

6. The White House, Office of the Press Secretary, "Remarks by the President at a Campaign Event in Roanoke, Virginia,' Obama White House Archives, July 13, 2012, ObamaWhiteHouseArchives.gov/thepressoffice/2012/07/13/remarks-president-camign-event-roanoke-virginia.

7. Capra, and Luisi, *The Systems View of Life*, 317.

8. Capra, and Luisi, *The Systems View of Life*, 316.

9. Holgate, M., "Self-awareness is underrated: Why the conscious mind leads to happiness," Lifehack.org. https://www.lifehack.org/629038/self-awareness-is-underrated-why-the-conscious-mind-leads-to-happiness

10. Spenser, Nick., "Machiavelli's the Prince: the two sides of human nature," *The Guardian*, May 27, 2012.

11. Schnabel, Dan., "How Will You Measure Your Life?" Forbes.com, from Clayton Christensen, June 5, 2012.

12. Barrett, Richard., *Building a Values Driven Organization – A Whole System Approach to Cultural Transformation*, (Elsevier Inc., 2006), 20.

CHAPTER 12: A MESSAGE TO WOULD-BE LEADERS

1. Drucker, Peter, in HBR On Leadership, "What Makes an Effective Executive?" p.19 Harvard Press, June 2004.

2. Kouzes, and Posner., *The Leadership Challenge*, 386.

3. "Boyan Slat," Wikipedia, https://en.wikipedia.org/wiki/Boyan_Slat. See www. theoceancleanup.com/updates for information on the Great Pacific Garbage Patch and the Ocean Cleanup

4. " Alexandria Ocasio-Cortez," Wikipedia, https://en.wikipedia.org/wiki/ Alexandria_Ocasio-Cortez.

5. Gladwell, Malcolm., *The Tipping Point*, (New York: Little, Brown and Co., 2000), 38.

6. Collins, and Porras, *Built to Last*, 53.

7. Collins, and Porras, *Built to Last*, 238.

CHAPTER 13: FIVE SIMPLE (BUT NOT EASY) 'HOW-TO' STEPS

1. The Peter F. Drucker Foundation, *The Leader of the Future: New Visions, Strategies and Practices for the Next Era*, eds. Hesselbein, F., Goldsmith, M., and Beckhard, R., (San Fransisco: Jossey-Bass, 1996), xiv .

2. IBM.com/ibm/values/us

3. Collins, and Porras, *Built to Last*, 99.

4. "10 Visions Statement Examples to Spark Your Imagination," Fit Small Business, Fitsmallbusiness.com/vision-statement-examples, Kotter, J.

5. "McDonald's Mission Statement & Visions Statement: An Analysis," Panmore Institute, last updated February 20, 2019. Panmore.com/ McDonalds-vision-statement-mission-statement-analysis

6. Barrett, *Building a Values Driven Organization,* 21.

7. Kotter, John, PhD., *Leading Change*, (Boston: Harvard Business Review Press, 2012), 126.

8. Rock, David, "SCARF: A Brain-Based Model for Collaborating With and Influencing Others." 2008 https://davidrock.net/portfolio-items/ scarf-a-brain-based-model-for-collaborating-with-and-influencing-others-vol-1/

9. Heifetz, Ronald, PhD., *Leadership Without Easy Answers*, (Cambridge, MA: Belknap Press of Harvard University Press, 1994), 37.

10. SWOT analysis: https://en.wikipedia.org/wiki/SWOT_analysis

11. Porter, Michael, Harvard University, en.wikipedia.org/wiki/ Porter%27s_five_forces_analysis

12. Kouzes, and Posner., *The Leadership Challenge*, 267.

13. Seppala, Emma., "What Bosses Gain by Being Vulnerable," *Harvard Business Review,* December 11, 2014.

CHAPTER 14: A NEW ZEITGEIST OF CONSCIOUS AWARENESS
1. Ghislain Coutard, Gilets Jeunes Movement http://bit.ly/2ZaLuIG

2. At the End I Ask Myself Why I Work Just to Survive' man who had 'yellow vest' idea tells Euronews," Euronews, last updated December 9, 2018. Euronews.org/2018/12/09/at-the-end-I-ask-myself-why-I-work-just-to-survive- man-who-had-yellow-vest-idea-tells–eur.

3. Euronews, 2018.

4. "Emmanual Macron Enlists French Business to Quell 'Gilets Jaunes,' *Financial Times*, December 14, 2018,

5. "Me Too Movement," Wikipedia, https://en.wikipedia.org/wiki/ Me_Too_movement.

6. Architects & Engineers for 9/11 Truth; www.ae911truth.org/grandjury

7. 9/11 WTC demolition; https://www.youtube.com/watch?v=YW6mJOqRDI4

8. Streubi, Patrick., "A New Zeitgeist Has Arrived. Are You Part of It?" *Huffpost*, September 24, 2015,

9. Streubi, *Huffpost*.

10. Collins, *Good-To-Great*, 83.

11. "Dunkirk Evacuation: World War II," Brittanica, last updated February 15, 2019. Brittanica.com/event/Dunkirk-evacuation

ACKNOWLEDGEMENTS

I AM VERY FORTUNATE TO WRITE MY FIRST BOOK IN AN AGE where technology permits anyone to publish and facilitates the process. Electing to use a hybrid, assisted self-publishing approach, I am extremely grateful for the efforts, expertise and guidance I received from my partner firms. Matt Stone and design team at 100 Covers showed patience, savvy and creativity in the design, listening carefully to my ideas and requests until we got it right. Publishing Director Helen Hart and her editing team at Silverwood Books also showed great patience and meticulous attention to detail as they tediously revised my layman's references and footnotes into standard professional formatting. Karen Schober-Maneely, Lori Stabile, Colleen Kelley and the Design team at Bookbaby did the required hand-holding and patiently guided me through the process of getting the book published. Emma Boyer at Smith Publicity was instrumental in teaching me the details of social media marketing.

I owe debts of gratitude also to family and friends, without whose support the book may not have materialized. My son Liam has always stood steadfastly by my side through many years of difficulty and disappointment, supporting my multiple attempts to discover my true purpose. Thank you, 'little tree'. My sister Catherine Marsh provided me with a stress-free environment in which to do the work, as well as feedback and enthusiastic encouragement. My sister Dianne Dancy spent many tedious hours copy editing the first manuscript, and offered literary and syntax suggestions that significantly improved the book. Long-time friend Andrew Laffey was first to read the initial manuscript, and insistent that I persist to the publishing finish line.

His early belief in the book, encouragement, critiques and suggestions were a constant source of energy and support. David Hopper played sounding board for many of the ideas, challenging them with his usual contrarian perspective and offering a grounding source for some of my more 'out there' thoughts."

Not trained as an author, I have never considered myself a writer, and thus never considered writing a book. It was the support of these people who knew how passionate I am about the subject matter, and offered whatever I needed and when I needed it, that brought the book to fruition. I will always be grateful, and hopeful that the thoughts in the book will help incite positive action from readers during these treacherous times. May our children, grandchildren and all future generations look back on this time with pride and gratitude that we placed their happiness and interest ahead of our own selfish agendas.